Henry M'Manus

Sketches of the Irish Highlands

Description - Social and Religious

Henry M'Manus

Sketches of the Irish Highlands
Description - Social and Religious

ISBN/EAN: 9783744666626

Printed in Europe, USA, Canada, Australia, Japan

Cover: Foto ©Thomas Meinert / pixelio.de

More available books at **www.hansebooks.com**

SKETCHES

OF

THE IRISH HIGHLANDS:

Descriptive, Social, and Religious.

WITH SPECIAL REFERENCE TO

IRISH MISSIONS IN WEST CONNAUGHT SINCE 1840.

BY

REV. HENRY M'MANUS,

First Irish Missionary of the General Assembly Presbyterian Church in Ireland.

ERIN MY COUNTRY

LONDON:
HAMILTON, ADAMS & CO. 33 PATERNOSTER ROW.
EDINBURGH: ANDREW ELLIOTT.
DUBLIN: J. ROBERTSON & CO.   BELFAST: C. AITCHISON.
1863.

TO THE

REV. THOMAS GUTHRIE, D.D.,

Moderator of the Free Church of Scotland.

Rev. and Dear Sir,

In soliciting for these pages the honor of your name, one reason that has influenced me is your well-known sympathy with suffering humanity of every class and clime; of which the system of "Ragged Schools" founded by you will remain an imperishable monument. Another reason—very unequal in importance, I admit, but still interesting to an Irishman—is, that in adopting the Total Abstinence principle many years ago, you were not ashamed to ascribe the change to the example of a poor Irish peasant. When many others—your inferiors in talent and worth—find nothing in the character of that people but subjects for ridicule or censure, not taking into account their many disadvantages, such a compliment on your part has still further endeared you to one who rejoices in being of that race, and whose lifetime has been mainly spent in endeavouring—however unworthily—to promote their spiritual welfare.

That the Lord may long spare your useful life, is the sincere prayer of,

Rev. and Dear Sir,

Yours truly,

THE AUTHOR.

PREFACE.

THE writer's best apology for thus venturing into print, is a simple statement of the Providential circumstances which have led to it. Laid aside by a tedious illness, he was applied to by his esteemed friend, Rev. H. MAGEE, Editor of "PLAIN WORDS," for a few articles on Irish Missions, to be inserted in that useful periodical. This subject, being the work of his life, grew under his hands until at last, contrary to expectation, it swelled into a volume.

To prevent serious misconception, however, he begs it to be understood, that this Book professes not to be a history of Irish Missions—not even of those connected with his own Church. It is not even a connected narrative of his own poor labours. It is simply, as it professes, a series of Sketches illustrative of that work; and these are selected exclusively from his own experience, because that of it only is he qualified to speak. If it be objected that his labours deserved not such notice, he freely admits that; but he hopes, at the same time, they may be allowed to serve for illustration—just as leaves of trees or blades of grass are introduced into pictures. If this plea do not satisfy, he can adduce another. His labours—such as they are—were amongst the first—in some places, the very first—of modern Protestant Missions to Irish Roman Catholics. At the least, then, they have the same claim to notice as Flynn's Inn had to be marked in the old maps of Connemara. In itself, this was only a common farmhouse; but it obtained that honor because, for a long time, it was the only place of entertainment in a vast wilderness.

In drawing up this narrative, great pains have been taken to ensure accuracy on all points; but amid the multiplicity of details, some minor errors may have been fallen into, the correction of which, by any friendly hand, will be gratefully received. But this remark applies only to matters of fact; it does not extend to the plan of conducting Missionary operations, unfolded in this Book. That must stand or fall on its own merits, and is not submitted here to discussion; for in past time, the writer has been nearly overwhelmed by the number of advices he received on that subject, most of them from parties utterly inexperienced in the work. Would it not be better for the advocates of these various plans to test their merits by at once carrying them into effect, for which, alas! there is yet too much room—remembering that "all knowledge is lost which ends in knowing, and that every truth we know is a candle given us to work by"? Instead, then, of useless debating, let us "be doing;" knowing that "the Judge standeth at the door," and will soon require from us an account for our means of usefulness. To forget this solemn fact, were unpardonable in the writer at all events, as most of his book has been written after his life had been given over by his medical friends.

Finally, the Author has to express his sincere gratitude to the many kind friends — some of them beyond the Atlantic — who have so promptly come forward as Subscribers. Amongst these friends, a special tribute of thanks is due to ROBERT KANE, Esq., author of the admirable translation of the New Testament into the Munster dialect of the Irish language. Never will the writer forget the disinterested kindness, on various occasions, of that worthy brother and true Christian patriot.

CLONTARF, October 19, 1863.

CONTENTS.

CHAPTER I.

PHYSICAL FEATURES OF CONNEMARA AND ITS NATURAL HISTORY.

PAGE.

First Visit to Connemara in 1840 — Road to Outerard — Traditions of the Past — Scene at a Holy Well — Outerard Described — First View of the Mountains — Grandeur of the "Twelve Pins" — Evening Scene — Roundstone Described — Story of a Jew — Statistics of Connemara — A Strange Wolf — Red Deer, &c. — The Country irreclaimable — Wild Badgers — Barnacle Geese, &c. — Curious Mode of Catching Seabirds — The Herring Fishery — Seals — Story of One — A Day alone in the Wilds — Utter Absence of Life — Scene on Orras Beg — Reflections — Connemara in Winter — Poetry . . 1

CHAPTER II.

ITS PEOPLE — THEIR MANNERS, CUSTOMS, AND LANGUAGE.

No Middle Class in Connemara — Injurious Effects of this, and of their attachment to old customs — Their Dress — Story of a Bonnet — Their Cabins — Anecdote of a Bedstead — Smuggling — Litigiousness — Dialogue on the Road — Pious Phrases — Want of Thrift — Intemperance — Evil of it — Dances — Practical Jokes — Trick of Shan na Geos on a Pedlar, and "Outwitting the Gauger" — The Irish language — Its Resemblance to Hebrew — Its Extinction still distant — Why its Bible so attractive — Orthographic Reform — How far Irish is useful — Samples of bad English — Anecdote of an Umbrella — A Solemn Thought in Conclusion . . 29

CHAPTER III.

THEIR RELIGION.

PAGE.

Value of the Soul—Importance of Missions—Need of in Connemara—Apostasy of the first Protestants—How a Poor Roman Catholic Widow received the Gospel—Discussion with a Devotee—The Two First Converts in Connemara—Their Sufferings—Lines to the Snowdrop—Extracts from an old Irish Catechism—Dr. Gallagher's Irish Sermons—A Wonderful Legend—Superstitions—Charms—A Chapel-Scene—Anecdotes of Penances 64

CHAPTER IV.

CONVERSATIONS AND DISCUSSIONS WITH ROMAN CATHOLICS.

Ireland a wide field for Protestant Missions—Duty of the Presbyterian Church in regard to it—The Late Revival—Verses on it—List of Presbyterian Missions—My Irish-preaching very successful at first; but greatly opposed afterwards—Obliged to change it to Irish Conversations—Examples of these, showing the Ignorance of the People—Their Ideas of the Virgin—Priests' Miracles, &c.—No Irish-speaking Roman Catholic ever referred to Scripture—Their Poverty—Scene of Misery in a Cabin—Mental Derangement from Eviction—Poetical Aspiration for Christ's Kingdom . 95

CHAPTER V.

CONVERSATIONS AND DISCUSSIONS CONTINUED.

Use of these Conversations—Openness of Romanists to conviction—Turf-cutters taught Repentance and Faith—A Man goes on his knees while taught Salvation—Another receives the Truth on Baptism and the True Church—Ribaldry Rebuked with good effect—A Tradesman Denounces the Reformation—A Devotee vilifies the Protestant Bible and Discusses in the open air at night—Love of Learning in Boys—A Professed Romanist, and yet a True Believer in Jesus—His Experience, and several interesting Conversations with him 126

CHAPTER VI.

IRISH PREACHING IN WEST CONNAUGHT IN 1841.

Best means of Ireland's Elevation is the Gospel—Irish Sermon at Galway, and Good Results—Visit to the Isles of Arran—Intolerance there and Superstitions—Joyce's Country—Great Ignorance—A Strange Congregation—"Patterns"—"Joyce's Will"—Recess—Lough Ina—Meeting at the Marble Quarry—Conversation with a Smuggler—Roundstone - Opposition—Clifden, good reception at first—Personal Assault on a subsequent visit—The Killeries—Scenery—Poetry—Improvement of the Country—Irish Sermon at Salruc—Sunrise on the Killeries—End of the Tour—The Missionary Future of Ireland—Great Opposition to be expected—Grounds of Hope—A Missionary's Comforts—Testimonies to this Mission and to that in Kerry—Concluding Appeal 175

SKETCHES

OF

THE IRISH HIGHLANDS.

CHAPTER I.

PHYSICAL FEATURES OF CONNEMARA AND ITS NATURAL HISTORY.

First Visit to Connemara in 1840—Road to Outerard—Traditions of the Past—Scene at a Holy Well—Outerard Described—First View of the Mountains—Grandeur of the "Twelve Pins"—Evening Scene—Roundstone Described—Story of a Jew—Statistics of Connemara—A Strange Wolf—Red Deer, &c.—The Country irreclaimable—Wild Badgers—Barnacle Geese, &c.—Curious Mode of Catching Sea-birds—The Herring Fishery—Seals—Story of One—A Day Alone in the Wilds—Utter Absence of Life—Scene in Orras Beg—Reflections—Connemara in Winter—Poetry.

IT was in the year 1840 that the writer first visited the mountainous parts of his native land. About midsummer of that year, after a brief sojourn at Galway, he passed on westward to the famous Connemara. This region, once so inaccessible, has been wonderfully opened up since that time. In consequence, its wilds have lost that garb of mystery and romance in which they were once invested. Of that romance, however, much remained at that date; and the writer being then fresh from a college, and at a time of life when the mind is most susceptible, felt on the occasion an exciting interest, such as few could sympathize with in this more "locomotive" generation. The main object of his journey, indeed, was more important than sight-seeing; but happily, in this case, both objects could be united.

Starting that morning on the "Bianconi Car," which even then plied regularly between Galway and Clifden, the writer found himself seated beside two intelligent fellow-travellers. One of these, as he afterwards ascertained, was an Augustinian monk, who was civil and communicative. The other turned out to be the Sub-Inspector of police at Clifden, who, in parting with the writer, kindly invited him to pay him a visit before returning from Connemara.

As far as Outerard the road possesses little interest. The country around is bare, and the fields are disfigured with piles of shapeless stones, "doing duty" for fences. Much of the surface, too, seems a pavement of rock, though deeply fissured at intervals. In the interstices some sweet herbage struggles into light, while the land capable of cultivation waved with a luxuriant crop of wheat. In such a soil, and so near the mountains, one would not have expected such fertility. Looking beyond the line of our route, we see to the north-east Lough Corrib, with its winding reaches and wooded islands. This lake is a noble sheet of water; but its shores being flat and stony are not picturesque.

In the absence of other attractions along this road, a stranger may be interested on learning, that at the first stage —Moycullen—was fought, in ancient times, a great battle, in which a native Prince defeated and slew Mahanon Mac Lir, celebrated as a Sea-king and as the Legislator of the Isle of Man. From this conqueror the place derives its name, and not, as some suppose, from the Irish name of the holly-tree.

Some miles farther on, the road passes over what was at that time a natural bridge, near which stands the ruined Castle of Auchnanure. For ages this was a stronghold of the O'Flahertys—a powerful clan, who were the possessors of this country, and the plunderers of the surrounding districts. In fact they were the Mac Gregors of the west; and the traditions regarding them would supply an Irish Walter Scott with materials for volumes. In their forays, they sometimes attacked the town of Galway itself; and so unmerciful were they to the citizens, then mostly English, that the latter inscribed on their western gate the pathetic prayer —" From the ferocious O'Flahertys, good Lord deliver us."

If we may credit other traditions, this old castle was the scene of similar outrages. They relate that it had a trapdoor, through which unsuspecting victims were precipitated into the river on which the castle was built; and there the dead bodies were caught in an iron grating, from which they were privately carried off and buried. In allusion to these stories, an Irish distich describes Auchnanure as not only "a castle of wine," but also "a castle of sighs," and "a castle of plunder."

In justice to the O'Flahertys, however, we must add, that at an earlier period they had themselves suffered from similar maltreatment. In the thirteenth century their fathers were expelled by the De Burghs, or Burkes, from their ancestral estates, east of Corrib. The fugitives had no alternative but to cross the lake, driving before them the weaker tribes, and seizing their lands. Thus, then, the O'Flahertys, like many other offenders, were " sinned against" as well as sinning. And when we of the present day reflect on the mutual outrages characteristic of those old times, we may thank God that our lot is cast in an age when equal laws throw their protecting shield round all classes of the community.

Quite close to Outerard, there was at that time, in a pleasant green field, a celebrated holy well. It was dedicated to a St. Cummin. At a subsequent visit to this place, I had an opportunity of witnessing the devotions performed there. Assembled around it for the purpose, I found about a hundred individuals of both sexes; but some of them were only spectators, and others were mendicants, who, with their usual sagacity, had flocked here to make "capital" of the occasion. As to the ceremony itself, as far as came under my observation, it consisted in repeating on the beads a certain number of "Paters" and "Aves." While thus engaged, they walked quickly in a circle round the well, their heads and their feet being bare. It was said that at other times they performed this ceremony on their bare knees, thus enhancing the merit; but the great number present to-day necessitated despatch; for I noticed that, whenever one devotee dropped from the circle, another instantly stepped into his place. As to the object of these devotions, it is generally understood that they were intended as a satisfaction to God for sin; and as such, the Roman Catholic clergy often made their performance a condition for "absolution."

At present, however, all over the west, the practice is on the decline; and, as to this particular well, it has been long since closed up. May we not hail this change as a sign of progress? We Protestants believe, as well as Roman Catholics, that if we injure our neighbour in his character or his property, we are bound, as a proof of our repentance, to make reparation. But as to "satisfaction" for sin to God, who is the party chiefly injured by it, and who hates it infinitely—such a thing we consider impossible. Indeed that is the very thing for which Christ died, and which He alone could accomplish. For us, then, to attempt such satisfaction in our own persons, were virtually a denial of the sufficiency of His atonement. In other words, by so doing, we would reject the Saviour altogether. Oh! that this solemn truth were made known to these poor devotees at St. Cummin's Well; who were sincere, no doubt, in their own way, but alas! on this vital point, fatally misguided. Could they only be induced to look for salvation to the merits of the Saviour alone, how soon would they experience the power of His blood to cancel all their past guilt, and of His Spirit to subdue all their present corruptions—the two-fold blessing constituting the Gospel, and the unfailing source, when fully embraced, of peace with God now, as well as glory hereafter.

Earnestly desiring that this precious truth might be known to those frequenting this well, I would have given much for liberty to clear away from a flag beside it the votive offerings of pins, rags, and nails, and to inscribe in their stead the life-giving words—"He was wounded for our transgressions; He was bruised for our iniquities; the chastisement of our peace was upon Him; and with His stripes (not our own) we are healed."

Outerard is a pretty village. All must admire its views of the bright lake on one side, and of the dark mountains on the other; also its beautiful river, celebrated formerly for its pearls, and now for its picturesque waterfall. Another of its attractions, more homely indeed, but more valuable, is the neatness of its houses, as compared with most other western villages; while in the vicinity there are several fine villas, embowered in trees, the want of which, as we go westward, sadly detracts from the scenery. In addition to all this, Outerard could boast, in the last generation, of being an important military station, being then the chief pass into lawless Connemara. Nor should we omit, that here began Mr. Martin's celebrated avenue to his castle at Ballinahinch, of which he boasted to one of the Royal Georges that, while the avenue to Windsor Castle was only a mile long, this was no less than twenty! So it was; and in its entire length it ran through Mr. Martin's own estate. But alas! his hundreds of thousands of broad acres have since passed away from all his race. How are the mighty fallen! According to the old classic adage—"*Sic transit gloria mundi.*"

Fresh horses being here attached to our vehicle, away we start into the real highlands, leaving behind us, as soon as we pass the village, all traces of civilization. Instead of cultivated fields or comfortable houses, we now behold, far as eye can reach, only a waste, heathery wilderness. Often before had the writer beheld similar scenes, but none on a scale so wildly magnificent. The distance from this to the western ocean is fully twenty-six miles; and yet, all the way there is one interminable succession of dark moors, lonely lakes, wild glens, heath-clad hills, and "cloud-capt" mountains. Occasionally, indeed, we find some cultivated patches, with a few thatched cabins; but amid the surrounding wilderness, these seem mere dots on the surface. Nay, the very road itself which we travel is peculiar, having no ditches nor hedges on either side, and frequently winding in graceful curves round the margins of the lakes and the spurs of the mountains. Altogether, to a stranger having a taste for such scenes, this region is a theatre of wonders. It might almost be called a new world, being a panorama of the wildest, strangest, and sublimest objects in nature.

Happily, too, on this occasion, its beauty was enhanced by a blaze of heaven's "living light," which silvered the otherwise dark solitudes, and caused the grim wilderness to smile. Nor is the effect less picturesque when this brilliancy gives way to the sober "hues of eve." Indeed that is the very best time to see the magnificent mountain-cluster, generally called the "Twelve Pins," this latter word being a corruption of the Irish *bin* or *ben*, which signifies a precipice. To these hills the mingled lights and shades of evening impart an indescribable charm, specially by the singular contrast between their sunlit and shaded outlines. Like "things of life," these vast shadows sweep their dark wings across the subjacent ravines and lakes, and the distant moors. Amazingly grand are the "dissolving views" thus formed. And what in connection with them most impressed my own mind, was the solemn silence with which they gradually spread over the landscape. It reminded me of the Nightly Heaven unveiling her worlds of light without noise. Poor man, when he does any thing great, "makes a fuss" about it; but these bright orbs, in obedience to their Creator's will, are content to shine unobserved. Mortal, "go thou and do likewise."

Since the writer thus made his acquaintance with these mountains, twenty long years have elapsed; still he can say, without affectation or exaggeration, that the impression then "photographed" on his mind has never been effaced; proving that, in the poet's words,

"A thing of beauty is a joy for ever."

Nor was the effect merely æsthetic. Mountains, with their heaven-pointing summits, are the true temples of the Eternal. They lift the soul, unless altogether debased, above the perishable things of time, and point it forward athwart the mists of sense to the ever-during realities of eternity. Hence in all ages the partiality of God's people for such scenes. Carmel's top was the favourite oratory of Elijah. On Moriah, Abraham offered his memorable sacrifice. And of the Holy One Himself it is said—

"Cold mountains and the midnight air
Witness'd the fervour of His prayer."

Not unnaturally, then, was the writer's mind imbued with religious feelings by gazing on these mountains; and, in this way, Carmel, Moriah, and Tabor were associated in his reflections with Knockhiggin, Lettery, and Bengower. Nor is he without hope that these grand old Celtic hills, second to none in displaying the glory of God as Creator, will yet be identified also with His glory as Redeemer; being made the scene of the same pure faith and spiritual worship which have shed such a halo round the Hebrew Highlands. Beyond all Greek, all Roman fame, is such a glory. "The Gospel is the jewel of which the whole universe is but the setting."

Changed is the scene. Let the reader now fancy me settled down for some months at the small village of Roundstone. Circumstances wonderfully affect the importance of places; otherwise this little village would seldom see itself in print. Such as it is, however, Connemara, with an area as extended as that of some eastern counties, can boast of no other town except Clifden. Besides this, Roundstone then presented the *beau ideal* of a mountain hamlet. It consisted of one street, running alongside the bay of the same name, and flanked on the land-side by a dark mountain, rather broad than lofty. The slated houses might be near one hundred. Behind these houses, on the land-side, were small gardens, producing potatoes and cabbages; and further back were some cultivated fields. All else was an unbroken desert of heath, which, after spreading into vast moors, terminates towards the north in the stupendous "Twelve Pins," the finest view of which is seen from Roundstone. Thus the narrow strip of tillage around the town, as contrasted with this ocean of heath, resembled a piece of green selvage on a web of black cloth.

Towards the sea the view was not less singular in its own way. The open ocean was not visible; but in its stead a number of zigzag bays and rugged promontories, intertwining each other in all directions, as if land and sea contended for mastery. The tide was arbiter between them, each reflux turning the scale of victory to one side or other. Of these promontories, the aspect was very desolate, presenting only rocks, or mud, or heather. But the bays looked very gay in the sunshine, resembling long bars of molten silver; and they appeared quite animated when traversed by the numerous fishing-boats under full sail, in the management of which the natives exhibited no small dexterity.

To complete the picture of this strange village, I may add, that having been recently built at the time of my visit, it had then an air of freshness, very unlike its present appearance. For its size, too, it possessed a considerable trade, being the centre of an important herring fishery, which, though even then on the decline, was still so valuable, that many poor people subsisted all the year round on its profits, though the fishing lasted only six weeks at Christmas. Thus, with little labour, every man had the means of subsistence; and if he wished to be industrious, he could get waste land cheap, while every sea-beach furnished the means for reclaiming it, in the shape of sand and sea-weed. Altogether, then, the prospects of the little community were not unpromising. But, alas! since that time the herring fishery, not only there, but all along the west coast, has proved an utter failure. In consequence, Roundstone has rapidly gone downhill; and at present it is the very picture of desolation.

Of this village, the founder was Alexander Nimmo, Esq., the celebrated engineer. He had died some years before my visit; but I found there two of his brothers. Since then they also have gone the "way of all flesh." But I cannot refrain from a passing notice of one brother. He was Mr. George Nimmo. Though advanced in years, yet loving wild scenery, and being of a kind disposition, he sometimes accompanied me in my pedestrian excursions. To beguile our way, he used to relate to me on such occasions anecdotes of what he had seen in foreign lands, having been a great traveller. Of these narratives I may give an example. He had gone to

Germany to purchase timber in the "Black Forest." While riding about there, his horse rubbed his foot against a tree, severely bruising it. In consequence, he could not return home that night, and was obliged to ask lodging at the first house that came in sight. The owner, after hearing his story, made him welcome, gave him supper, and then showed him to his bed-room for the night. Mr. Nimmo, before retiring to rest, happened unconsciously to pray so loud as to be overheard by the family in another apartment. Instantly, to his surprise, the host rushed to the door; and, in a great passion, ordered him not to repeat again that name in the hearing of his family,—meaning the name of Jesus. "If you do," said he, "I will expel you from my house." The man was a Jew.

Alas! how fearful the undying hatred of that race to

> "Jesus, the name that charms our fears,
>   And bids our sorrows cease;
> 'Tis music in the sinner's ears—
>   'Tis life, and health, and peace!"

From the great Engineer, we borrow the following statistics, which will give a good general view of this country. In its utmost extent,—that is, from Galway in the east to Slinehead in the west,—it stretches fully fifty miles; and in the other direction,—from Galway Bay to the Killeries,—about thirty miles. Its most remarkable feature is the number of its lakes, being emphatically what Carlyle calls "an amphibious country." In it there are "twenty-five navigable lakes of a mile or more in length, besides hundreds smaller." "With its islands, it has four hundred miles of sea-coast"—"perhaps as many miles of shore of the sea or navigable lakes as there are square miles of surface;" with "upwards of twenty safe and capacious harbours fit for vessels of any burden." Its superficies, Mr. Nimmo estimates at 350,000 acres.

Of these, in 1814, there were 25,000 arable, 120,000 mountain, 200,000 upland pasture, and 5,000 rock. Its population, including that of Arran, then numbered 76,189. As to its climate, it is mild, there being little snow; but "the summers are wet, and it is exposed to heavy western winds." The latter are the more felt, owing to the total want of trees. And yet, according to Mr. Nimmo, "the country possesses an extensive stool of timber: for in almost every dry knoll or cliff the oak, birch, and hazel appear shooting in abundance, and require only a little care to rise in valuable forests." The beautiful natural wood of Kylemore is an example of this peculiarity of the soil. It is also a fact that forests once abounded here, but they were recklessly "used up" in iron mines, and for "pipe-staves," of which great quantities were exported. This Gothic clearance was complete, not sparing a single tree of the ancient woods; so that an American backwoodsman, on catching a distant view of Connemara, exclaimed, "That is the best cultivated country in the world!"

Of the state of this country in 1685, a curious description is given by Mr. O'Flaherty, in his "Iar-Connaught," to which Mr. Hardiman, the well-known historian, has added valuable notes. Mr. O'F., in his list of its wild animals, specifies "wolves, deere, badgers, hares, rabbits, squirrels, weasels, martens, and the amphibious otter." Of rats he makes no mention; they had not yet gone farther west than the "liberties of Galway." Amongst otters, he notices a "white-faced species," which is "never killed, they say, but with the loss of man or dog; and its skin is mighty precious." Of the wolves, one was very wonderful, according to the annals of Clonmacnoise; for "it was seen and heard to speak with human voice!" But this story is outdone by that of the modern fox, which was said to read the newspapers to find out the "meets" of the hounds. At all events, it is now too late to inquire into the vocal powers of these wolves; for the last of them was killed in Joyce's country in 1700. Still later was the disappearance of the red deer; for Mr. Hardiman knew "an old man in Ross who had seen them grazing among the black cattle on the hills." In Erris, again, they were common till 1752; and in Kerry till 1760. One cause of their destruction, Mr. H. thinks, was a species of murrain, which is still common amongst the deer in Lapland.

Amongst the birds, O'F. mentions "barnacles, wild geese, swans, cocks of the wood, woodcocks, choughs, rooks, Cornish choughs, with red legs and bills," &c. Nor is Connemara ornithology without its marvels. "Here is the bird engendered by the sea out of timber long lying in the sea: some call them clakes, or soland geese; some puffins; others barnacles, because they resemble them. We call them girrin." Not quite so incredible, yet still doubtful, is what he adds concerning the "black eagle;" that it "kills the deer by grappling him with his claws, and forcing him to run headlong over a precipice."

Whales were then common on the coast. One of them being killed at Bunown, and left to rot on the shore, "the surface of the bay was dyed with a rainbow tinge from the floating particles of the oil." Of another, the body measured "thirty-three yards." Much of their "ambergrease," also, was thrown up by the sea, sometimes in masses from sixty to two hundred and twenty-five pounds, which, according to O'F., sold enormously high.

The chief agricultural products were, "as much corn of wheat, barley, oats, and rye, as was enough to sustain the inhabitants and furnish the markets besides." But as yet there is no word of potatoes. The other products were, "beef, tallow, hides; and of late, cheese out of Arran." At present, its beef is neither good nor plentiful; but its mutton is excellent. Many strangers consider the latter a delicacy, together with the salmon, white trout, and turbot; the two last of which are exceedingly cheap in the season.

Of the extensive territory described by Mr. O'F., the western division constitutes Connemara proper. It is far the smaller; but, as regards scenery, the more interesting. Between its views of the Twelve Pins, on one hand, and of the Atlantic on the other, it is indeed the very region of the sublime. And yet, though so mountainous, three-fourths of its surface are not a hundred feet above the level of the sea. This follows from the absence of table-land; and constitutes its greatest agricultural disadvantage. Weeping skies above, and a deficient drainage beneath, form an impassable barrier to the farmer. Spots there are, indeed, which are more favourable for cultivation, and there industry has triumphed over the wilderness. But, for the reason mentioned, agriculture can never be extended over a wide area. Evidently Nature intended this country to remain uncultivated; but is it therefore useless? By no means. While the world lasts, its magnificent scenery will expand the souls of its visitors, and inspire them with thoughts that wander through eternity. It is no waste, then, though it bears no crops. Who finds fault with a picture gallery for not being a dining-room?

To the above statistics, we shall add of our own a few particulars of its Natural History. They were picked up incidentally from the people when learning their Irish; but we cannot vouch for their correctness farther than the fact that they were told by persons who ought to know, and who would not intentionally mislead.

Of its present wild animals, the most numerous are badgers. They abound in the mountains, but are sometimes found in the valleys. Their chief food is grass or hay. This they gather in summer for a winter store, rolling it in balls to the mouths of their holes. They never go out in frost or severe weather; nor in the daytime. During most of the winter they hybernate; but on the approach of May, they return to activity, first clearing out their burrows. The latter they make only where they find previously existing clefts or openings. These they extend inwards to sixty feet or more; and near the end of their gallery, they elevate it several feet, thus giving themselves vantage-ground in case of attack. There posted, they bid defiance to other animals; their teeth being sharp as needles, and meeting an enemy like so many "fixed bayonets." It is said, too, that their front claws are formed like fish-hooks. Thus guarded, their hole is their castle. But if attacked on the hill-side, the case is very different. Then, instead of fighting, they gather themselves together like a ball, and roll headlong down the precipices; nor are they often injured by the fall. Lastly, their flesh is said to be palatable, and is sometimes cured like bacon.

On the coast is a great variety of wild fowl. But some species that were once common, are said to have since disappeared, like the wolves and red deer on land. Of this kind are the barnacle geese. These came in the winter from the countries north of the Baltic, and left again in the spring. One season they were detained beyond the usual time by contrary winds; and, in consequence, they dropped their eggs on the shore. Whether it was for this reason, or more probably from the encroachments of man, at all events they soon after sought other winter quarters.

To another bird I allude because of the singular way in which it is killed. This is a large kind of diver, and is called in Irish *cailleach dubh;* but its English name I know not. Its colour is black; and it is eaten, though its flesh is said to be hard. In taking these birds, the plan adopted is, to row out in a very dark night, carrying in the boat a bag of sand. Approaching noiselessly the low islands on which they roost, handfuls of this sand are thrown over them, which they take to be hail or snow, and so shelter their heads under their wings. In this state they are quietly seized one after another, and their heads are instantly wrung off, lest they should scream, and alarm the rest of the flock. From this custom, I suppose, has originated the phrase of " throwing dust in people's eyes."

Of the herring fishery a few words may be said in passing. Its great value at one time may be learned from the single fact that a gentleman living on the coast told me that he had put up six hundred barrels in one season! Again, in the space of two hours, a fisherman once caught five thousand two hundred fishes. On another occasion, in a quarter of an hour, he took eight thousand; and afterwards, with two boats, he took in two nights, fifteen thousand, and twenty-one thousand, respectively. Equally successful, also, were Scotch fishermen who then fished off our western shores every winter. Indeed the difficulty at that time was, not to catch the herrings, but to find salt for them. There were only two salt-pans adjacent, one at Westport and the other at Galway; so the supply fell far short of the demand. Sometimes £20 were paid for a single ton; and yet the profit realised by it was a hundred per cent! Besides the fish that was barrelled, a great deal was carried away in baskets on horses' backs by cadgers who, in the season, swarmed on the shores and mountain-roads. Still, after all this consumption, in great takes, thousands of herrings were thrown on the shore, as useless, from the want of salt; putrifying in large masses, out of which there ran streams of rich oil.

Seals are still common in their favourite haunts. It is not easy to shoot them, as they are remarkably quick of eye, diving the moment a gun is levelled at them; so that the only way to secure a good aim, is to divert their attention to some other object. But the more successful plan is to attack them wholesale at night in their haunts, and kill them with clubs. On such occasions they sometimes show fight. Once a seal seized in its mouth the stick of an assailant, and flung it so high up a cliff that it remained there inaccessible, till it rotted. If they get the limb of a man between their teeth, they never relax their hold till the bone is heard to crack. When wounded, their cry resembles that of a human being. Contrary to what I had imagined, their flesh is said to be good for eating; but so closely does it adhere to the skin, that as long time is spent in flaying one of them as a cow.

Most readers have heard of the ingenious seal on the coast of Mayo, which, when attacked, exclaimed, "Don't kill me; I am your grandfather." Nor is this Pythagorean opinion of the animal confined to that country. In Connemara, also, they were believed to be a nation under enchantment. In illustration, take the following curious story, which I give in full, as I believe it has never before appeared in print.

A party of fishermen were out one night plying their vocation between the Killeries and Westport, and there they took refuge for some hours in a sea-cave. One man, having fallen into a deep sleep, remained behind after the others had left. He was awaked by the entrance of seals, ignorant of his presence. To his surprise, they all, after some time, assumed human shapes, and cast their old skins aside. They also conversed together, but the burden of their discourse was sad; they bewailed their slain relatives. One of them, holding up a piece of flesh, said—"Ah! this is Winny's hand!" (Winifred's.) Another—"Ah! this is Eva's foot!" "Oh, big Miles, didn't you watch badly yesterday," &c., &c. Having thus for a while indulged their grief, they resumed their skins, and, with them, their former shapes, and then plunged back into the sea. But not all of them; for the fisherman, having admired one of the females, sprang after her from his hiding-place, and seized her just before her metamorphosis. In vain she strove to get free; he held her fast, and brought her home, carrying also her former habiliment. They were married, had a family, and lived happily together. But, in course of time, the thatch of the house took fire, which soon communicated itself to the old sealskin hid there by the husband. No sooner did she smell it burning, than she sprang to the place, and seizing it, put it on her. She then became a seal once more, and fled to the sea. Afterwards, as they say, she was often seen swimming near the shore; and, in keeping with maternal love, she would warn off any of her children who might approach too near it.

According to tradition, this is the pedigree of the tribe of the Coneelys, of whom there are still some in that country; and, till a late period, it was often cast in their teeth by their enemies that they were, "*d'chineal na róntigh*," "of the race of the seals." Such is the story, a very wild one, no doubt—the creature of an oriental imagination; and yet it contains some touches of nature, which, to the simple fisherman, give it the semblance of truth.

To complete this brief statistical sketch of Connemara, we shall describe a day spent alone in its wilds, believing that there is no other way of pourtraying so vividly its peculiar features, and the impressions which they are calculated to produce. The locality selected for this purpose was a wild, desolate moor, to the north-east of Roundstone, and off the line of the roads. My express object in going there, was to test the truth of Dr. Johnson's remark, that a man's feelings in a wilderness are such as could be understood only by experience. Nor can any remark be more correct. In truth, such experience resembles a new window broken into the soul, or a new sense imparted to it. Or, to speak more soberly, it is the waking up of a mental faculty previously dormant for want of its proper stimulus, showing that the human mind is endowed with untold capabilities, which, perhaps, eternity alone can fully develop. Is this the language of æsthetic enthusiasm? We reply that it is not; it is matter of fact. Nor should it be objected that some travellers are not conscious of these impressions. No doubt of that; but let them not apply their experience as a test to that of others differently, and, as we think, more happily constituted.

After this preface, let us briefly describe the scene. As usual in Connemara, it was one wide expanse of heath. To the west, it was bounded by the ocean, which, however, was not visible; and several miles distant, in the opposite direction, towered the grand "Twelve Pins." Vast was the space within those bounds; and yet my eye could discern in it no house, nor other trace of man. Not one acre of tillage was to be seen, though I believe there were patches of it hid in some sheltered valleys. Nor did any domestic animal enliven the cheerless waste. The very birds were gone—both the dumb and the tuneful. The common crow—a ubiquitous bird—was absent here; and so was the sparrow, which, I am told, is found high up, even on the Himaleys. Unrepresented also were the insect tribes. Not one was seen of any species; though I afterwards found at Recess, twelve miles distant, swarms of midges, which, for number and tiny ferocity, outdid their co-geners in any other part of Ireland.

But here were none even of them; in a word, *not one living creature.* All that breathed the breath of life had fled these wilds, or had been starved out of them! reminding me of the satirical verses on the sterility of the Scottish Highlands—

"The plague of locusts they secure defy,
For in three hours a grasshopper would die."

As a small set-off to this utter absence of life, I may mention that afterwards I discovered in this same place one species of bird. And none could be more in keeping with such a scene. It was the carrion-crow, or, as it might be called, the Irish vulture. These birds are found here in pairs, standing moodily on heathery hillocks; and, when disturbed by the unwonted presence of man, they flit away so noiselessly that I do not wonder at their being mistaken by the superstitious for troubled spirits, doomed, for their sins, to spend a certain period in this melancholy shape. This superstition may seem strange, bearing so close a resemblance to the Hindoo transmigration of souls; but I can vouch for the fact of its having been believed by the old people.

Being so cheerless, the scene before me would seem ill-calculated to cause such deep impressions on the mind as I have already stated. But that very desolation itself, being so profound and novel, was deeply impressive; while the less pleasing details were swallowed up in two elements of the sublime. One was—a boundless expanse of surface below; and the other was—a boundless expanse of sunshine above. The effect of these on the mind excluded every other feeling, and filled it with pleasurable emotions. Instead of hedges bounding your view, as elsewhere, with only a narrow strip of sky visible above you, here you behold at one glance hundreds of square miles, spanned at their extremities by the whole concave heaven, filled of a fine day with a blaze of living light, indescribably glorious. To such sunshine on Lebanon the Psalmist alludes, when he describes the Eternal "clothing Himself with light, as with a garment." Magnificent were the robes of oriental monarchs, encrusted all over with precious stones, glittering like stars. But it is with the light itself—and such light as that of a mountain region—that God "clothes" Himself; thus, as an old sage expressed it, "having truth for His soul, and light for His garment."

Let us now ascend Orras Beg, which is close by. This mountain stands quite alone; and though not high compared to the "Pins," yet, being contiguous to the ocean, a grand view is obtained from its summit. At every step upwards, new prospects are presented to us—not yet of the sea, however, for we have taken the opposite or eastern flank. In ascending all the Connemara hills, one is disappointed at finding a series of swampy flats, like terraces, which greatly incommode progress—it being often necessary to "fetch a compass" round them, in order to escape floundering. But those who will rise in the world must expect difficulties; so on we go, taking things as we find them. After much circumnavigating and clambering, we think we have reached the top; but "Alps on Alps successive rise," mocking our hopes. The day being hot, it is wearisome work. But, lo! at last, the *cairn* is in prospect. With quickened step, we clear the last height, and what a glorious view! Before us is spread the great Atlantic. It was the first time that I had obtained a full view of this ocean; consequently, the sight of it was to me most impressive.

Sitting down on a stone, I gazed long on this wondrous scene. But to attempt describing it were vain. I shall only say, that next to the grandeur of the ocean, the most remarkable object in view was the singular zigzag coast-line, being indented by the violent action of the waves to a degree quite wonderful. The shore itself is mostly flat; and often shoots into the sea in long, narrow headlands. Of these, the largest is Sline Head, far away to the north-west, with its two lighthouses; the most westerly point in Ireland. Nearer lie a number of islands; of which, as I was afterwards told, the names are—Innisnee, Innislaccan, Mac-Dara, &c. Again, towards the south, lie the three Isles of Arran in the mouth of the Galway Bay. In clear weather, even Brandon Head, in Kerry, is said to be visible; but that I doubt, from the great distance.

Many were my reflections amid such scenes; but the following alone will be recorded here. Assuming that the Phœnicians were the earliest navigators of this sea, I wonder what were the feelings of their first explorer, who, with bold prow, like another Columbus or Cook, discovered these hitherto unknown coasts; and I admired the enterprise of these ancient mariners who so early overspread all the seas of the world, "as if they had dropped from the clouds." Half amused, I then recollected the statement of a Roman historian—I think Tacitus—who says that, beyond Hibernia, the setting sun, which they fabled as a god driving a fiery chariot, was seen sinking with burning wheels, into the western waves! Such was mythology, deifying everything—specially the heavenly bodies. No doubt, this idolatry was very dishonouring to God; and yet I think it is not half so bad as our modern atheistical-scepticism, which finds God nowhere—

> "Great God, I'd rather be
> A Pagan suckled in a creed out-worn;
> So might I, standing on this pleasant lea,
> Have glimpses that would make me less forlorn—
> The sight of Proteous coming from the sea,
> Or hear old Triton blow his wreathed horn."

Amid these reflections, it were strange if I should forget our own Celtic tradition, that far away in these waters lay Hy-Brazil, or the Isles of the Blessed. Of this, wrote Mr. Roderick O'Flaherty, in 1684—"Whether it be real, firm land, kept hidden by special providence of God, as the terrestrial paradise, or some illusion of airy clouds appearing on the surface of the sea, or the craft of evil spirits, is more than our judgment can sound out." (sic.) But not doubtfully, like Mr. O'Flaherty, felt millions of his untutored countrymen on the subject; and one of them—Morogh O'Ley—positively affirmed that he had spent two days in it; and as a relic of it, brought back a beautiful book. This is, at the present moment, preserved in the Royal Irish Academy. It is a medical work; "contains forty-six large quarto folios, very well written in Irish and Latin; each page presenting the appearance of a complex astrological figure." The diseases, with their cures, are "arranged in parallel columns, headed, Prognostics, Region, Season, Age," &c.

Without testing Mr. O'Ley's story, it is certain, at all events, that for ages this Hy-Brazil was believed to be the abode of departed spirits. Thither, on the setting sunbeams, I suppose, disembodied souls winged their flight, and there rejoined the spirits of their ancestors; and there, too, in never-ending bliss, they ate the ambrosial fruit, and the enchanted apples of the Hesperides. It was a pleasing dream; the relic (though greatly disfigured) of man's primeval bliss; and an aspiration after the restoration of that happy state. And are not all similar aspirations proofs, apart from revelation, of our being outcasts from a higher existence? And, in still cherishing these feelings, do not mankind virtually yearn after that Divine Restorer, who, alone, having expiated their guilt, is able to satisfy such longings. Hence, He is called in Scripture, the "Desire of all nations." Not as if they literally desired Him ; that they do not, but rather hate Him. But what they do desire to make them happy—what their fables of " Happy Isles" symbolized only to tantalize them—all that is treasured up in Him. And when the " veil is taken away from their hearts," then they will desire Him really and fervently, and not as now, blindly and instinctively, as the young lions are said " to seek their food from God."

Reader and fellow-outcast from Paradise, do you wish to know the way to this Holy One—our great Restorer? That way is meritoriously by His blood—efficiently by His Spirit—and instrumentally by His Word. And with this great thought, we close the scene on Orras Beg.

Such is Connemara in its best aspects ; but it has its dark side too. And both are in the extreme. Nowhere else does a fine day appear to such advantage ; but nowhere else is the storm so terrible.

In my past life I have known cases in which a very plain human face looked beautiful, because lit up by a brilliant intellect. The mind within, like a lamp behind a picture, made the features luminous and attractive. Such also is the effect of sunshine in Connemara. But without that attraction, it is a very gloomy place ; thus accounting for the diversity of opinions regarding it. And if even in summer it is dull of a misty day, what is it in winter, when, for weeks together, dark clouds obscure its sky, and pour down torrents of rain, which turn it into a marsh ? At other times, as already remarked, fierce westerly winds off the Atlantic sweep it with a fury unknown to the rest of the island, reminding one of Virgil's cave of Æolus. When overtaken by these storms, I have found it difficult to keep my feet; and I was told an instance in which a woman was raised from the ground by the wind, and blown against a house. As a protection against these winds, the houses are sometimes defended with double doors and windows. It has also passed into a malicious proverb, "*Go mbheith d' theach air ard*," "May your house be on a height:" implying that this would be a calamity. Hence, too, a fact which has surprised many strangers—that districts which at first appeared uninhabited were found nevertheless to contain a considerable population. The explanation is, that to escape these high winds, the villages were built behind sheltering hills, or in the bosom of the valleys.

In such a wet climate, during the winter, I seldom enjoyed even a dry walk. Nor was my imprisonment in the house relieved by congenial society, or by a sufficient supply of books. In a word, there was the absence of all ordinary comforts, which might be endured with equanimity for a time; but, when long continued, it was very depressing.

To these discomforts may be added that of the house in which I dwelt. Finding the inn too public a place to lodge in, I was obliged, in want of a better, to put up with lodgings as miserable as need be. Outwardly the house seemed good enough, being two storeys and slated. But it had never been finished inside; and thus resembled a large barn. Of the interior, a part was enclosed for me, forming a small sitting and bed-room. So far so good; but, alas! the roof was not staunch. Through chinks in it the sky was visible, and when the winter set in, I had to "rough it" in earnest. To keep off the drops, my host covered my bed with plates and dishes; but the moisture would not take the hint that its presence was unwelcome; so on my awakening some mornings, I saw pools of it on the earthen floor! In this wretched abode I spent four months. A brother minister, who was appointed to take my place for six weeks, actually wept when shown his quarters. And yet many Romanists, who saw me endure all this, and more, will not be persuaded that in voluntarily undertaking it for their good, I was not actuated by sordid motives.

Such was my first winter in the West; reminding me of the remark of an English gentleman, to whom I had observed that it was a nice country. "Yes; a nice country to *visit*." That was the truth, as I now found to my cost. But I reaped one benefit from such experience; it cast me more on Divine comfort, and thus prepared me for subsequent trials. This will appear from the following verses, which were composed at that time, but not being intended for the public eye, are now, after a lapse of twenty-two years, published, only as illustrative of Connemara life in winter. If the longings there expressed for home seem excessive, let it be remembered that I was very young at the time, and had never before lived out of my native Ulster. And if the religious allusions appear to some readers as "cant," or the like, I beg to set myself right once for all on that point, as similar professions will occur again in the subsequent pages. With this view, I shall repeat a brief conversation which I once held on the subject with a fellow-traveller on a stage-coach. It was introduced by his reflecting generally on religious people.

"Why, so, may I ask?"

"Because they are always making themselves out better than they really are." Of this he gave an instance which had recently come under his observation.

"Now, Sir, I profess to be a religious man, and perhaps you will allow me to explain what I mean by that. I believe that if I get my deserving, I'll be put in a pit of fire, to burn there for ever. You do not know my personal character; but if you did, I do not suppose you would think worse of me than that?"

"Certainly not."

"Well, but suppose that from this deserved punishment a Friend delivers me merely out of his own kindness, do you think that it would be presumptuous in me to mention the fact to his honor, and from a feeling of gratitude? Now, that is what I mean by making a religious profession."

"Well, I must candidly say that I never took that view of it before."

That he spoke sincerely appeared from his giving up his prejudices, and treating me kindly to the end of our journey. May I not hope, then, that the recital of this conversation will obtain for me from the general reader an equally charitable construction of the religious profession made in these verses, or elsewhere in the volume?

MUSINGS

During a moonlight walk on the heath, alone, in winter—the ocean in the distance, on which a storm is rising.

'Tis silence around me—the sleep of the dead—
Save the ocean's hoarse voice, from its oft-heaving bed;
Or portentous sounds, where storm-clouds fly,
On dark rustling wings, through the western sky.

Ye spirits of storm! to you, oh, I call—
My voice do you hear from your blustering hall?
Ah! pity these hills, and spare these sad plains!
Shall winter for ever thus blast your domains?

Your wild blasts call off; cease rain, hail, and snow;
For once let the Spring her balmy gales blow;
And over these wastes—a bare wintry scene—
Let her cast her soft robe of the purest of green.

Let her spread far and wide a forest of shade,
Where now blasted heath-stems eternally fade;
And lonely and sad—thin sown in the vale—
The long, spiky grass shakes its head in the gale.

Let Pansy and Primrose their bosoms unfold,
And blush to the sun in their petals of gold;
While Daisy and Bluebell combine to adorn,
And drink in their cups here the dews of the morn.

And here—Ah! cease, fond fancy, I pray,
Nor thus lead my mind far wand'ring away;
'Twas my home that I wish'd—but wish'd it in vain—
To bloom far away on this desolate plain.

How sweet, yet how sad, like the moon's silver beam,
That plays on the face of yon mountain stream:
'Tis thus, oh! my home, 'tis thus you appear,
And call from my eyes the fast-falling tear.

* * * * * *

Ah! no friend can I see—no brother is near;
No hand to grasp mine—no greeting I hear;
No happy fireside, with friends seated round;
But the stormy sea-cloud, with its unearthly sound.

And careless and cold, the moon hides her head;
And 'tis silence all round me—ah! silence how dead!
While over the deep, and across the lone heath,
The blast still is sighing a lone knell of death.

And life is extinct; and each living thing
Has fled far away from this desolate scene.
Here bird, beast, and insect, all—all are unknown—
Nought but a stranger wand'ring alone.

What a wanderer I, ye mountains know well;
That I've traversed you oft, each of you can tell.
With you I've conversed, and conversed with the deep—
While with joy I now smile—now with sorrow I weep.

Oft lonely and sad in the dim twilight eve,
When the sun was just touching the western wave,
You have seen me to wander the trackless heath o'er,
Or sit watching the waves on the surge-beaten shore.

Here, with soul wrapp'd in thought, my eyes back I cast
On times that are gone—on scenes now long past;
Of a Saviour I've thought—of the grave's narrow bed—
Then of friends dearly loved, who now sleep with the dead.

The world has vanish'd away from my soul—
Its pleasures, and cares, and vanities all;
While, wearied of earth, to my Saviour I'd pray
For the wings of a cherub to bear me away.

This bright hope it was that check'd my sad sigh,
And dried up the tear that stood in my eye.
By this, heath-clad hill and wild lonely sea
An Eden of bliss were made unto me.

Such joy did I feel, though friend I knew none—
But in desolate scenes I've wander'd alone—
Methought that some times, in the shades of the even,
The angels unbarr'd the portals of heaven;

While, sweet and enchanting, I thought I could hear
Voices celestial salute my glad ear;
And Bethlehem's plains display'd to my sight
The glory Divine of that sacred night.

Next to Calvary's hill I'd turn my eyes—
Now gushing tears stream—now raptures arise—
Till, able no longer my soul to restrain,
Forth bursts to the wilds the heavenly strain.

Farewell, then, ye wilds, grim and sad though ye be,
Yet Jesus has given you charms for me;
With Him each lone hill-top a ladder supplies,
Like that seen in Bethel to mount to the skies.

CHAPTER II.

ITS PEOPLE—THEIR MANNERS, CUSTOMS, AND LANGUAGE.

No Middle Class in Connemara—Injurious Effects of this, and of their attachment to old customs—Their Dress—Story of a Bonnet—Their Cabins—Anecdote of a Bedstead—Smuggling—Litigiousness—Dialogue on the Road—Pious Phrases—Want of Thrift—Intemperance—Evil of it—Dances—Practical Jokes—Trick of Shan na Geos on a Pedlar, and " Outwitting the Gauger"—The Irish Language—Its Resemblance to Hebrew—Its Extinction still distant—Why its Bible so attractive—Orthographic Reform—How far Irish is useful—Samples of bad English—Anecdote of an Umbrella—A Solemn Thought in Conclusion.

AFTER saying so much of the country, I come now to speak of the people. In so doing, however, I shall at present content myself with first impressions, such as might occur to any stranger. More important information will turn up afterwards, when I come to describe my intercourse with them on religious subjects.

We have before remarked of Connemara, that its most prominent feature, physically, is its being all mountain or plain, and having no table land. A similar remark may be made of its social state. In common with the South and West generally, it is composed of the highest and lowest, and has no middle class. This was the case in 1840; and to a great extent it is so still. Of this want the injurious effects are manifest. A middle class, combining the intelligence of the higher order with the industry of the lower—equally removed from the harassing cares of the one, and the enervating luxuries of the other—are the bone and sinew of any land—the inheritors of its virtues, and the guardians of its liberties. Whenever, then, such a class is wanting, the keystone of the social arch is wanting; and no laws or political constitution can supply the loss. As a necessary consequence, the rich and poor being too widely separated for sympathy or co-operation, become mutually estranged, and prone to collisions, of which we have seen so many examples in the Continental revolutions. But of such a catastrophe there is no danger in Connemara, and that for other reasons. The Celt is not a revolutionizing animal; and still less the Celtic mountaineer. He is only too wedded to old customs, and too inclined to content himself with his lot, however miserable, consoling himself with the thought that it is hereditary. His ancestors were no better off: why, then, should he complain? In India trades are hereditary: a tailor inherits that employment from his father, and thinks no more of forsaking it for another than of changing his planet. Somewhat the same is the feeling of the old Celts, who, in other respects also, prove themselves to be an oriental race. This principle, being founded on love to ancestors, is so far good; but in the excess it is ruinous. It hopelessly conflicts with modern civilization, of which the great law is progress: nor is there any resisting this law, more than a railway train in motion. So the uneducated Celt, by clinging to the past, and falling behind his countrymen in their onward march, is either thrown into the ditch, or obliged to fly for bread to foreign lands. This is a terrible calamity to him, with his strong attachment to his native hills and fathers' graves. Alas! that it should be often the result of the want of a right education, and of an undue attachment to old customs.

The extent to which antiquated social notions are still entertained in the remote districts is astonishing. Thus some old people, like the fossils of a past age, imagine that because the land once belonged to their fathers, they are entitled to share its fruits, no matter who tills the soil, or how often it has since changed hands by lawful purchase—a delusion incompatible with the first principles of civilization. Under the influence of this feeling, a woman once bitterly complained to me that she could not get a comfortable house for herself, owing to the influx of strangers; thinking that none of them should be served till after the natives, whether the latter paid the proper rent or no! It never occurred to her that respectable strangers coming to spend their incomes among them, confer a favor rather than receive one. Still more outspoken was a virago, who in a workhouse headed an outbreak against the dietary, and whose watchword was—"My forefathers ate beef and mutton, and I must get the same." This notion, ludicrous as it may appear, is a serious matter in its results, being the source of many social outrages. Let us, then, implore all who have influence over our lower orders, to disabuse their minds of such a delusion; and in its stead, to inculcate the great Christian and common-sense principle, that if a man has got a mouth to be filled, he has got also two hands to work for it; or as Scripture says, "By the sweat of his face, he must eat bread till he return unto the ground;" and "If any man will not work, let him not eat;" that is, give him nothing to eat. By this Divine law, which is as unchangeable as that of the tides or seasons, men must work or want. The idler, like the sea-weed, is the sport of every wave, till cast on some foreign shore to rot; while the industrious man strikes root in his native soil like the oak. In other words, as Scripture affirms, "The hand of the diligent maketh rich." Nor is there any other way: for all "short and easy methods," for wealth national or individual, resemble Dean Swift's ingenious plan "for defraying the national debt without the payment of a farthing."

The want of a middle rank was brought out painfully by

the famine. Elsewhere this class, besides largely employing the poor, and thus lessening the mass of want, formed themselves into relief committees for the collection of subscriptions, establishing soup-kitchens, &c. But in most of Connemara such useful philanthropists were not forthcoming. The inhabitants were all on a level. None could help the other, and there were few men of mark among them to seek help from abroad. The clergy alone could not overtake a tenth part of the misery, specially as the parishes were large and the population thinly scattered. Thus, multitudes perished unknown in their wretched cabins; and very often, the survivors had none to assist them in burying the corpses. A poor girl had to carry on her back the remains—first of her mother, and then of her brother and sister, and to scrape with her own hands graves for them in the garden! What a melancholy funeral! In what a fallen world do we live, and what fallen creatures we be! What a lesson, also, to the poor elsewhere not to hate the rich—and to the rich everywhere to help the poor! We need each other's sympathy; and, according to God's law, the rich or poor shall have "judgment without mercy who have showed no mercy."

Except in time of famine, however, the condition of this people was not so bad as might be supposed. Of land, such as it was, every one could have a little, and without much trouble he could convert part of it into a potato-garden, and the rest of it into turbary. Thus, he was sure of the Irish necessaries of life—potatoes and turf. And, after all, good potatoes all the year round, with a blazing fire in the winter, were not to be despised. At the time we allude to, he might also calculate upon a cheap luxury in the shape of fish, either from the herring-fishery, which was then most flourishing, or, before the introduction of fishery laws, by angling for himself in the streams and lakes. In the latter way, by the use of cross lines, I have heard of a person taking, in one day, "eighteen dozen of trout." To crown his comfort, he might also keep a cow, which, if she gave no butter—a rare thing on such pasture—supplied him with abundant milk. The cheapness of her keep may be inferred from the fact, that a farmer once offered me grass for a pony at a shilling a month!

Another thing that reconciled them to their lot, was their ignorance of a better. Seldom did they see a home more comfortable than their own. Of the slated houses, or lordly mansions, there were then few; nor was there, as in large cities, the tempting sight of grandeur, flaunting in her silks, or reclining voluptuously in her gilt chariot. Neither were they tantalized by the display of luxurious food or dress in shop windows, in regard to which few can moralise with Socrates, after his seeing such displays at Athens—"How many things are here which I do not want." On the contrary, the sight of such things generally produces a feeling of covetousness. A child of my acquaintance, in repeating the Lord's Prayer, unconsciously interpolated in one of the petitions, "Give us this day our bread and butter." That is human nature; its fall began in desiring more earthly good than God gave, and it evinces the same propensity still. And though Divine grace can overcome it in any circumstances, as Daniel was incorrupt in a luxurious court; yet, ordinarily we are safest when altogether removed from temptation. Nor do we know how much of our integrity is owing to our path being providentially so ordered, agreeably to what God said to Abimelech—"I have withheld thee from sinning against me."

Taking a closer view of the Connemara people, the first peculiarity that strikes us is their dress. In some countries the dress is quite as characteristic as their language or religion. Such is the toga of the Romans, the turban of the Turks, and the kilt of the Highlanders. But here such a national costume is wanting; and instead of it, a nondescript thing, as unmeaning as it is unpicturesque. The men seemed to have borrowed the cut of their clothes from sailors; for they wore only a loose jacket and trousers. The material was home-made flannel, undyed, and therefore not becoming. Unknown amongst them was the comfortable frieze surtout of the inland peasantry; and so also their dress suit, consisting of a body coat of the same material, and corduroy breeches buttoned at the knees. This latter fashion, by the way, though now despised as vulgar, was the ancient court dress of England! Truth is stranger than fiction. So to this day the peasantry keep up a fashion which their ancestry first learned, near three centuries ago, from the Irish gentry who attended the levees of the great Tudor Queen.

Of the females the dress was still more singular. At chapel or market, some of them wore round their shoulders the quilt taken off the bed! But this was owing to poverty. Again, instead of a cap or bonnet, the older women wrapped round their heads a small shawl, tied under the chin, thus sacrificing the graces to comfort. But the most remarkable part of their costume was a flaming red petticoat. This was manufactured by themselves, and dyed with madder. Cloaks of the same kind were sometimes used; and contrasted oddly with the dark colour of the heather. Thus attired, a party of old women would pass, at a distance, for so many dismounted dragoons: begging pardon of my military readers for so undignified a comparison.

That the deficiencies of the peasantry, in dress or otherwise, were not owing to a want of natural taste on their part, appeared from their rapid improvement when favoured with ordinary advantages. Young persons who obtained situations in respectable families, or who emigrated to America, very soon abandoned their old habits, and excelled in the neatness of their persons as well as in general intelligence. In many cases this metamorphosis was complete. A few days ago, a poor woman showed me a photograph of her daughter in America, who had married comfortably there, and whose elegant attire differed most singularly from what she had been accustomed to in her native cabin. Not greater the contrast between the painted wings of a butterfly, and its original grub habiliments. This is not said in admiration of mere dress, which all classes prize too highly, but to show how quickly this people improve under favourable circumstances.

That they do not improve equally at home is owing, as we before observed, to their absurd antipathy to innovation. Of this, an amusing case came to my knowledge at Galway. There a servant-maid obtained a situation on condition of wearing a bonnet to which she, with others of her rank, had a great objection. The next Sunday, when going to Mass, was the first time in which she had occasion to appear with this new-fangled article, and she did put it on; but no sooner was she out of sight of her master's house, than she hid it in a grove till her return.

Of all the instances of their improvement which came under my observation, the most remarkable was at the Ballinahinch Fishery. There, within three miles of Roundstone, a Scotchman had set up an establishment for curing salmon, by enclosing them hermetically in tin cases, in which state they would keep fresh for many years. This process requires no small skill on part of the workmen; and yet, some of them, who were intelligent and well dressed when I saw them, had come there only a few years before girdled with straw ropes to keep their rags together. And in that wretched state they would have remained, only that they were here supplied with a stimulus to work. And after all, without that, who will work more than the Celts? No man will work for work's sake. But when remunerative employment is given, what people have done more than our countrymen, specially our emigrants, who at home, indeed, were idle, or industrious only by fits and starts, but beyond the Atlantic have performed prodigies of labour—felling the forests, digging canals, and levelling railways? What a pity that such industrial capabilities were not utilized at home in developing our own resources—agricultural, mineral and commercial.

From cases like that at Ballinahinch our people are learning to give up former prejudices against strangers; and it is for their own interest to do so. Of course all strangers are not such as should be desired; but those who introduce capital, or, what is the same, industry guided by intelligence, are our greatest benefactors. And if, in developing our resources, they at the same time enrich themselves, that is no loss to us, as they circulate amongst us ten pounds for one which they pocket; and the money which our poor thus honestly earn is a greater gain to them than would be ten times the amount of charity: it is a perennial fountain, as compared with a passing shower. If, then, our people are wise, they will welcome such strangers among them, and sternly discountenance all interference with them. If they do not, let them no longer complain of want of employment. Besides, if they give way to such prejudices, where are they to stop? Our only native fruits are sloes, haws, and the like. Our very cereals are importations. It is a disputed point whence we get them; but certainly they are not indigenous. Even our Christianity is the gift of strangers; for whether St. Patrick was a Scotchman or a Frenchman, at all events he was not an Irishman.

The transition state of this people was evidenced, not only by their dress, but also by their houses. Some of these seemed relics of a remote antiquity. They were half cave and half hovel. In making them, a hole of the requisite dimensions was dug in the side of a dry hill, the depth ranging from four to six feet. Over this a low roof of sticks was thrown from side to side, and afterwards thatched with sedge. Wall there was none, except what enclosed the front; and thus the habitation was complete! Such huts are still found in the remoter districts. Even in the immediate vicinity of Roundstone I found one, which laboured under this great disadvantage, that it was excavated, not in high ground, as elsewhere, but in a low mud bank! How it escaped being overflowed by the mire in winter, I could not conceive; but I resolved to inquire; so descending through the door, which resembled the mouth of a cave, I ventured into the smoky apartment below. No one appeared inside, but a few children, who could not speak a word of English; so, without further examination of this place, I returned to the light of day. What a wonderful place, thought I, for human beings to live in!

Of the best class of cabins, one description will suffice, as they are all built on the same plan. The side walls are formed of rough stones, put together without mortar, or only with mud; and they rise generally to about six feet. The gables are built of similar materials, and are generally rounded at the top. The thatch is composed, not of straw, but of a long wiry grass called sedge, which grows along the mountain streams. To bind it on, ropes are thrown across the roof, and tied on each side to heavy stones at the eaves, resembling a string of beads. For a chimney a hole is left in the roof; its proximity to the thatch exciting the stranger's surprise that conflagrations are not of daily occurrence. This, however, is accounted for by the fact, that the chimney has quite a sinecure of it; for the smoke, following its own fancy, generally makes its exit through the door! But when I say door, I do not use the word in the ordinary sense. Properly speaking, it was a mere aperture, of which each house had two; so that, in the great winds peculiar to this country, one of them could always be open on the sheltered side. But as to a regular door, the primitive cabins had none, using a straw mat instead. And what is very remarkable, considering the wildness of the country, this frail defence was quite sufficient at night for the safety of the inmates. House-breaking was unknown. Even at present, some respectable families, whose houses have strong doors, never lock or bolt them; and experience proves that there is no need. In this world of ours what extremes meet! Here is a district famous during many ages for its lawlessness; and yet, in regard to burglary, it has enjoyed an immunity, which a small army of constabulary cannot secure for highly civilized Dublin or London. Surely, after all, there is something to love in a patriarchal state of society.

Let us now take a peep into the interior of a cabin. The Connemara people are hospitable, and will not count us intruders, especially as our visit is made with no unfriendly intent. In some cabins, alas! the first glance shows, by the pools in the floor and the green streaks along the walls, that the roof is not staunch. This is wretched in so humid a climate; of which a native wit once remarked, "In Connemara it rains thirteen months in the year!" And yet it is wonderful how habit reconciles people even to this discomfort. With great coolness a poor cottier once replied to a gentleman who complained, after flying to his house for shelter, that the rain followed him there; "Why then, Sir, the way here is, when it's fair without, it's fair within; and when it's wet without, it's wet within!"

The difficulty of tidiness in such houses was increased in other ways. The pig claimed the "run of the house;" while the roof was occupied by the "hens, the crathurs." In former times, too, the cattle were domiciled in the kitchen. Of course, under such circumstances, cleanliness was a rare attainment. But a change for the better has set in, and I trust will increase; for after all, Liebig's assertion is true, that the amount of soap consumed by any people is an index of their civilization.

Let us now glance at the accommodation for the night. That a little room was generally set apart for this purpose is true; but alas! for a bed. Instead of it, we only find a heap of rushes! When I was in Recess last summer, I was informed of a farmer there who possessed a whole herd of young horses, and yet had never used a better bed. But about that time he began to think that in his improved circumstances he might treat himself to a bedstead. It so happened, however, the very first night he slept on it, that one of his ponies was smothered in a marsh. Superstitiously ascribing the accident to the new article of furniture, he indignantly ejected it from his house, and left it to rot under the rains. Then, with a relieved mind, he returned to the rushes on which, without any disaster, he had so long luxuriated, in what a sleepy author calls "sweet horizontal enjoyment."

Having thus sketched the costume and the habitations of Connemara as late as 1840, I shall, with equal brevity, describe its other social peculiarities, arranging the different illustrative particulars in the order in which they came under my own observation.

Of all their strange notions, the most singular was their

opinion of the excellent roads made through the district some years previously. Considering the engineering difficulties which had to be overcome, these roads form an imperishable monument of the skill of Mr. Alexander Nimmo, by whom they were planned and executed. For this service alone, indeed, Mr. Hardiman, the historian, justly pronounces him the greatest benefactor to Connemara that has ever existed. But what was the opinion of the natives themselves on the subject? Why, some of them openly denounced these roads as a curse! Their saying was—" There is no luck in the country since they began to make the roads, and to build the big (slated) houses!"

An opinion so odd amazed me; but, on further acquaintance, I ascertained their reason for it, and certainly it was a substantial one. While the district remained inaccessible, it formed the emporium of a smuggling trade with America and the West Indies; and this, to many of the inhabitants, was a mine of gold. In carrying on this traffic, a whole district clubbed together for the purchase and freight of suitable vessels, each contributor receiving an amount of profit proportioned to his investment, but sharing also in the risk; for the invariable proviso was—" barring capture and dangers of the sea." But capture was a rare occurrence at that time, as the Government kept no strict watch on the numerous bays of the west coast; consequently the whole district was filled with valuable contraband goods, such as sugar, rum, brandy, tobacco, and wine. By stealth these imports were disposed of to the shopkeepers of the neighbouring towns. Still a surplus remained in Connemara sufficient to reduce their price there to a minimum; and so this sterile country abounded in the luxuries of life! Not without truth, then, did an old man tell me in Irish, that "there was not at that time so plentiful a country for a poor man in all the nine regions!"

The making of the roads, however, put to flight these illgot gains; and on their departure, like other demoralizing practices, they left the country poorer than they had found it.

A few weeks after my arrival at Roundstone, a court happened to be held in the village. This developed another trait of their character—I mean litigiousness. In former times their boast was that the "king's writ did not run in Connemara!"—in other words, British law possessed there no force whatever. But at the time of my visit, they went to the opposite extreme, and invoked the law on all occasions. It would seem as if their fighting propensities, which formerly vented themselves through the stone or the cudgel, had now transmigrated into the entangling meshes of "Nisi Prius" and "Fieri Facias." But be that as it may, the court on this occasion was crowded. That all present had business on hand, I do not believe; no doubt, many attended merely to "learn law" for future use. Great, also, was the energy of the litigants; for sometimes, after the magistrates had decided the case, they retired to the street, and there, with great clamour, discussed the whole affair over again. Their earnestness was the more remarkable, as, in some cases, the interests at stake were small. Thus, a plaintiff, seeking compensation for damages, on being pressed by the court to state their amount, estimated them at sixpence! Another case reminded me of the old state of things. A quarrelsome fellow, convicted of an assault, was fined in the sum of half-a-crown. He paid it; and then raising his fist, in the presence of the magistrate, he struck the plaintiff another blow! Again he was fined the same sum as before; and again he paid it. Then, rushing to the door, he shouted triumphantly to the crowd outside—"Oh! boys, don't spare one another; fight away as much as ye plaze—'t will be only half-a-crown a-piece to yees!"

It were a mistake, however, to infer from this case, that the law did not soon obtain a salutary influence over the popular mind. It certainly did; restraining by fear those who were inaccessible to higher motives. In consequence, the well-known lawlessness of the district has gradually given way to habits of peace and order. Of this wholesome fear of the law, one instance was narrated to me, which, though partaking of the ludicrous, supplies a case in point. A quarrel happened to take place between an old pensioner and a neighbour. The military man ran in for his gun, and presented it at his opponent. The latter, nothing daunted, raised a stone; and boldly facing his armed antagonist, cried out in Irish—"*An maitheadh tu an dlighe*"—"Will you forgive the law?" As much as to say—"I, with my stone, will fight you with your gun; only first promise that if I beat you, you will not prosecute me at the law." Thus he was more afraid of the law than of a loaded musket! A proof that good government was effectually subduing the turbulence of the people, to their own great advantage, temporal and eternal.

It may be more satisfactory to the reader if I now permit a Connemara man to speak for himself; presenting, in substance, a conversation which I had with him on the road to Ballinahinch. The individual referred to was a total stranger to me; but, from his dress, I conjectured that he was a fisherman. In the sentiments expressed by us, of course, there is nothing remarkable; but they will exemplify the kind of converse usual here amongst strangers when meeting by the wayside:—

"This is a fine evening."

"A fine evening, glory be to God, sir."

"I hope it will do good to the crops."

"They want that, sir. It's not in this part of the country you live, sir?"

"No; not in this country, except for a short time. I hope the crops will be good this year."

"I hope they will. Will you stay long in this country, sir?"

"No; I think not."

"I'm thinking that you're from Leinster, sir?"

Finding that this question must be answered, I gave the desired information, and resumed.

"How is the land set here?"

"They set it with a spade, sir."

"No; that's not what I mean. How is it set by the acre?"

"We have no acres here at all, sir."

This was true, as land is still set there by the bulk. Thus, a farmer says, I have twenty pounds worth of land; meaning, I pay so much rent.

"What time in the year does the herring fishing commence?"

"A little after Christmas, sir."

"Does it continue long?"

"Sometimes for two months, and sometimes less."

"And what do the fishermen do all the rest of the year?"

"Sometimes they take other fish; but often they do nothing at all. Most of them have little gardens to work in; but fishermen seldom mind such things."

"Well, now, that's a great wonder; and many of them almost starving."

"True for you, sir."

"And why do they not lay up in winter for the scarcity of the summer. Sure they ought to work as well as to fish, and keep themselves from want."

"Oh, when they have enough, they never think of want. They sometimes, in the fishing season, catch five pounds' worth of herrings in one night, and that in one boat; but when they have it, they're never *asy* till it's spent; and, signs on them, they're now in black want."

"They deserve it, too, if they act in that manner. Surely, when they have a superabundance to-day, they ought to lay aside something for to-morrow."

"Oh, yes, sir; but they trust God for to-morrow."

During the rest of the conversation, he informed me that he had travelled that day twenty-eight miles, to "take the pledge" from Father Mathew, who, however, did not appear as expected—that his Reverence had wrought a great many miracles, and by that means had converted many Protestants—and that the infraction of the pledge would certainly be followed by some awful judgment from God.

In the above dialogue the reader will notice the frequent allusion made by this fisherman to the Divine name. The same feature runs through all their conversations. In their forms of salutations they constantly refer to God; and to Him they invariably ascribe every blessing, temporal and spiritual. Again, in praising any person or animal, they always bless the same in the name of God; and they never enter on any undertaking, however trifling, without invoking "*cungnamh De*"—that is, "the help of God." This custom, though disapproved of by many pious strangers, on the supposition of its being insincere, and engendering an unbecoming familiarity with sacred things, forms, nevertheless, a relic of a purer and Scriptural faith in ancient times. Thus, according to O'Donovan, our greatest Irish philologist, the common salutation, *Dia dhuit*, equivalent to "God bless you," was originally, *Aon Dhia dhuit*, or the "One God bless you." He adds that this phrase dates as far back as the introduction of Christianity into Ireland, and that it was adopted by the early converts as a watchword by which to discover each other. Such being the case, I confess that I am partial to these pious old expressions; and as to the charge of their being insincere, surely it is not a *necessary* consequence they should be so. That a time is coming when true religion will sanctify all social relations, and pass downwards to the most ordinary affairs of life, is what most Christians understand by the Scripture prophecy, that, "on the bells of the horses will be written, Holiness to the Lord." Instead, then, of condemning the Irishman's pious phrases, let us rather try, by Scriptural means, to imbue his soul with their sacred import; and then this custom will be at once consonant to Scripture, profitable to society, and pleasing to God.

Another observation suggested by this dialogue is the want of thrift. This is a homely virtue; but, for the poor, a most important one. On it depends their comfort, more than on the amount of their earnings; for, "without thrift, their wages are put into a bag with holes," disappearing they know not how. In this case, the absence of such a virtue is partly excusable on the ground that the people are generally fishermen—a class always improvident. But the other classes, also, were the same, proving that the source lies deeper. Accordingly we find that thrift is a concomitant, and therefore a consequence, of true religion. For forethought, which is the basis of it, will not be exercised as regards earthly things, unless it has been previously exercised as regards the eternal. And false religions, by discouraging reflection, and encouraging slavish dependence on the clergy, destroy that industrious self-reliance which is the spring of all social progress as well as financial foresight.

Such being the true view of the matter, what are we to

think of an English tourist who ascribes the superior comfort of the northern peasantry solely to "Scotch thrift." This is shallow philosophy. By digging deeper he would have found that such thrift is not inherent in the Scotch nature. When the Reformation, another name for primitive Christianity, dawned upon that nation, they were as deficient as others in this virtue; and at the present, whenever they fall away from their religion, they make shipwreck of this, as well as their other virtues. That this is the fact is seen in their mining and manufacturing districts, which, unfortunately, are hotbeds of infidelity, and in which, consequently, a reckless wastefulness is quite common. In one such locality, according to that eminent philanthropist, Rev. Dr. Guthrie, every fourth house is a whiskey-shop! And so, also, in England, amongst a similar class. Well authenticated cases have been cited of skilled workmen there, earning from one to two pounds a week, and yet, for the reason assigned, as wretched in their homes as an Irish peasant on a shilling a day. Their wives and children were half-starved; their clothes were ragged or pawned; and their houses without ordinary furniture. Why do we dwell on this unhappy state of things? Certainly not from any unkind feeling towards the sister countries; but to impress upon all, the great truth that domestic comfort, with other blessings, depends chiefly on the possession of true religion. That it does not generally secure great wealth is true; but it secures a little; and by thrift it makes that little go a great way; verifying the Scripture that, "a little that a righteous man hath is better than the riches of many wicked."

Of intemperance, happily, I saw but little in Connemara. Whatever its prevalence formerly, or at that time privately, at all events it gave no public indication of its existence. During all this visit I do not remember once meeting a drunken man! Then, indeed, was the great temperance era from which there was subsequently a general falling away; but still a great social reform had been achieved. The habits of the people were changed; and the beneficial effects remain to this day. Though the motives leading to this change may not have been of the most enlightened character, yet, on the whole, it forms a fair subject of rejoicing to the Christian patriot, and should encourage him to labour for the expulsion of this demon vice from all parts of our land. Once in passing through a midland county I had the curiosity to visit a large distillery, in which I found that on the same day there had been "steeped" no less than 150 barrels of barley! Is any calculation necessary to show that in this way, over all Ireland, there is consumed of human food what would support the entire poor of the land, thus superseding our workhouses, with their heavy taxation and demoralizing influences. Only let Ireland cease for a year from intoxicating drinks, and this miracle would be accomplished! The Creator, in His bountiful providence gives enough for all; but man, in his folly, wastes a large proportion of it on— what? A poison. Alchohol, the product, is, no doubt, medicinal in some cases; but as a beverage it is, in the opinion of the best judges, a poison. Whether or no it possesses any nourishing properties we do not inquire. That is a matter for the doctors, many of whom answer in the negative. But probably the true view of the case is, that in combination with other ingredients, which is the form in which the Creator gives it to us, it is both nourishing and wholesome; but not so in the elementary and unmitigated shape to which distillation reduces it, converting it into a stimulant too strong for frequent use. As some one has well said, it resembles the rays of the sun, which in their natural combination are most beneficial, but which concentrated in a focus only burn and destroy.

So far as regards the economic and physiological argument against this vice; but who can paint its baneful effects morally and spiritually! Suffice to say, that intemperance fills at once the jail, the workhouse, the grave, and another place!

The abandonment of drink by this people was the more remarkable, considering not only their past habits, but also their want of education. That intemperance is often the result of mental stagnation there is no doubt; yet here that predisposing cause was universal. Of the entire population, not one in a hundred could read; and if they could, they had no books. What would the English mechanic do without his newspaper? But here was nothing of the kind. During his many idle weeks the Connemara peasant had absolutely no intellectual recreation to fill up the blank—nothing either new or important to think of. "What a waste of the thinking principle!"—yes, a waste greater than that of land or of gold.

Of the various expedients employed to cheer this monotonous existence a chief one was dancing. In winter it was held in private houses; but in summer in the open air, specially at "patterns" or religious festivals. At Leenane I once saw a dance in a fair, and with difficulty I made my way through the gay crowd. Their music was the pipes, and the players were often strangers from Munster, who were well paid, and wherever they went, gratuitously lodged and feasted. I happened once to meet one of them; he was very intelligent, owing, perhaps, to his constant travelling. He told me that besides his wanderings in Ireland, he had visited the Scottish highlands, and played at their merry meetings; that he liked them much; and, having attended their worship, he thought well of it.

Intermingled with their amusements was a custom of practical joking. I have read of old men flying kites in China; but such ill-timed juvenility is not confined to the "flowery land." Of these jokes, a curious one was formerly practised in Connemara at the dances of which I have spoken. These were sometimes held in uninhabited cabins, round a great turf-fire, kindled in the midst, and serving at once for heat and light; while the smoke escaped through a hole in the roof—that is, so far as it chose to go out, for in Connemara it shows great repugnance to ejectment. Here they danced gaily, till by degrees the fire died out for want of fuel. Then in the dark the real fun began. This consisted in flinging at each other small missiles, such as turf, or clay, or mud, and sometimes stones. Of course contusions and cut heads were the necessary consequences. But the joke was, that when any one was hurt, he could indemnify himself by flinging more vigorously at his fellows. And another part of the fun was, as I was told, that the sufferer could feel no enmity, not knowing who had struck him. In all this the reader may fail to see any joke, but that is his affair, not mine. I simply relate the affair as it was told me, with this gratifying addition, that such fun has passed away for ever.

We have heard of "the ruling passion strong in death." In circumstances little less solemn this vice of practical joking was once practised in Connemara. The perpetrator of it was a singular being, surnamed "*Shan na gcos*," or "John of the feet." He was a great swearer; and his favourite curse suggested this curious soubriquet. At one time he caught a fever, was forsaken by his friends—if he had any—and having on a pair of new brogues his swollen feet were so compressed by them, that on his recovery the feet literally rotted off! Thus was his own curse inflicted on himself! But did that reform him? Not at all. This will appear from his treatment of a pedlar to whom he owed some money. The latter, after being put off on various pretences, called one day at Shan's cabin, where he lived alone, and hermit-like, and insisted on immediate payment. Shan turned the subject to the annoyances he received from rats, bewailing his inability to hunt them, as he was a cripple. He then begged the pedlar to be kind enough to collect a heap of stones with which he might pelt the vermin. No sooner was this done than with the same missiles he attacked the obliging pedlar himself, and forced him to fly for his life.

Only one more of these anecdotes will be added, as this book aims at a higher object; but not to give some, would resemble the omission of bogs from a map of Connemara. This occurred about forty years ago. At that time the chief seat of illicit distillation was an island in a remote lake in Joyce's country, where there was no danger of government interference, though there was great risk in carrying the poteen to purchasers in the surrounding country. One day a young man who was sent with a keg to Ballinrobe, had the misfortune to meet the gauger on the road. It was too late to retreat, and what was he to do? He put the best face on the matter, advancing cheerfully to meet the officer, and saying to him, "Your honour, I have brought a keg of the real stuff as a present to you." The gauger, not unaccustomed to such bribes, accepted the present graciously; and, pulling a key out of his pocket, said, "Give it to my wife at my house in Ballinrobe, and tell her to put this keg in the room of which this is the key, and where the other keg is." The young man took the key; but, on entering that town, first sold the poteen on his own account; then calling at the gauger's house, he presented the key to his wife, saying, "Mr. —— sent you this key as a token for you to give me the keg that is in the room that it opens." She gave it, nothing doubting; on which he went away, and sold it also.

From these anecdotes—which of course we do not commend in a moral point of view—we turn to the Irish language, the study of which was our chief motive in visiting this country. How far this language deserves cultivation on its own account, we need not ask, as our object with it was not philological, but practical. Consequently, it would have made no difference to me, even though the Irish were as barbarous as many suppose it to be. But to this opinion I am very far from assenting; indeed, I believe the very opposite. And, in corroboration of my view, I might cite some of the greatest Continental philologists, especially the German; but it will suffice to quote the well-known testimony of our own great Usher, who pronounces the Irish as "both elegant and copious;" and of Rev. Mr. Shaw, author of the Gaelic Dictionary, who considers it "the greatest monument of antiquity which the world ever saw;" adding, that, "the perfection to which the Gaelic attained in Ireland, in remote ages, is astonishing."

That the undeserved contempt for this language at home is owing in part to the extravagant claims put forward on its behalf by some native philologists, I do not doubt. But let us avoid the other extreme; and, at least, do common justice to this venerable relic of ancient Ireland. Perhaps, too, we shall find on examination that all these claims are not unfounded. Take, as an example, the resemblance which they trace between it and the Hebrew, and which to many, appears so absurd. Though I am not a professed Hebraist, yet I know enough of that language to enable me to form an opinion on this analogy, and perhaps to supplement the usual arguments in its favour. These, so far as I have seen, have been founded chiefly on verbal resemblances, which I admit may be accidental. But the case is very different as regards idioms, which constitute the essence of language, and consequently are not variable, like their vocables. Indeed, hundreds of changes may take place in the one, without the slightest alteration in the other. Therefore, a resemblance of idiom is an argument of great weight.

But are there any such in this case? Let us see. The Hebrew has a curious mode of expressing those numbers in which ten occurs. Thus, instead of saying twelve men, it says two men ten; putting the small number first, and then the noun, and last the decimal. Now, the case is exactly the same with the Irish. Is not this a striking coincidence—and the stranger this idiom seems to us, the stronger the argument. Another idiom common in Hebrew, and found in no modern European tongue, is the union of the personal pronouns with prepositions, forming new compound words. The same is true also of the Irish. Nor is that all. By a very singular usage, the Hebrew employs one of these compounds to express possession; as, *li ha sepher*, "the book is mine;" literally, "the book is with me." Precisely the same is the idiomatic usage of the Irish *liom ;* as *'s liom an leabhar*, "the book is mine," or, "with me." These coincidences may seem strange, but at all events they are not imaginary.

Philology apart, however, we shall view the Irish solely as a medium of religious instruction, which is the only way in which we have to do with it at present. How strangely it has been neglected in that respect by Protestant Churches need not be stated. And though some years ago a vigorous effort was being made to atone for that neglect, yet at present a re-action has taken place in the old direction. Whether this be owing to disappointment—perhaps an unreasonable one—for want of greater success, or to the decline of the language itself, which is the reason more commonly assigned for it, we need not stop to inquire. For these circumstances make no material difference as regards our object, more than the merits of the language itself. Enough for us that this language is still actually spoken by a large body of our countrymen, many of whom cannot—while others of them will not—receive Protestant teaching through any other medium. If any man questions this, he is not to be reasoned with; and if he admits it, we require no more to prove the duty of availing ourselves of so important a means for benefiting these thousands of precious souls.

Such being the true state of the case, most of the objections usually made against us are answered by anticipation. Some of them assume that our object is to perpetuate a worn-out language; while, as now explained, we mean simply to use it for Gospel purposes. If it is replied that our object is impracticable, we point to the fact that most of the late accessions to Protestantism have taken place in districts where Irish was less or more made the medium of Scriptural instruction. If this is true—and we are not aware of its being denied—then surely no professing Christian should disparage such an instrumentality. For our part, we would dread to discourage any well-meant attempt to do spiritual good anywhere, but specially where it is so deplorably needed. And if it is again replied that parties anxious to "magnify their office," have made too much of this language, we would like to know what means of usefulness has not been sometimes over-estimated. In this, as well as other respects, poor human nature ever runs into extremes. For, as Baxter remarks, how apt are we to overrate a gift if we have it, and to underrate it if we have it not.

But the chief argument against us is the anticipated speedy extinction of the language. That it will come to this ultimately, no one doubts. For while it is true that, for two centuries at least, this vaticination has been repeated without accomplishment, yet undoubtedly there are influences now at work which will accelerate the decline of the Irish—such as the depopulation by the famine, with the effects of the railways and the National Schools. The language, then, seems doomed. And, all things considered, this is not to be regretted, as, on the whole, the advantages to the people would greatly preponderate.

It does not follow, however, that its extinction is imminent. Generations may pass before it altogether disappear, like the language of the Indian tribes amongst whom Elliot laboured, andw hose only monument is the Bible he translated into it. What a comment on the text, "All flesh is grass; and all the glory of man is as the flower of grass: the grass withereth, and the flower thereof falleth away; but the word of the Lord endureth for ever."

That the Irish will survive for a long time, appears from three considerations. First, because languages are tenacious of life; secondly, from the number who still speak it; and thirdly, from their attachment to it.

How long-lived languages are, history proves. Great conquerors, while overturning empires, have never destroyed a single language. Analogy bears a similartestimony. See Wales, separated from England only by hedges and ditches, and having every inducement to abandon her Welsh, yet still retaining it with a determined grasp. Even the little Isle of Man has not yet altogether abandoned her Manx. And as to the Scottish Highlanders, they have actually transplanted their Gaelic beyond the Atlantic; so that, according to a good authority, there is more of it now spoken in America than ever was spoken in Scotland! And what is still more singular, it is not confined to their own descendants, but has been communicated to some of the coloured race. Hence the story of a countryman of ours, who, on landing in Canada, was surprised at being accosted in Gaelic by a negro. In reply, Patrick eagerly inquired how long he had been in that country, and then turning to his wife, exclaimed—" He's only a few months here, and yet see how black he is! Arrah! what will we be when we're here for some years?" He inferred from the negro's Celtic tongue that he was a countryman, blackened by the climate!

That the Irish will not soon die, appears, secondly, from the number who still speak it. On this point we have no certain data; but the estimate of a leading religious society makes them a million and a quarter. This may be over the mark, but no doubt it is near the truth.* Now it is generally supposed, that the whole Irish nation exceeded not that number at the period of the English invasion. If so, then, the language, notwithstanding its great decrease geographically, still maintains its ground numerically, as compared with remote times—a very curious circumstance truly. At all events, the number of its speakers still equals that of some nations. It exceeds that of all the South Sea Islands, for whose spiritual benefit so many missions are actively and laudably engaged. But, while not forgetful of these distant tribes, shall we neglect so many of our countrymen? And we do neglect them so long as we refuse them the Gospel in their own language.

The third reason is the well-known attachment of this people to their language. That this is the fact requires no

* Since the above was written we have seen the census of 1861, from which it appears, that the exact number of the Irish-speaking population is 1,105,536, of whom 163,275 speak it exclusively. This is precisely the number which we had supposed probable from other sources.

proofs, being well known; but we may give an illustration of it. When studying the Irish, we received from a Roman Catholic farmer the loan of an old book of Irish sermons. The volume was worn and blackened with smoke, which greatly detracted from its marketable value; but when we sent to inquire if he would sell it, what was his reply? "Tell the gentleman that he is welcome to the use of the book as long as he pleases; but as to selling it, I would not take a cow for it." For this attachment to the language, there are two reasons—one from the nature of the language itself, and the other from its associations. As to the first, it is well known that primitive languages address themselves with peculiar power to the affections, like ancient melodies, which are so much more touching than modern set music. Of this we have an example in the celebrated Gaelic song, "*Cha till, cha till, cha till, me tuille.*" Literally translated, these words signify no more than "I'll return no more," thrice repeated; but all Celtic speakers know, that the original possesses a force and pathos of which this translation is only the shadow, and which could not be transfused into English. Hence the hold which the Celtic, "with its wood-notes wild," has taken on their affections. Nor is this feeling peculiar to Roman Catholics. Presbyterian Highlanders have been known to walk several miles to hear a Gaelic sermon in preference to an English one, even when they understood both equally well. And one chief reason, adduced several years ago by the Welsh Methodists against joining the Irish Presbyterian Church—as otherwise they felt strongly disposed to do—was an apprehension that the union would interfere with the use of their own tongue in their worship.

This attachment is increased by the power of association. The Celt, as far as he knows English, associates it with the foreigner, and with painful effort to learn or speak it; but the

Celtic, he identifies with his home, his ancestors, his ancient songs, and his summer rambles.

A naturalist once remarked of himself, that "the chirp of the field cricket, though harsh and stridulous, imparted to his mind exquisite pleasure, because it was accompanied by a host of summer ideas." On the same mental principle is the Celtic endeared to its speakers. It is associated by them with all that is pleasing, and thus forms, in the words of a Scotch clergyman, "the romantic avenue to a highlander's heart."

Illustrative of this is an anecdote which was told me many years ago in Glasgow. A Highland servant girl there having fallen sick, a chapter of the English Bible was read for her, but it seemed to produce no impression. When, however, the same chapter was read in the Gaelic, she exclaimed, "Oh! that is the pretty Gospel!"

Why the Gaelic Scripture should be so attractive may not be easily understood by the English reader. But he may form some idea from a few examples, showing how it invests sacred things in Gaelic imagery. Thus Mount Olivet is called "Sliabh" Olivet, which is far more significant to a Highlander, and more suggestive of home scenes. In like manner the hills of Lebanon are called "bens;" Tiberias, a "lough;" Bethlehem, a "bally;" and Jehoshaphat, a "glen." Nor do I know any name for God's people so expressive as the Celtic—"the clan of God." And what English phrase can describe so well the assembling of the tribes of Israel as the Gaelic "gathering of the clans"? Again, no English word unless "razzia," borrowed from the Arabs through the French, describes so well the ancient foray as the Celtic "creach." And as to "eiric," another of its peculiar terms, its existence in the language is a matter of great theological importance, it is so admirably illustrative of the doctrine of the atonement. It meant originally a fine, into which, by the old Irish laws, the punishment of death for murder was commutable, and which was paid to the relatives of the deceased as an atonement for the crime. So well established was this custom, that when Maguire, a chieftain of the sixteenth century, was told that an English sheriff would be sent into his country, he eagerly inquired, before promising to receive him, what was the amount of his "eiric"—that is, the fine for killing him; implying, of course, that such was no unlikely contingency! This was a sad picture of the times; but the custom itself strikingly illustrates the substitutionary character of our Lord's death. And the word is so employed by the Irish translators in Matt. xx. 28—"To give his life as an 'eiric' for many."

We need not multiply examples under this head. The Irish Scripture is full of them: such as its calling "the wise men of the East," "Druids," and the worship of Baal in the old time, "Druidism," which I believe it really was. Again, the book of Judges is called the "Book of the Brehons," who resembled that class in ancient Israel much more than our English judges. And the tribute which Solomon imposed on the Canaanites is significantly called "black mail," or "dubh-cios." With equal expressiveness an Irish teacher once translated "our earthly house," as "our mud cabin;" and "he will destroy the husbandmen"—"he will rack the farmers;" "he rebuked the winds"—"he threatened the winds," &c. Lastly, Ps. xxi. 3, "Thou presentest him with the blessing of thy goodness," is more happily rendered in Irish, "Thou givest him the blessing of thy goodness before he asked it."

The above examples will show how suitable this language is for the religious instruction of its speakers; and that is all that we contend for. Of course, between it and the

English we institute no general comparison. That were out of the question; for the English, though only at first a conglomerate, has been, during several centuries, receiving from learned men, a polish and perfection, while, for its copiousness, it has, like British commerce, laid under contribution all other lands. Still more, in its noble literature, it is the intellectual Pharos of the world: so that it is a happiness to any man to have English for his mother-tongue. But let the Irish also have its due. And certainly we cannot but think, in common with many others, that, as the vehicle of primitive ideas, and of ardent affections, it is unrivalled; thus faithfully reflecting the character of its speakers.

But that the Irish labours under some disadvantages for religious instruction must also be admitted. These we shall allude to, as they do not appear to be known to its disparagers, whose knowledge of it seems only at second-hand. One of these disadvantages is its cumbrous orthography, and another its various dialects. The former was caused by the bards, the only literati in the early ages, who, for the sake of their metre, added unnecessary consonants. Thus the name for Lord, which ought to be *tirna*, being derived from *tir*, (land,) was lengthened out into *tighearna*. But from the same defect English itself is not free. There is, for instance, the constantly recurring word "though," with its useless *gh*; and the fantastically-spelt "tongue," for plain *tung*. If it be said that the general application of this principle to the language would destroy its etymology, we answer that the advantages in other respects would be immense. Many hope that English will yet be universal; but how can that be, whilst its anomalous orthography places so many needless difficulties in the way of its acquisition by foreigners, eliciting from one of them the sarcastic remark that "the rules for writing English are all exceptions." Well might Dr.

Rapp of Germany say, "that out of Europe English might become a universal language only for its absurd orthography." Consider further, that on the phonetic system children of six years have been taught to read in a week. Why not, then, for their sakes also, adopt so needful an improvement, thus saving them a year or two of useless labour. What a golden age would that be to teachers, wonderfully economising their patience and their birch. Nor would any tyro in orthography need any longer to blame a bad pen for his bad spelling. In a word, the path to learning would have become smooth, and the horror of a school be erased from the youthful brain. That this is no fancy picture is proved by the effect of the phonetic system in the South Sea Islands, where it was introduced by the missionaries, who were the first to reduce their languages to writing. All the words being spelled as spoken, reading is an easy task, costing almost no trouble. Were the same system, or even an approach to it, introduced at home, how wonderfully would knowledge spread with all its attendant blessings! But it is feared that this reform is hopeless. Many of our large towns owe their best streets to conflagrations, which, though otherwise disastrous, gave an opportunity for improvement, by sweeping away the old crooked lanes and alleys. But we fear that, at this stage of our national existence, no opportunity of any kind will ever occur for the much more needful rectification of our orthography.

As to the other drawback—the difference of dialects—this must necessarily be greater in Irish than in other languages, because that for centuries it has had no literature to form a standard. In consequence the verbal divergences are very great. But they do not consist, as I once thought, in new vocables, so much as in the retention by each dialect of a different part of the original tongue. That these form, however, a serious obstacle in the way of its use for religious purposes, is undoubted. But they are compensated for by an advantage of another kind; that is, its supplying its own compounds, which, for intelligibility, is a matter of the greatest moment. Thus, reconciliation, which in English is composed of two Latin vocables, is expressed in Irish by a compound of its own, meaning "second friendship." To the Irish, then, may be applied Origen's remark concerning the Scripture, that "it contains within itself the keys of its interpretation;" whereas the keys of the English are to be sought for "beyond the four seas"—chiefly in ancient Greece and Rome.

Enough, we hope, has been said to show, that even with these drawbacks, this language is an important means for advancing Ireland's evangelization, which is the object we have had in view in dwelling on the subject. And if so, the duty of using it is specially incumbent on ministers residing in Irish-speaking districts. Many of them cannot become fluent speakers of it; but they may learn enough to commend them to the people. I have seen a bigoted Romanist disarmed by quoting a single Irish text; and in most cases it exercises some influence. My worthy friend, James Campbell, Esq., of Galway—to whom every good cause in the West is indebted—has learned Irish phrases for the transaction of business; and surely most ministers could do the same for so holy an object. On this point let them learn from the priesthood. Thus, Dr. Gallagher, in his preface to his Irish sermons, presses his brethren, if only able "tolerably to pronounce the Irish," to read a portion of the book for their flocks every Sunday—even a "point or paragraph." "Rather than they should fast," says he, "give them a portion of the loaf." Shall we ministers not take equal pains to break to them in their own tongue a portion of the "bread of life"?

At the same time, to prevent disappointment, let us not expect too much from the mere language. Only God's grace can change the heart. All that the language can be expected to do is to gain for us a hearing. But is not that a great deal? If any think otherwise, let them just try to accomplish the same end in some other way. A true estimate of the value of the language may be learned from a Scripture example. Thus, Paul's preaching to the Jews in their own vernacular, as recorded in Acts xxii., did not prevent their afterwards assaulting him when he offended their prejudices; but at the same time it is said, that when "he spake in the Hebrew tongue to them, they kept the more silence." Now, was not that a great point gained?

Is it replied that most of this people now know a little English—we admit that. But they do not know enough to enable them to learn through its medium, for they still think in Irish. That this is the fact appears from their many ludicrous mistakes when they attempt to speak English. Thus, I have heard an old woman complain of a pain in "the big finger of her foot"—the Irish word for finger and toe being the same. Again, in rebuking their children, they will say, "you'll do good makings," meaning, ironically, you'll do well. "Wait till I tak you," for overtake you. "I will dead a goose for you!" for kill a goose. A little boy shouts to his father in the garden, "Arrah, father, the bread at the fire be boiled," (baked); "say not boiled, cries the father, but roasted!" Another man, whose son was ill of small-pox, said of him—"He be boiled, burned, and blowed up." This was a too literal translation of the Irish phrase, which expresses figuratively the heating and swelling effects of that disease. But of all their blunders, the one that most amused me was that of a servant girl, whom her master had sent for the loan of an umbrella. This word being new to her, escaped her memory before she arrived at her destination, so she could only stammer—" My masther send me for loan of—of—a brolee brella ;" of course, this was not understood. She then called it the "sheet—the sheet;" but this, too, was unintelligible. At last she carried her point by waving both her arms over her head, and exclaiming—" 'Tis what be'es over them entirely."

This being the amount of their English, it is a mistake to infer that they need no more teaching in Irish. But this mistake is not unnatural to tourists and other visitors, on their finding, in the western towns and along the roads, that the peasantry can answer simple questions in English. They would change their opinion, however, if they travelled in the remote districts; or if they noticed, at fairs or in shops, how commonly this same people must have a bargain explained to them in Irish before they close with it, or how often, when anything confuses them, they are instantly forsaken by their English.

But why dwell any longer on a matter so plain? We are shut up to this language if we wish the salvation of its speakers. They, or most of them, will not hear us in any other, and that decides the point. Nor does it make any material difference to us when the language may die; for in matters of duty, we are not to be guided by future contingencies, but by present circumstances.

Suffice, then, that for the present, Irish is the only way of access to the Celtic heart, which, with its priceless affections, we wish to win for Jesus. In such a case, to dissuade us from using it, because it may soon die, were as wise as to tell a person, who held in his hand the key of a precious casket, that he should not use it, but wait till the lock should rust and fall to pieces of itself. But when that happens, where will the present generation of Irish speakers be? And where will we be—where?

CHAPTER III.

THEIR RELIGION.

Value of the Soul—Importance of Missions—Need of in Connemara—Apostasy of the first Protestants—How a Poor Roman Catholic Widow received the Gospel—Discussion with a Devotee—The Two First Converts in Connemara—Their Sufferings—Lines to the Snowdrop—Extracts from an old Irish Catechism—Dr. Gallagher's Irish Sermons—A Wonderful Legend—Superstitions—Charms—A Chapel-Scene—Anecdotes of Penances.

WHAT has been said of the social state of the Connemara peasantry is only introductory to a higher subject—their everlasting welfare. With all their rudeness, every one of them, in the view of the missionary, lodged within his breast a gem of inestimable worth, through which he was capable of receiving the Divine image, and of participating in the Divine happiness, and by means of which, for weal or woe, he was destined to live for ever. In illustrating this noble attribute of our nature, a modern divine well remarks: "Behold the child born last night—that child will never cease to be; that child will outlive the hills; that child will 'hear the heavens and the earth pass away with a great noise,' and behold the great 'white throne placed in heaven,' &c." Such is the ennobling, because undying, principle with which, in common with all our race, each denizen of these wild mountains is invested. But alas! many of them—

> "Unconscious as the mountain of its ore,
> Or rock of its inestimable gem—
> When rocks shall melt and mountains vanish,
> These shall know their treasures—treasures then no more."

Now, to raise this gem, or immortal principle, from the mire of sin—to cleanse and polish it, so as to reflect the beams of the "Sun of righteousness"—that is the object of the Christian missionary—a work, indeed, for which he has no power of himself, but in which, nevertheless, it pleases God to use his instrumentality, if he employ the divinely-appointed means. Of such a work, surely, the importance cannot be over estimated. Its value will be fully understood only when we stand in that place, where "we shall hear the songs of the redeemed on one side, and on the other the groans of the damned."

But even here on earth the importance of the work is partly seen in the peace of conscience and spiritual comfort imparted by it, whenever it is made effectual. In visiting the Killery Bay, to the north of Connemara, I was shown a valley into which, during the entire winter, the sun never shines, its beams being intercepted by a high mountain. What a privation, thought I, to the inhabitants of this valley! But alas! infinitely worse is their want of that Sacred Book, through which "life and immortality are brought to light by the Gospel." An open Bible, shone upon by God's Spirit, and scattering beams of truth and comfort over the homesteads of a country, and thus lighting up this world with the glory of the next—that is the true sun of the firmament. And inconceivably wretched are they from whose eyes that light is excluded by a dark mountain of error. Or take another illustration, borrowed from the same district. High up the sides of the "Twelve Pins" I was shown some cottages, the inmates of which, for several months in the winter, are enveloped in fogs, so that they rarely see a clear sky, or enjoy a dry day. I am ashamed to say that I felt more for these people, than for the millions who live all their days in the mists of spiritual ignorance, not knowing the way to peace with God, or to a happy eternity, and to whom, consequently, life is

"A vapour that gleams o'er a hidden abyss."

Is it objected that there is no help for this people, our efforts to enlighten them having met so little success? We reply, that in all ages pure Christianity has had a small beginning, and that, in other missions as well as ours, "the same sun that shines on the fruits of a missionary's toil, shines also upon his grave." Nor let any one imagine, if a missionary in his first efforts be thwarted or crushed, that he has necessarily failed in his object. According to a most expressive similitude of our Lord, " a grain of wheat, before it bring forth fruit, must die;" meaning that temporary defeat usually precedes permanent success. Let not the world, then, be in haste to taunt the Gospel labourer with failure. If he has sown even a few seeds of truth, God will look to the result; and if God wills that fruit shall follow, neither man nor devil can prevent it. Such being the case, the missionary, though single-handed amid a host of enemies, becomes, through the truth which he advocates, and as regards the object for which he was sent, invincible and invulnerable. Over his grave, like that of his Master, "vain the watch, the stone, the seal," of his foes. In his principles he rises again, and perpetuates his influence. Across a bend of the river Bann a farmer once cut a small dyke. Through this, at first, only a few drops of water made their way; but, as it lay in the direct line, the whole river, in course of time, forsaking its ancient bed, rolled through what was once only a shallow ditch. So the missionary who sees but a "few drops" flow in the ditch he has cut, may rest assured that these drops will yet swell into a mighty stream.

In order to decide the question raised so often by Romanists, and sometimes by careless Protestants, whether or no a mission was really needed in Connemara, we shall inquire into its then religious condition—that is, in 1840. In so doing, we shall consider first its Protestantism, and then its Romanism.

Owing to its former lawless condition, no Protestant settlers had made their way into it until about eighty years ago, when Colonel Martin introduced a colony. These, from their names, appear to have been English; the principal being Coneys, Corbet, Baker, Powall, Dissel, Disney, Cottenham, &c. They settled chiefly at Clifden and Ballinakill. For their spiritual oversight, a minister was brought with them, whose name I do not mention, for he was an unworthy pastor. The Sunday service was his whole work; on week days he never visited his people, nor did he provide a school for their children. On the contrary, his activities were absorbed in the then fashionable occupation of—smuggling; and, being detected at last, no less than £300 worth of contraband tobacco and whiskey were seized on his premises. But, alas! there was then no authority to punish his neglect of souls, or other minister to supply his lack of service. And what was the consequence? In course of time the entire colony, with only two exceptions, lapsed to Romanism.

Many are the lessons taught by this sad history. We cannot stop to dwell on them; but shall only remark in passing, the advantage to our common Protestantism of there being now several branches of it at work through the land, one supplying the defect of the other, and thus preventing such lamentable defections as the above. Let it also be learned from this case, how powerless is dead Protestantism to cope with a sincere Romanism; and how indispensable, for the very existence of a Church, is a pious Gospel ministry, and therefore how ill-advised are those who, because of the abuses of the office, would abolish it altogether.

To the Romanist, also, this incident illustrates one great difference between his religion and ours. The one exists only by instruction; the other flourishes best without it. An untaught Protestant lapses to Rome; but an untaught Romanist does not lapse to Protestantism. Thus Romanism proves itself to be the natural religion of mankind; it is that in which they are born, and to which, unrestrained by spiritual influence, they tend. At Recess, in Connemara, is a tract of land which was reclaimed in last generation; but now, from the discontinuance of culture, it is fast lapsing into its original wildness, and the grass giving way to heath. So of our fallen nature; without constant Gospel culture, it ever tends to error. Consequently, it is no objection to Protestantism that its nominal professors so often fall away from it. This tendency is what Bossuet calls "the variations of Protestantism;" and on it he founds his great argument against it. But if he had studied the Scriptures better, he would have learned that, in the visible Church, as distinguished from that which is spiritual, this propensity has always constituted the chief difference between it and other religions. Thus, in Jeremiah ii. 10, 11, the Lord Himself asks—"Pass over the isles of Chittim, and see: and send unto Kedar, and consider diligently, and see if there be such a thing, Hath a nation changed their gods, which are yet no gods? But my people have changed their glory for that which doth not profit?" Here, according to God Himself, a tendency to apostasy from their religion is peculiar to His own professing people; and it is owing to the very excellence of that religion which makes it distasteful to our fallen nature. Thus, too, we account for the fact that the Jews, who were prone to apostasy in old time, are so steadfast now. The reason is, that their religion has changed; it is now corrupt, and so they like it. May not the same be said of the Church of Rome also?

Though Connemara had not at that time become the field of any regular mission, yet its Protestantism had considerably revived since this unhappy defection. This change was owing chiefly to the influence of the then Archbishop of Tuam—"the good Archbishop," as he is still affectionately called. After his own conversion to God, which occurred after his elevation to the Episcopate, and in a remarkable manner, he set himself energetically to repair the waste places of his diocese, and sent to the west some excellent curates, whom he required to study the Irish language. The good results of this will be noticed in a subsequent part of this volume; for it is really a pleasure to acknowledge worth in any denomination.

At the same time, on my entering this field as an Irish missionary, I found almost the entire Roman Catholic population unvisited by any Scriptural agency; nor did I hear of any Irish missionary having preceded me in Connemara, except in one place, where the Rev. Mr. Coneys, afterwards Professor of Irish in Trinity College, had preached in Irish. These facts will demonstrate both that my mission was needed, and that I did not build on any other man's foundation.

To complete the religious delineation of Connemara, I need only add, that a little before my arrival, a small settlement of Presbyterians had taken place at Roundstone. As they were without a minister, I volunteered my services, and conducted for them a service every Sabbath. Amongst the worshippers on the very first occasion, appeared a middle-aged gentleman and two ladies, who turned out to be the celebrated Thomas Martin, Esq., of Ballinahinch Castle, with his wife and daughter; they were disposed altogether to join our Church, but afterwards drew off, owing, it is supposed, to their aristocratic connections. At all events, they made no secret of their preference for our doctrines; and this was the more gratifying, as Mrs. Martin had been brought up a Roman Catholic.

There being, then, no other congregation of Protestants in Connemara but those connected with the Establishment, or our Church, I turn in the next place to its Romanism, which was the prevalent religion, numbering a hundred to one Protestant. My first intercourse with this people showed me what, indeed, I had previously believed, that, if left to themselves and kindly treated, they were generally accessible to the Gospel. This fact will be still more apparent from the following incident, which was the first attempt I made for their enlightenment. Having procured an Irish copy of the "Sinner's Friend," I called with it on a poor Roman Catholic widow, who lived on the sea-shore near Roundstone, and asked her permission to read a portion of it. This was freely granted; and so I read some passages, setting forth the atonement of Christ and the freedom of salvation. "How do you like that?" said I, when I had done. Her reply was emphatic. "*Go tuige nach dtainoch she liom ?*" "Why should I not like it, for it has sense and reason with it?" While she was speaking, a neighbour woman came to the door, but seeing me, drew back; on which the widow exclaimed to her in Irish, "Come in, for here is a gentleman that reads prayers as well as a priest or a friar."

This widow may be regarded as a fair sample of the peasantry generally, provided their minds be not perverted by calumny, or overborne by intimidation; for religious liberty, though happily the law of the land, does not exist here socially. According to the law, a man may hold and propagate what view he pleases; but society is not so liberal. Those who guide its opinions and sway its passions, do indeed generally permit a member of a different creed to worship God quietly in his own way; but should he attempt to disseminate his views, however mildly, then woe to him and his disciples! Without being once heard in their own defence, and all pleas of conscience in their case being scouted, they are instantly ejected from the bosom of society; and, where felons would be screened, they are hunted down like wild beasts! That there are exceptions is true, but unhappily that is the rule. Nor, in such a social state, can human law be enforced for their protection; verifying their own Irish proverb, *Cineadh gnas tire air dlighe da geire :*—Social custom is sharper than statute law.

That this picture is not overdrawn—would that it were!—will be shown hereafter. Meantime, in answer to those who defend such intolerance on the ground that all such attempts at proselytism are wrong, I subjoin the censure cast upon us by a Roman Catholic author thirty years ago, for the very opposite reason. "With every respect to the Protestant Church of Ireland and its ministers," says Mr. Hardiman, the Galway historian, "it has been doubted whether the latter, as a body, really believed the doctrines they professed. The best proof of conviction in religious opinions, is an earnest endeavour to disseminate those opinions in order to bring people to the truth. This has never been attempted by Protestant divines in Ireland," &c.* Thus, as Mr. Hardiman here properly remarks, our not propagating our religion argues our disbelief of it. And yet such is the alternative to which those would shut us up who fiercely denounce what they call our proselytism! that is, our efforts to bring others to what we believe to be the way of salvation.

* Irish Minstrelsy, vol. ii., pp. 137, 138.

Though in years subsequent to the date of which I speak, I have suffered almost to death from this fell spirit of persecution, yet, at the time referred to, I had no cause of complaint in that respect. For this, however, the reason was, that having visited the place only to learn the Irish language, my desultory efforts in that way were really too unimportant to provoke opposition. Even controversy, which alone is the legitimate weapon in such a case, was seldom employed against me or my doctrines.

The only instance of the latter kind took place at a village near Roundstone. Here I was quietly addressing a few people one summer's evening, when a devotee, or "confraternity man," as the order is called, suddenly made his appearance, and at once launched into controversy. But the man was no fair representative of a Romish controversialist. Nearly all the argument he could muster in defence of his Church was its antiquity. It was the oldest, therefore the best—that was the sum total. In reply, I told him that the mere fact of a religion being old was no proof of its truth; and if it were, that the Chinese religion had the advantage over his Church. "You claim for your Church," said I, "only eighteen hundred years; but they claim for theirs five or six thousand. Therefore if yours be good, theirs is three times better, because three times older! This way of putting the question amused the listeners, who had eagerly gathered round us. Though all Roman Catholics, they laughed at the argument; and seeing that, he gave up the discussion.

Should a more intelligent Roman Catholic than my opponent wonder at my admitting, even for argument's sake, that Romanism was so very ancient, let me state, that I meant not Romanism in its *present state*. In that respect it is no older than the year 1854, when the system culminated in the doctrine of the "Immaculate Conception." But as to Romanism in its elements, I really believe it to be as old as the apostolic days. Thus in the Galatian Church—who were of Celtic origin like ourselves—there was even then a lapsing from the doctrine of salvation by faith to that of salvation by works. And elsewhere we see in these days a "cropping up," as geologists would say, of the "worship of angels." And above all, an apostle complains that the elements of Antichrist were developing themselves, even then, (2 Thess. ii. 7.) That such poisonous "tares" should so soon appear in the Gospel wheat is a melancholy fact; and yet what else could we expect, from the known activity of the "father of lies," and the depravity of our nature. Besides this, the circumstance was overruled for good: an opportunity being thus given to the inspired teachers to brand these errors with the Divine reprobation, for the warning of subsequent ages.

Before I take leave of my opponent, I may mention, that afterwards he and I became personally acquainted, when he opened his mind freely to me on religious matters. One of his confessions may seem strange to my readers. It was, that he could love the Son of God, who died for our salvation; but could not love the Father. "I dread him," said the poor man. To dispel this sinful impression, I directed his mind to those Scriptures which declare that the "Father Himself loveth us;" and that so far from being an embodiment of severity, as he had been led to suppose, it was He who planned our salvation, and sent His Son to accomplish it: agreeably to that glorious text, John iii. 16—"God [that is the Father] so loved the world, that He gave His only begotten Son," &c.

Returning to the subject of intolerance, I shall give two examples of it in the history of the two first converts to Protestantism in Connemara.

Let the reader visit with me a poor cottage, which then stood in a lane ascending the hill behind the village. This cabin we enter; and within, we find only one apartment, nearly a half of which is occupied by a bed. On the latter lies a female, probably not quite thirty years of age, though she looks far older, being spent with long wasting sickness. The only other occupant of the house is an old woman—her mother—who sits on a stool at the fire-side tending the invalid. She also appears sad and care-worn. We inquire into the history of the family, and painful is the narrative that follows. This invalid, when a stout young girl about six years ago, that is, in 1834, had hired as a servant in a respectable Presbyterian family. Brought up a Roman Catholic, she was totally ignorant of God's Word. Her mother, indeed, was a Protestant, but her father was a Roman Catholic; and, as usual in the western intermarriages, the children were trained in the dominant religion. This girl had never been taught to read; so in every sense of the word she was ignorant. In her new situation, however, she obtained an opportunity of hearing the Scripture read at family prayer. At first, no doubt, the Bible seemed to her a strange book; for, according to its own avowal, "it is foolishness" to the natural man. By degrees, however, its life-giving words arrested her attention, and sank deep into her heart. With all her ignorance she could not but learn from it, that there was One Saviour, not many—One Mediator, and not a multitude—One Sacrifice for sin, not a succession of them, called "Masses." Truths like these, though as yet imperfectly comprehended, quite changed her religious sentiments. No longer, could she attend the Mass. She gave it up; and she concealed not her motives. This bold step set the village in a blaze. Again the furnace on Dura's plain was heated. To shake her steadfastness, menace and insult were first employed;

but these failing, a more dreadful ordeal was prepared for her. Going home one night to her parent's house, she was met in the lane by a tall man, whom she did not recognise. Without speaking a word, he raised his powerful arm, and with one blow felled her to the earth. While she lay prostrate at his feet, he kicked her in the back, and injured so severely her spine, that she could never afterwards stand erect. During the six subsequent years, she has lain prostrate night and day on that bed where we now behold her.

Her assailant was never discovered; but that was of no consequence, as in the temper of society at that time he could not have been convicted. But among the secrets of the great day this affair will be brought to light; and I cannot but fear that the Judge will then regard as his accomplices, all who now, by word or deed, abet such religious intolerance, or lend their influence to circulate those indiscriminate slanders against converts, which are made the pretext for such persecution.

Not quite so tragic was the second conversion. It preceded the other in the order of time; but became known to me at a later period. It was, I believe, the first conversion in Connemara.

But in adducing these cases I beg my Roman Catholic readers to understand that I do not thereby insinuate that all subsequent conversions were equally genuine. If the Apostolic Church itself was not altogether pure, why should perfection be expected of any modern community? There is no wheat without chaff; but what then? Because some of these converts turn out Judases—which is all that can be proved against them—does it follow that the others are equally bad? Yet this is the monstrous conclusion to which the great body of western Roman Catholics have come on the subject; and which they are not ashamed to defend. In doing so, I must tell them that their principle is uncommonly like that of the South Sea Islanders, who, if injured by any Europeans, think themselves justified in avenging the wrong on all other white men. We smile, perhaps, at so odd an idea of jurisprudence; but I defy my opponents to show any material difference between punishing all white men for the acts of a few, and their punishing all converts for the acts of a few. The cases are identical; and yet, hundreds of intelligent Roman Catholics defend this enormity, compared with which, the worst of the old "penal laws" was justice and mercy. In fact, the principle in question would, if fully carried out, destroy not only all civil and religious liberty over the world, but all law, order, and happiness. According to it, all men, including Roman Catholics themselves, would be responsible for the misdeeds of all their co-religionists! Down, then, with a principle so outrageous and so wicked.

The subject of our narrative was born about 1777; so he is now eighty-three or eighty-four years of age. His birthplace was Connemara. His parents were in comfortable circumstances; yet, they gave him no education. This, however, was not their fault, as there was no school in the place. "It is an ill wind that blows nobody good;" so our friend owed his knowledge of letters to the rebellion of '98. Many fugitives from the battle of Balnamuck took refuge that year in Cónnemara; and one of them, who was blessed with some learning, obtained employment from his father. This man initiated him, being then twenty-one years of age, into the art of reading, the unspeakable value of which only a person in his circumstances could appreciate. However, beyond mere reading and writing, his master could teach him little. And if he could, there were no books for the purpose. Grammar, geography, or history, there was none in all the district. And as to religious instruction, that consisted in his getting by rote an old Irish catechism, which has never been printed. Small, then, was the knowledge which he acquired; but in his case it was not the dangerous thing it is said to be. Quite the contrary—it excited a thirst for more. To satisfy this appetite, he used every means in his power to procure books; and he succeeded in purchasing, from the pedlars who then perambulated the mountains, Robinson Crusoe and Gulliver's Travels, with the Voyages of Cook and Anson. Such another library could not be found in the country.

After some time, he obtained a farm, and married. The farm consisted of forty acres, according to Government taxation; for at that time a direct tax was levied on land, and for its assessment, appraisers, or *measadorigh*, as they are called in Irish, were sent through the country by the Government. But these appraisers seldom measured any land but what was arable; so, including the mountain pasturage, our friend's farm consisted really of two hundred acres. And yet, in these "good old times," the rent for all was only twenty pounds a-year! Large, also, was his stock; it consisted of three horses, eight milch cows, and one hundred and twenty-one sheep; while of the dry cattle no account was kept. As to land-produce, it was thought little of compared to cattle and wool; and no wonder, when potatoes, if not given away, were sold for a penny a stone! Their only cereal was oats, and having no market for it, they were obliged to convert the surplus into *poteen*; the practice being so common that it ceased to be considered a violation of the law. But the fact that will seem strangest to us in those stingy days is, that no milk or butter was ever sold at that time! What could be spared of either was invariably given away to those needing it! To do otherwise would have been a lasting disgrace. Indeed a farmer's wife of those days would have preferred being charged with stealing a pound of butter, rather than with selling it.

In this primitive state of rude abundance our friend lived till 1820. Though not without his trials and losses, yet he was on the whole very comfortable as regards this world. Nor was he neglectful of the next; for, in addition to the ordinary observances of his Church, he performed certain penances and pilgrimages, usually left to "*voteens*." But it pleased God about this time to call him to a purer faith; and He did so in a way which at first seemed most painful to flesh and blood.

This trial originated in the reappearance of disaffection that year in Connemara. I have already remarked that, after '98, zealots of that party had made this district their rendezvous. Of these, fully one hundred still maintained their military organization; and they were often seen in arms in the middle of the day, "exercising" on Rosshill. Their captain was one Prendergast, who had been prior of a monastery near Westport; and by all accounts he became a desperate man. The band at first drew their supplies of food from the surrounding localities, specially County Mayo, to which Prendergast sent out plundering expeditions. At last, however, this resource began to fail, and then they resolved to levy a "black mail," even on their hospitable friends in Connemara—a lesson to many ignorant malcontents elsewhere, who "love to fish in troubled waters." But, happily for that country, it was saved from spoliation by some companies of Highlanders whom the Government sent down to the district. At the sight of them, the insurgents fled; and Prendergast, having concealed himself near Clifden till the proclamation of the amnesty, availed himself of its terms, and so obtained a full pardon.

After this brief retrospect, we return to 1820, when, as I

have already said, the old disaffection began to revive, and made our friend its first victim. His only crime was, that, on conscientious grounds, he refused to take the illegal oath by which members were enrolled into this secret confederacy. Their ostensible object was only to " cut down the tithes;" but there is no doubt that they contemplated a renewed rebellion. Secret societies are always despotic, whatever their pretext; so it was here. For refusing to swear, our friend was violently threatened; that failing, worse means were employed. The " Ribbonmen," as they were called, followed him in a boat, on New Year's night, 1821, into Leenane Bay, where he was fishing for herrings. Presented with the book for the last time, he still refused it; and they, getting enraged, struck him with the back of it on the mouth, causing the blood to flow in profusion. Then they violently seized his person, and attempted to cast him overboard, and drown him. Perceiving their intent, he threw himself with all his force into the bottom of the boat, and held the beam with both his arms. This hold they failed to loose; but in the struggle they bruised him dreadfully, and broke three of his ribs.

After this assault, he was confined to his bed thirteen days. On his recovery, dreading another and worse attack, he resolved to sell all he possessed, and to fly the country. His place of refuge was Westport; but even there he was not safe; for before entering the town, he was waylaid by some enemies unknown, who struck him several times, and would have done worse only he was saved out of their hands by friends, who came to his rescue.

Amid all this persecution for his loyalty to his earthly sovereign, he was still a staunch Romanist. But now an event occurred which changed his whole religious history. Visiting one day in the house of a neighbour in Westport, he saw a book on the table; he took it up, and asked what was the name of it. His friend said that it was a Bible, and offered to lend it to him. Having never seen the book before, he was curious to know its contents: so he accepted the offer. After reading a little, he lighted on 1 Tim. ii. 5, "There is one God, and one Mediator between God and man, the Man Christ Jesus." This verse startled him. "If this be true," said he, "I am all wrong; but I'll not take it on the authority of the Protestant Bible." So, to satisfy himself, he procured a Douay Bible also; and for fourteen months he devoted every spare hour to a comparison of the one with the other. In this way he often spent several hours at night, when his family were asleep; and hence he possesses to this hour a surprising amount of Scriptural knowledge. The result was what might be expected. Without the intervention of man, he was fully convinced by the Bible alone, that Rome was fatally wrong; and, accordingly, in the face of renewed persecution, he abandoned its communion. That he was sincere has been proved by a consistent life, and by a patient endurance of sufferings for forty years! Nor was the change merely from creed to creed. That were no better than the removal of a corpse from one coffin to another. With him, on the contrary, I believe that the change was one from the world and sin to Jesus and salvation, through his being "born again of the Holy Spirit." By "their fruits" we know men; and many believers, well acquainted with this man, testify that such is his character. He is now old and "full of years," but, in the Psalmist's words, "He is bringing forth fruit in old age." And often have I heard him declare with emotion, that the great object for which he desires to live longer is to see the conversion of his countrymen to Christ; after which he could say with Simeon, "Lord, now lettest Thou Thy servant depart in peace: for mine eyes have seen Thy salvation!"

As these converts were the "first fruits" to Christ in Connemara, I shall not be chargeable with over-estimating their worth, if I apply to them the following lines, which, at another period of my life, I composed for a flower which is no inapt emblem of a tried believer.

THE SNOWDROP.

A flower there is, of pure and spotless breast,
Born when nature's gayest scenes are waste,
Peeps smiling forth amidst the drifting snows,
And blossoms in the keenest wind that blows.

Sweet flower! with what an unknown power endued,
Canst thou defy the freezing blasts so rude?
And thy soft veins their tender currents pour,
When deepest streams are locked in ice all o'er?

Unable to endure the pelting storm,
The birds and beasts around the shelter swarm;
And man exposed—the vital spark flies fast—
"His pale corse bleaching in the northern blast."

But thou, with tiny stem and leaflet soft,
Dost venture forth, and smil'st unhurt,
Teaching me faith; since from a frozen clod
A flower can spring, if such the will of God.

In coming now to speak of Romanism as a system, we do not contemplate a general view of it; for, as Calvin says, "who can exhaust that ocean?" We only propose to give a few of its prominent features in this remote county.

Of these peculiarities the most remarkable were contained in an old unwritten Irish catechism, peculiar to the place, and which we took down from the lips of an aged man who had learned it in his youth. It began not with the usual question of modern Romish catechisms, but with the following:—

"*An Chriosduighe thu?*"

"Are you a Christian?"

"*She maille le grasda Iosa Criost.*"

"I am by the grace of Jesus Christ."

"*Go de an comhartha Criosduighe ta ort?*"

"What mark of a Christian do you bear?"

"*Comhartha croiche ceasda le na ndeanamuid ar gcosragan.*"

"The mark of the cross of Christ, by which we bless ourselves.

"*Go de an nigh an cosragan?*"

"What is it to bless ourselves?"

"*'S maith an comhartha Criosduighe.*"

"It is a good mark of a Christian."

"*Bfuil d' chial agad ann acht shin?*"

"Have you no other reason for it than that?"

"*Ta shin agus cial eile : Guibhmid ar d-Tigheama leis; agus abhdimid ar gcreidiomh leis; agus be she na sgiath dhidion agus na arm cosainte eidir shin agus cumhacht an Aibhersora.*"

"Yes, that reason and others too. By it we pray to our God, and by it we confess our faith; and it is a shield and weapon of defence between us and the power of the tempter."

After this follows the usual division of sin into mortal and venial. It does not formally define sin—at least in my notes of it; but that is the chief point of difference between Rome and Protestantism. Thus Donlevy's catechism—by far the best in the Irish language—defines sin in this peculiar fashion:—

"*Easumhlacht a naghaidh aitheantadh De, na heagluise no na nuachtaran.*"

"Sin is a disobedience to the commandments of God, of the Church, or of our superiors."

Now it is well known that this word, "superiors," commonly means the clergy; so this definition makes them not only the interpreters of the Divine law, but also a co-ordinate authority with God! At all events, disobedience to them is here represented to be a sin as much as disobedience to God. That the inspired teachers made no such claim on their part, all readers of the Bible know. Of course when they were commissioned directly by God to reveal any truth in His name, they claimed implicit credence to it; but, at the same time, they carefully distinguished between the authority of themselves and of their Master. And when in Corinth some unwise Christians, forgetting this distinction, paid undue deference to the persons of their teachers, Paul severely rebuked them, and repudiated the honour as an encroachment on the Divine prerogative. "Who then is Paul, and who is Apollos, but ministers by whom ye have believed, even as the Lord gave to every man? I have planted, Apollos watered, but God gave the increase; so then neither is he that planteth any thing, neither he that watereth, but God who gave the increase."

From this gross perversion of the very meaning of sin, let us remark what a blessing is God's Word, without which the very distinction between good and evil would be obliterated, and the human conscience perverted from the cradle. But is it objected that the above expression regarding the clergy is accidental, and not to be pressed, we answer, What is to be thought of its definition of the Pope?—"*Fear ionad De air a dtalamh*"—"He is the Man in the place of God upon earth." How awful such teaching!

This catechism need not be cited on the points in which it agrees with others of its kind. But we must cull a few of its more curious passages; such as its exposition of the doctrine of the Trinity, better if left unexplained.

"There are three joints in the finger, and yet only one

finger; three foldings in a web, and yet only one web; there are frost, snow, and ice, and yet in these three only water."

But a more curious part still is its explanation of baptism, which will surprise many readers:—

" What mean the three breathings, or puffs, *(seidioga,)* that the priest puts into the water? They signify the expulsion of the evil spirits.

" What mean the breathings into the mouth and nose *(sron)* of the child? The expulsion of the Evil One, and the introducing *(tabhart asteach)* of the Spirit of God.

" What means the spittle *(seilbh)* that the priest puts on the mouth and nose of the child? It signifies that his sight and hearing are opened to hear the commandments of God, and fulfil them; as Christ Himself restored the sight and hearing of the man born deaf and dumb.

" What means the cross that is laid on the face of the child? It signifies that he is made a servant of Christ by the mark of the Cross.

" What means the oil that is put on the palm of the hand and breast of the child? It signifies the strength and power to receive, to fulfil, and to defend the law of God.

" What means the white robe in baptism? It signifies the purity and holiness that he receives through baptism, which will be his ornament after the resurrection, if he fulfil the obligations of baptism."

On this travesty of Christian Baptism we only remark, how it again exalts the clergy—specially by investing them with the power of communicating the Holy Spirit through a mere ceremony.

When I first visited Connemara, other Irish Catechisms of an improved character had appeared in print; but that was after Protestant missions had been set on foot in other places. Consequently I need not quote them, not only because they are well known, but also because I am now illustrating the teaching of Rome only when she had the field to herself. In this point of view, the only other standard of her doctrines which need be referred to is, Dr. Gallagher's Irish Sermons. This work was not very generally known there, but some of the people had seen it, or at least had heard it read; and there was only one opinion amongst them as to its transcendent worth. Indeed I have known them to swear on this book instead of a Bible. Neither can it be denied that it has its merits, not only as regards style, in which it excels, but also in some instances as regards doctrine also. Of the latter, a remarkable example is supplied by the sermon on the duty of forgiving enemies. Let us quote a passage:—

"Oh! ye cursed people, who are wrathful and vindictive, whose heart is hard and merciless, behold to-day Christ on the crucifying tree! See His head pierced with the crown of thorns; see His side wounded by the spear; see His body torn by the scourges: see His hands and feet pierced by the nails; and yet listen to Him on that crucifying tree, praying the Eternal Father—'Forgive them, beloved Father—forgive them their sins.' Behold, ye people, see if there was one inch unhurt of His body—if it was not all, from the top of His head to the sole of His foot, covered with wounds and sores. For my part, I see no part of Him whole but His tongue, and that member never ceases praying the Father not to impute his death to his enemies."

To this, what a contrast is the following, from his sermon on the Virgin:—

"Jesus Himself went to meet her, [on her exaltation to glory, both body and soul, as Dr. G. says,] the rays of light and the effulgence of glory in His countenance. He received His mother kindly and cordially; He brought her by the hand into the presence of the Eternal Father, and said: 'Here, O Father! is the woman whom Thou from eternity didst choose to be my mother; here is the woman who always fulfilled Thy will, and never inclined to break Thy law; this is the woman who was a model and pattern of righteousness and integrity to all the men and women in the world.' 'Inasmuch,' replies the Eternal Father, 'as thou, O Mary! hast fulfilled my will on earth, and hast not, at any time, defiled thy conscience by any taint of sin, I grant thee, as a gift and reward, to be partaker of my power.' 'And I,' says the Son, 'grant thee to be mistress of my mercy.' 'And I,' says the Holy Spirit, 'grant thee to be partaker of my wisdom and goodness. We ordain thee, from this time forth, to be queen over angels and archangels—over all saints and all paradise.'"

That any professedly Christian teacher should preach such doctrine as this, must appear marvellous to one who derives his opinions from the Bible. And yet, the Church of Rome has never yet disavowed this gross Mariolatry.

But it was not from books that the Connemara people learned their religion, so much as from tradition. Stories supplied the place of sermons, and exercised on their minds an incalculable influence. One of these legends is as follows, though the place I heard it was not Connemara, but the southern outskirts of Ulster. There was a rich farmer, who, with his wife, was very worldly and uncharitable—that is, illiberal to the poor. One day a beggar called at his door, and asked alms for God's sake. The wife only was at home at the time; and, as usual, she gave a stiff refusal. "There is nothing for you, poor man," said she; "and so you may go away." "May be," said the beggar, "you could give me a drink of butter-milk, for I am thirsty." This, also, she refused; adding, in the name of the Evil One, that there was not a drop of it in the house. This was a falsehood; for she had plenty of it in the dairy; and there she went, soon afterwards, to get a drink for herself. On taking it up in the vessel, she noticed in the milk something like a small, black clock, which, in Irish, bears a very unsanctified name, and is not generally considered, in Scottish phrase, to be "canny."

This impurity she attempted to remove with her finger but failed, and thus she swallowed it in the milk. Immediately, strange pains seized her, and her body began to swell and turn black. In great haste her husband called in the doctor. But medicine was of no avail, and so the priest was then sent for. After serious deliberation, he set about her cure in the following manner. By his direction, a barrel was provided, and filled with water, over which he read in succession nine masses. Then he ordered the sick woman to be taken out of her bed by six or seven strong men, for she had become furious, like one possessed. She was then forced gradually into this water. As she sank, her limbs returned to their natural colour; and this process went on till nothing monstrous remained but in her head; one plunge more, and that, too, was submerged; but just at the moment, a fiery explosion shot through the house, and carried away the top of the gable!! Such was the story; and when it was told in due form, it would be wound up by the narrator solemnly exclaiming, "God bless the hearers," on which all present would devoutly cross themselves!

As might be expected, many were the Connemara superstitions; but most of them were similar to what are found in other parts of the country. Some, however, were peculiar to the place, specially those which concerned its geology, of which marvellous tales were told. Thus, the pass of Maam Turc, on the borders of Joyce's country, was said to have been formed by three great leaps of Fin-ma-Coul, when out hunting one day with his Fenians! Other superstitions related to the fairies, who seemed to make that country their favourite haunt, specially Knock Mah on the opposite side of Lough Corrib. Of their many pranks, one was to carry off young mothers to suckle their own children, to which allusion is made in a wild old Irish song that I heard in Kerry—

> "Mar sho cuirim mo leanbhsa acholladh
> Air barr na gcraobh 's a gaoidh da bhogadh."

> "Thus I put my child asleep
> On the top of the trees, shaken by the wind."

Sometimes, also, human children were taken, for whom blocks or stones, in their shape, were substituted. Only a Connemara imagination could have originated another idea regarding these aërial beings, which I have never heard of elsewhere. That was, that they were divided on religion—some being Romanists and others Protestants—and "sign's on them, they're always fightin'!"

Peculiar to this country was another curious superstition. It is called in Irish, "*urchoid a cnuic*," or "spell of the hills." The explanation of it given to me was, that in making a grave, if any of the dust of a former corpse should be disturbed, it would rise from its bed, fly through the air, and never rest till it reached the native place of the deceased. If it met man or beast on its way, it would do them some grievous bodily harm, unless immediate recourse were had to a priest for his blessing,

Allied to superstitions were charms, which here formed the system of therapeutics. They were very numerous, and much trusted in. In using them, certain ceremonies were observed, which savoured strongly of Druidism. Thus, when the herb, called in Irish "*luibh Eoin Baisde*, or "herb of John the Baptist," was employed for cures, it should first be pulled according to a certain ceremonial, with the repetition of Paters and Aves; then the leaves should either be carried direct to the sick person, or if the operator entered a house on the way, they must be left under a stone at the door till he came out again. After this, part of the leaves were bruised, and the juice given to the patient to drink. If the remaining leaves continued green he would recover; if not, he would die.

Other charms operated without any medium, solely by the use of certain words. Of these I took down a number as curiosities; but two specimens will suffice. One is called *airiod an fhiabhris*, or charm for the fever. The original is in Irish, of which the following is the translation:—" Oh! Anna, mother of Mary, and Mary, mother of Jesus, and Elizabeth, mother of John the Baptist, be between me and disease of the bed." (fever.) The other charm is for the tooth-ache—a great desideratum, when we remember the difficulty of its cure by the professionals:—" As Jesus and his apostles were walking together, Peter sat down. 'What ails thee, Peter?' said Christ. 'Oh, Christ, my tooth pains me.' 'Rise up, Peter, and be cured: and by repeating the charm I give thee to-day, your head will never ache again.'"

As the reader is not likely to desire more of such stuff, we shall, in the next place, glance at some peculiarities of Romish worship in Connemara. We begin with the following " chapel scene," which occurred long since on the southern shore of Galway Bay, and which we had from an eye-witness. This was an exercise of discipline by a priest, whom we shall introduce to our readers. He was a well-disposed clergyman, and very popular; but he had the weakness to wear, since his return from a French college, a three-cornered hat, peculiar to its collegians. When the bishop remonstrated, he replied that he thought it a proper symbol of his education, and a distinguishing mark between him and a layman. Remonstrance having failed, the bishop had recourse to stratagem; so he invited the priest to his house, and kept him over night. Next day, on his leaving, his hat was missing;

and in its stead was a new "Caroline," of the existing fashion. But the pertinacious priest would not accept the substitute, though informed by the servant that it was left for him by order of the bishop. He covered his head with his pocket handkerchief, and left. On seeing this, the bishop kindly sent the hat after him, and afterwards offered him a parish if he would abandon his odd fancy. But he still refused, saying that he did not care for a parish, or any worldly advancement; that, while he lived, he was sure the Christian people would give him "a bit and sup," (as the Irish phrase is,) and that he wanted no more. He spoke sincerely, for he was a very mortified man—spare in flesh, and very self-denying. When attending stations for confession, or baptism, at which time other priests were feasted, he made it a point never to eat any thing that cost money, contenting himself with the common fare. For this he was liked by the people; which was the reason, perhaps, why the bishop was so indulgent to him. It has been remarked that a ship is directed by a rudder, which is at the stern of it; and so, in both Church and State, the most despotic rulers often bow to popular influence, which they affect to despise.

Such being the clergyman, let us see how he maintained discipline in his parish. The subject of it was a tailor, a native of Loughrea; and his offence consisted in his pretending the miraculous cure of diseases. He also professed to hold communication with the "fairies," and to prevent their making away with the milk and butter of the farmers, for which larcenies they were in bad odour in that part of the country. This was all his crime; but really one does not see that it was very serious, when the priests themselves were accustomed to claim similar power. But that is an affair which does not concern us, outsiders; suffice to say, that one Sunday after Mass in M——, Father M'G—— cited the tailor to appear for this offence. He spoke in Irish from the altar.

"Are you here to-day, A—— D?"

"I am, Sir."

"They tell me that you perform miraculous cures."

"Yes, with the help of God."

"If your power is from God, you cannot be condemned; but I fear it is not. Who gave you the power?"

"It was a priest, who gave me 'seven orders,' and at the same time gave me the great wafer." (or host.)

"Is it the same wafer that we priests get?"

"Yes; and I think it was even bigger."

"Don't you see the fairies too?"

"I do."

"In what shape do you see them?"

"In the shape of men and women, like the congregation here to-day."

"Where do they appear?"

"Along the walls of the house, and up in the roof."

Here the priest remarked, that, in such a case, it was indelicate of the tailor to look at them; on which the whole congregation burst into laughter, in which the priest himself joined. Having waited a few minutes for the laughter to subside, he resumed—

"'They tell me you bring back butter to the people who lose it. But I think you make more holes in the butter tubs than you fill up—(you steal it.) Now we priests have a chapter *(leighion)* that expels the fairies; but you have not got it, nor any other man not in holy orders."

Then, addressing the congregation, he added:—

"I will tell you what it is, my friends; I will not curse this creature; but let none of you receive him into your houses henceforth, and let him go home to his own country."

The poor tailor expostulated. "But, sir, there is money owing to me for work done in the parish."

"Well, do you go to the people who are indebted to you, and stay at their fireside till they pay you; but after that, let no one in the parish have any more dealings with you."

This denunciation annihilated the poor tailor. For no sincere Romanist thought of resisting a priest at that time. Instances, however, were not wanting, in which they evaded what they durst not oppose. This was the case specially in regard to the payment of dues, of which an amusing instance occurred at my first visit to Roundstone. There it was the custom for the priest himself, with his clerk, to go round the parish levying these contributions. At one cabin where he called, the owner, to avoid meeting him, hid herself in her bed-room, and told her daughter to say that she was not at home. But this trick was ingeniously defeated. On the "dresser" there happened to be a nice gilt jug, the treasure of the child. This the priest seized, saying that he would take it away. As he anticipated, the girl got alarmed, was thrown off her guard, and then shouted to her mother to come to the rescue:—"*Gabh niar a mhathair.*" "Come forward, Mother." The rest of the scene may be imagined.

Even in penances the same deception has been played off on the clergy. A Kerry man, with several others, was required by his confessor to walk up the side of Magillicuddy's Reeks with peas in his shoes. He astonished his fellow-penitents by his agility in so doing, while they plodded their way in pain. After a time he divulged his secret: he had boiled his peas. Another penitent was required by the priest to stand before the congregation in a white sheet. He sent to his reverence for a loan of one, saying, that he had none of his own; and when the penance was over he refused to return it, pleading that it was little enough to compensate him for the public disgrace. A third—a Connemara man—was ordered to perform a pilgrimage to the "Rick," as Croagh Patrick is called in Irish. This he evaded by repeating his *Paters* round a rick of turf in his own yard. But the most ingenious, as well as creditable, of all the evasions of sacerdotal commands was that of a Kerry woman, whose priest had forbidden any one to give a drink of water to the Scripture-readers. Being asked soon after by one of them for that small favour, she replied, " No, I dare not, for the priest forbad it; but here is a drink of milk for you: he did not forbid that."

These reprisals on the priests by the laity are borne by them more patiently than we would have expected from their severity against Scripture-readers. They seldom notice such peccadillos at all; and when they do, they vindicate their dignity solely on the ground of their office. It is their office, they say, that is insulted, and through it the Almighty Himself. So common is this plea, that in Kerry the offender against a priest begs pardon, not of him, but of his "vestment." This distinction is very convenient for the clergy, as it preserves their credit no matter how culpable they may be personally. They are careful, then, to uphold it. A Mayo priest, after receiving some affront, said, " I do not care for the disrespect to myself, but to Christ that I carry in my pocket." He alluded to the host, or consecrated wafer, which a priest carries about with him in a little box, in order to administer it in case of emergency. This box is called a " pix;" and when I was in Kerry I heard of an instance in which a priest's nephew, in cleaning it, found a host decomposed, which so shocked him that he at once turned Protestant. And no wonder: for can any idea be more revolting than that our Lord's blessed body should suffer corruption?

Our space obliges us to close; but before doing so we

shall narrate one more "penance," which appears to us the most judicious of its kind. A blacksmith who lived near Tuam was notorious for a habit of profane swearing. It is said that every sentence was accompanied with an oath. Having confessed this sin to the priest, the only penance imposed on him was to put a stone in his pocket every time that he should swear for the future. This he promised faithfully to do, glad, no doubt, to get off so easily. At his next confession the priest asked him if he had performed the penance enjoined. "I did," said he; "I put a stone in my pocket every time, but the pocket did not last long; the stones soon tore it away from me." "Well," replied the priest, "that is the way, unless you give up your sins, that they will drag your soul down to hell." After that the blacksmith was never heard to swear again.

CHAPTER IV.

CONVERSATIONS AND DISCUSSIONS WITH ROMAN CATHOLICS.

Ireland a wide field for Protestant Missions—Duty of the Presbyterian Church in regard to it—The Late Revival—Verses on it—List of Presbyterian Missions—My Irish-preaching very successful at first; but greatly opposed afterwards—Obliged to change it to Irish Conversations—Examples of these, showing the Ignorance of the People—Their Ideas of the Virgin—Priests' Miracles, &c.—No Irish-speaking Roman Catholic ever referred to Scripture—Their Poverty—Scene of Misery in a Cabin—Mental Derangement from Eviction—Poetical Aspiration for Christ's Kingdom.

AFTER six months' study of Irish in Connemara, I was ordained by the Presbytery of Dublin, in accordance with the solemn forms of the General Assembly, as their first Irish Missionary. This took place in February, 1841. One remark made to me during this service I have never since forgotten. It was that of the Rev. Dr. Kirkpatrick, to whose kindness and counsel I have often been indebted. "Perhaps," said he, "your mission may be one link in the chain of Ireland's conversion." Twenty years afterwards, by a singular coincidence, this very remark was again made to me, when set aside from labour, by the worthy Rector of Athlone, the Rev. Mr. Murray. How far this anticipation has been realised, God only knows; but if it should happen to be the case in the slightest degree, my most sanguine hopes have been fulfilled. At all events, this aspiration on my part will not appear presumptuous to any generous reader, who knows what I have endured in the work; for it is natural for us to value highly what costs us much. Neither should any well-meant effort of the kind be despised;

for in the end it may be found to serve some important purpose, perhaps the least expected by us, and yet not the less valuable on that account—agreeably to the saying of Dr. Vinet—"Man accomplishes in this life, not his own individual plan, but the plan of God, who triumphs to the end."

Roman Catholic Ireland presents a wide field for Protestant missions. Notwithstanding all that has been done for it, the vast majority of Romanists have never yet had the Gospel explained to them. There is no need then (rather it would be a positive sin) for any one Church to monopolise such a work. Nor is there any necessity for one interfering with the labours of another. Let each take up a part of the moral waste for itself, and cultivate it for Christ; and then, the more agencies at work the better. But while we rejoice in good done by any evangelical body, we shall be excused if we covet much of the honour for our own Church. Probably there is no other which has, in all respects, the same advantages. We willingly acknowledge the great, and not unsuccessful efforts, lately made by the Established Church to recover lost ground in this work; while minor sects, also, are awakening to a sense of what they owe to our perishing countrymen. In thinking, however, that the Presbyterian Church is specially called to this great enterprise, we adduce the following facts, which we cite, not as things to boast of, but as precious talents entrusted to our care by our Master, and involving serious responsibilities to our beloved land.

One fact is, that the Presbyterian Church is herself Irish, and therefore free from the objections naturally entertained against foreign churches. Though of Scottish origin, as in all probability the Irish Apostle himself was, yet, a sojourn of two hundred years has naturalized her in the Irish soil. Small at first, she now embraces within her pale about one-half the whole church-going Protestant population of Ireland; while her people include a great proportion of the industrious classes—agricultural, manufacturing, and commercial—the very classes that are most wanted for the prosperity of Ireland. What a noble character would be produced by the grafting of their industry and steadiness upon the warm-hearted, emotional temperament of the south!

That Presbyterianism has been hitherto confined chiefly to one province is true; but that state of things is changing every day. Increased intercourse is rapidly uniting the whole island. Old people in Kerry remember when it required six whole days to travel from it to Dublin, and when the adventurous travellers, before starting, usually "made their wills," and were then escorted to the coach-office by weeping friends! Even when I first visited that county, I reached my destination only in the evening of the third day. Now, by rail, it is the journey of hours instead of days. Thus, then, the four provinces are becoming the streets of one city; and all the Irish people are brought into juxta-position, from which an interchange of religious ideas must follow. That this anticipation is well grounded, and that our Church is likely soon to extend, less or more, over the whole island, appears from the single fact that, during the last twenty years, she has built no less than one hundred and thirty new Churches, of which a large proportion are in the South and West.

Another qualification of our Church for this work is, that besides a Scriptural creed, which she holds in common with all the Reformed Churches, she also possesses a Scriptural form of government and worship. This we believe to be her peculiar excellence. We do not put the form before the Church; still it is important, as has been proved by the painful experience of other Churches, whose reformation was not carried equally far. Of this Scriptural Church-government, two points are remarkably adapted to Ireland at the present day. One is its harmonizing the authority of the clergy with the freedom of the people; and the other is its giving the laity a voice in the election of their pastors. When Romanists were deprived of the elective franchise, we know how bitterly they felt the disability. But here is a more precious privilege, which is theirs by a Divine charter. That it was also the custom in the early Church, even at Rome, history testifies. So Presbyterianism, in restoring it, resembles the builder, who, when lately excavating a foundation for a house on the side of Mount Moriah at Jerusalem, uncovered the remains of the ancient temple wall. Now, what that wall was to the temple, Scriptural government is to the Church—its guard and ornament—though it is not the Church itself.

But the chief qualification of all is her late blessed Revival. Though true doctrine and Scriptural government are very important, still, unless the Spirit's influence descends upon them like the refreshing rain, they are wells without water. This truth, alas! has been exemplified by the past experience of our Church; for she, as well as others, has had her season of spiritual declension, during which, though still retaining the form of godliness, she felt not its power, and, in consequence, many of her congregations became "valleys of dry bones!" What a sad fall from her life and energy in a former age! But, at the worst, her spiritual children could plead for her, "This Mount Zion, wherein Thou hast dwelt." And the Lord did hear their prayers, the result of which, in the late remarkable Revival, is known over the world. It is said that this movement has subsided, and, in many respects, so it has; but its effects remain. It has subsided only as the high spring tide, which some years ago buoyed up and floated into the open sea "the Great

Britain" steam-ship, after she had been stranded on the beach of Dundrum. In like manner, the Revival, before its reflux, floated into spiritual activity a Church, which for a long time, alas! had been stranded on the rocks of worldliness and formality. But what then? Is this blessing to rest with her? Was it not intended for the good of others also? And who should be invited to share in it so much as our own less favoured countrymen? And from them, may that blessed movement extend to other lands; thus realising an anticipation which, on its first appearance in America, I published in a local paper; and which, being the first poetical contribution to it from this side of the Atlantic, I shall be excused in transferring to these pages. The verses are founded on the suggestive incident of Humboldt, in his travels on the Andes, being awakened by his Indian guides with the cry—"The midnight is past; the cross (a southern constellation) is bending."

"THE CROSS IS BENDING."

Their snow-crown'd heights the Andes rear
  'Mid azure fields of cloudless light;
While lightning's flash or thunder's roar
  Can ne'er ascend their lofty height.

Here Night her ebon throne had spread
  On snows untrod by human feet;
And all was dark save where were shed
  Dim beams of starry radiance sweet.

Upon a cliff a voice is heard,
  Where silence deep had slept before;
Unbroke but by the conder-bird,
  Or eagle from his aerie-tower.

It is an Indian guide, who, 'cross
  Night's twinkling fires has cast his eye;
Then cries—"Awake! for lo! the cross
  Is bending in the southern sky."

> Oh! ye, on Zion's walls who watch,
>   Learn from this simple mountaineer
> To turn your eyes to heaven's high arch,
>   And read the signs that there appear.
>
> Sublimely o'er Columbia's strand
>   Bends not the Cross with kindling light—
> Herald of dawn to many a land
>   Long buried in the shades of night.
>
> From Britain's shores to climes remote
>   Nations behold the new-born star;
> Its trail of light along the sky,
>   With wond'ring eyes, they trace afar.
>
> Speed on, O Cross, thy glorious way,
>   Through all the world thy radiance shed,
> And usher in the latter day,
>   Like " morn upon the mountains spread."

So far, as regards the duty of our Church to Roman Catholic Ireland, and which the general reader will excuse for the sake of such Presbyterians as may read these pages. He will also permit us to subjoin a brief list of our different missions, both at home and abroad. With one exception, these missions date subsequently to the happy merging of the two Synods into one General Assembly, which took place in 1840. Cotemporaneously were established the missions to the heathen and the Jews. Of the first, the founder is the Rev. Dr. Morgan, of Belfast, who, for usefulness and devotedness, during a long life, is not surpassed, perhaps, by any other minister in Ireland. Its chief sphere of labour is the province of Katiawar in India. Of the Jewish mission, the fields are Germany and Palestine, and its first promoter was the late amiable and useful Rev. D. Hamilton, also of Belfast. A third mission, which, however, was not founded till long afterwards, is that to the colonies, which is ably superintended by the Rev. W. M'Clure, of Londonderry. By its instrumentality, sixty missionaries have been sent out to these young nations. Thus, the sun never sets on the mission-work of our Church; and, in a still higher sense, may her "sun no more go down, and the days of her mourning be ended."

It only remains for us to speak of her mission to the Irish Roman Catholics. This has not had one founder, but has been the work of several agents. The first impulse to it was given as far back as 1833, by an address from a worthy clergyman of the Scottish Church, Rev. Dr. M'Leod, to the Synod of Ulster, who, in consequence, passed a law requiring their students to study the Irish language. Soon afterwards, the Rev. J. Fisher, Minister—then in Galway, now in London—warmly took up the cause; and as far as his duties to his congregation permitted, both studied the language and carried on mission work among the Roman Catholics of his bounds; specially through Irish Schools, which he established westward, even to Connemara.

About the same time, the Rev. Robert Allen, Minister of Stewartstown, introduced the same agency into many parts of the north-west, and thus contributed greatly to the opening up of that country to the Gospel, being a man of much prudence, and quiet persevering energy. Both these labourers, with others afterwards, were greatly aided by Miss Charlotte Pringle, of Edinburgh, who, for near a quarter of a century, has collected funds for this work, and in every other way in her power has promoted the spiritual regeneration of Ireland.

As yet no missionary had been sent forth by the Assembly to preach the Gospel in Irish. To this work the Lord called me in 1841: at all events, if I had not so believed, I would never have undertaken it—feeling my incompetence, and foreseeing its dangers.

About the same time, an interesting mission was organised at Parsonstown, amongst the English-speaking Romanists, by the late intellectually-gifted Dr. Carlile and his sainted wife, assisted by a devoted medical missionary, Dr. Wallace. There they had obtained a good opening, by the secession from Rome of the Messrs. Crotty—two priests; one of whom, with a considerable portion of his flock, joined the Presbyterian Church. This was Rev. William Crotty, a talented man of spotless character, who afterwards laboured many years, amid much persecution, at Roundstone and at Galway.

Five years after Dr Carlile and I had thus entered the field, the Rev. Mr. Branagan, a convert from Rome, and a very laborious missionary, set on foot another mission in Mayo; and during the famine year, was temporally as well as spiritually, a messenger of mercy to many. He was ably supported by the Rev. Dr. Edgar of Belfast, who having chosen this field as his peculiar province, raised for it large means, and sent into it many useful labourers, educational as well as missionary. Mr. Branagan was still further aided by the Rev. Mr. Allen, who was at that period relieved of his pastoral duties, that he might devote his whole time to the superintendence of the mission schools in the west.

Such, in the order of time, were the several individuals in our own Church, who, I hope, were called of God to seek the salvation of our Roman Catholic countrymen: and if I do not include in the list various others who have since trodden in their footsteps, it is because my subject is the origin of our mission, and my space is limited, not permitting me to say more. It were wrong, however, not to pay a special tribute of respect to the talents and usefulness of the late Dr. Dill, who, while pastor at Cork, was always a warm friend to missionaries in the south, and who himself, after the famine, laboured for some years efficiently in the Kerry mission that

I had opened in 1842. A similar acknowledgment is due also to the Rev. Dr. Kirkpatrick of Dublin, who, though never a missionary himself, has greatly aided the work by his sympathy and counsel. And, of late years, his amiable and talented son-in-law, the Rev. Mr. Magee, has organised a promising mission in Dublin; and in connection with it has started a useful publication for Roman Catholics, called, " Plain Words."

We now return to the personal narrative. After appointing me as their Irish missionary, our Church left me entirely to my own judgment, as to the mode of conducting my mission. Preaching in Irish was new, not having been tried by any of our ministers; so I was wisely permitted to make the attempt unfettered by any regulations as to place or time. Two courses were open to me. One was to itinerate, and the other was to concentrate my labours in a given locality. Both I have tried. But the latter having been carried out, not in Connemara, but in Kerry, does not fall within the province of this volume, though it will be glanced at towards the close.

The chief advantage of itinerating was, that it enabled me to forestall the opposition of the clergy. By coming so suddenly, they had not time to warn the people against me; and in that case, the attraction of the language generally gained for me a favourable hearing. This was the fact to an extent that neither my friends nor myself had anticipated. Wherever I went, with few exceptions, Romanists attended my preaching, not only in school-houses and court-houses, but sometimes in our churches, to which ordinarily they have a great objection. This is attested by our mission reports at the time.

Useful, however, as such itinerating was at the beginning of a mission, it sufficed not for permanent success. For that there was needed a persevering work in one locality. And here I came in conflict with the full opposition of the priesthood, which was indeed most formidable, and though it did not expel me from my post, it prevented the people from hearing me. If they did so, they would be exposed to a species of martyrdom. Under these circumstances, I was obliged to change Irish sermons to Irish conversations in the cabins or by the way-side. This plan was more tedious; but while the persecution lasted, there was no other. Besides, that pressure may not last; and were it once removed, Irish preaching would again have free course, with the best results.

Generally this conversational preaching has been left to Scripture-readers, and supposed not to be suited to Ministers. But that, I think, is a great mistake. From my own experience, I can testify that the explanation of saving truth in this way to the very ignorant is more difficult than public preaching to well-taught congregations. It is also more trying, because the hearers are not restrained by conventional forms from interrupting, contradicting, or insulting the teacher; and when they are inflamed by altar denunciations, then the difficulty and even danger of the work are immeasurably increased. Is such a work, then, to be committed altogether to Readers? Very different was the opinion of our great Master, if we may judge from the fact that He Himself taught individuals by the way-side, and that the record of such conversations occupies much of the sacred page; thus putting the Divine stamp on the practice.

Such being the case, I am encouraged respectfully to commend to my brethren this mode of instructing Romanists; and perhaps the following conversations may direct some of them how to begin. At all events, they are faithfully reported just as they occurred. There is no colouring; which will be still more evident when I pledge my word that originally they were not written at all for the public eye. Neither, in transcribing them for the press, has any change of consequence been introduced. The alterations consist chiefly of verbal corrections, and the condensation or omission of unimportant details, with a few words of explanation interspersed for the general reader. In other respects, they remain as when written for private use.

In candour, however, I must add, that these specimens are the most encouraging that I met with for a long time. They are not the average; very far from it. But what is a missionary to do? If he dwell on his discouragements and persecutions, he is charged with affecting to be a martyr; and if he give only the bright side, he is charged with embellishing. Now, I want to do neither. Therefore, as a general preface to these conversations, I state, once for all, that at first almost every Romanist was willing to converse with me in Irish on religion; but after opposition had arisen, not one in five would do so otherwise than to insult me; that those who were better disposed were closely watched by the clergy, and, as I have reason to believe, cross-examined and threatened for it; that to stop the work altogether, persecutors sometimes placed themselves in my way, and, without the slightest provocation, poured on my head the vilest epithets that the expressive Irish could supply, not without threats and stone-throwing. What! some Protestants will exclaim. Surely it is not a minister's duty to submit to such maltreatment. Quite apostolic, we answer; for they, too, were "treated as the filth and offscouring of all things." And for my own part, I can truly say that I found all this easier to bear than the ill-natured remarks of some who ought to be friends.

That I felt even a liking for the work, with all its drawbacks, will appear when it is known that I then served chiefly as a volunteer, not being directly connected with any mission. I was also in broken health, which had obliged me to resign a pastoral charge. By bearing all this in mind, while looking over these conversations, the reader will have before him the dark as well as bright side; at least, he will have the two sides, as far as I can present them.

These extracts being varied in character, will not, it is hoped, prove wearisome. At all events, there are positive reasons for giving them at such length. One is, that great difference of opinion has existed respecting what the western Roman Catholic laity really believe. Here they are allowed to speak for themselves, which is surely the most satisfactory mode of settling the controversy, and it will show whether they needed a mission or no.

From these extracts also Romanists too may learn what is the doctrine of the missionary, and how far it deserves the charges and denunciations which their clergy hurl against it. In a word, these conversations are so many facts illustrating the present moral and religious condition of our countrymen in the West. And after all that has been written respecting them, perhaps there is no great superabundance of such facts. Of opinions and theories we have had enough; but in this practical age we prefer facts. Consequently, these imaginative writers, who have speculated so often on the subject, will soon share the oblivion of all other romancers.

In arranging these extracts, we shall adopt the following order:—

1st—Those illustrating the popular ignorance.

2nd—Their poverty and misery.

3rd—Their openness to conviction.

4th—The arguments of educated Romanists.

5th—Their appreciation of knowledge.

1st—*Their ignorance and superstition.* The first conversation under this head took place with a farmer, who may be regarded as a representative of the past generation. He resided on the northern shore of Galway Bay; the place I do not particularize, not desiring, for obvious reasons, to furnish a clue to his identification. His hale appearance would indicate him to be about sixty years of age, but his own statement was, that he was "four score." In that he may have erred, as the old people here are not accurate as to dates; nor do they calculate by the year of grace, but by some epoch of their own, as "the year of the great frost," or of the "dear summer," or the "year of the French,"—that is, 1798. Possibly, however, he was as old as he said; and if so, his present vigour shows the sanitary value of pure air and temperance; not forgetting exercise, for I have known him to walk ten miles before breakfast. That he was uneducated, might be expected from the state of the country in his youth; but it followed also from his not speaking English. And yet, in all matters with which he was conversant, he evinced much intelligence. Withal he was kind and generous, of which he gave me an unequivocal proof. Though my acquaintance with him consisted only of a few religious conversations—begun at first on occasion of a small business affair—yet of his own accord he brought me a horse ten miles, that I might visit him at his own house!

In our first conversation, he denied most positively that "he had ever broken the law of God." By this, however, he must have meant that he had not committed any crime, for at other times he admitted that he was a sinner; but he did not appear to think that he was so in any sense which should cause apprehension. With this prefatory remark we introduce our second conversation.

This morning had another conversation with F., the farmer from S. Notwithstanding what I had formerly told him of our lost condition by the fall, he told me twice that "we would get heaven if we earn it." I reminded him that we are sinners, and that one sin alone would prevent the possibility of our entering heaven in our own name, and by our own good deeds. He admitted all this, but I fear only to deny it the next minute, by again leaning to "good works." How deeply seated in our nature is that old error!

But afterwards he showed me that he had a better insight into the nature of good works than I had anticipated. This appeared from a story which he told me of a lady who was remarkable for her charities to the poor, but after her death, having risen from her grave, she told a friend that the only real "charity" she ever gave was to a poor outcast woman who had taken refuge in her stable, having been refused lodging by all the neighbours because she was excommunicated by the priest. "This," said the ghost, "was all the 'charity' I ever gave; for it was all I gave without it being known; the rest was given in pride. And now get three masses said for my soul, and I'll be received into heaven." "So you see," said F., "that it's only the charity that's given privately *(gan fhios)* that is of use." A true principle, certainly, though invested in strange drapery.

He then related to me several stories of miracles performed by "blessed priests," all of which he appeared implicitly to believe. But he spoke Irish so fast, that I could not follow him in all the particulars. Nor was his faith in these priests at all shaken when he admitted that one of them was a drunkard! He said, too, that a schoolmaster who lived there could do one of these miracles by his learning: and he asked me, quite seriously, could I not do the same myself! "*Nach bhuil an leabhur agad ?*" said he. "Have you not the book?" He seemed to think that miracle-working constituted a necessary part of a learned education. I know other districts in which no schoolboy was supposed to have finished his education till he had composed a song!

After discussing several other points, he summed up our

differences by saying—"You have God, and we have the Virgin Mary." In reply, I told him that we honoured the Virgin as a holy and blessed woman. He was rejoiced to hear it, and said, "Ye do right in that." "But," I added, "we do not worship her. It was not she who died for us, but Jesus; and His blood only can cleanse us from sin. And if the Virgin were on earth again, she would send us to Christ; and Christ Himself says, '*I* am the door,' &c. He maintained, however, that the Virgin was God's mother, and asked if I would not honour my mother. I said that it was only as a man Jesus had a mother, for as God He had made all things, and could have no mother.

In order to give the conversation a profitable turn, I told him twice that if we believe Jesus Himself, no one can enter heaven without a "new heart;" that none can make this change in himself; that we should ask God's Spirit for it; that by it we repent of all sin, and love God supremely. I then quoted some expressions of Dr. Gallagher on the alarming state of a sinner, and repeated in Irish John iii. 16, "God so loved the world," &c.

Another Conversation on the Virgin.

The person referred to in this case was a poor widow who also spoke Irish, and was illiterate. Temporally, she was less fortunate than F., for she depended for subsistence solely on her labour, and sometimes was unable for that by sickness. In consequence, she was very poor, and destitute of every comfort. In hard frost, I have seen her out barefoot—which, indeed, is quite common amongst the poor of this place. In attempting to direct her mind to Jesus, the chief obstacle, as in other cases, was her trust in the Virgin. Her reasons for this I need not give at length; but one of them was so curious that it should not be omitted.

I asked her if Christ were on earth would she not go to Him first. She said that still the intercession of the mother was of use with the Son; and, in proof, told me a wonderful story that she had heard read out of a book, of the Virgin's having saved a soul at death from a host of devils. According to her version of it, no less than "five miles of devils," were watching for this poor soul as soon as it should leave the body; but the Virgin being invoked, came to the rescue with "four hundred angels," and saved the soul from their fangs, bringing it straight up to heaven. All this she narrated with the utmost solemnity, and she seemed to expect my credence also.

On another occasion this conversation was renewed at a well, where she was filling a vessel with water. The subject was the same as before, and it elicited another curious argument. She said that at one time the devil came to tempt our Lord, and for this purpose changed himself into an eel; and that the Virgin, detecting the imposture, put her foot on his head, and crushed him. Saying that, she "suited the action to the word," by stamping with her foot on the ground. Suspecting that she alluded to the fall of man, I asked her was it not into a serpent that the devil had changed himself; but she maintained that it was not, but into an eel.

Most probably, however, the story is a corruption of the third chapter of Genesis. A similar travesty of Scripture I find in another part of my journal. On my speaking to a Roman Catholic woman, (a different person from the above,) of the great error here prevalent, of trying to earn heaven by our good works, she assented, and gave me, in corroboration of my view, a singular version of the parable of the Pharisee and the Publican. One of these men, said she, bragged of his not cursing, &c., and the other confessed his sin; and, after leaving the church, one became an angel, and the other a devil. This metamorphosis she understood literally!

In further conversation, this widow mentioned Eve's eating the apple as the origin of all sin. And when I spoke of Christ being now the only door to heaven, she replied, very politely—"Don't the catechisms say, sir, (begging your pardon, as you know best what is right,) that there are three keys to heaven—prayer, alms, and fasting?" In opposition to this, I told her that the only true key of heaven is the merits of Jesus; that His blessed hand alone can open the door; but that, after its being opened to us by Him, our good works follow us as evidences of our being His, but they do not go before us to merit heaven. She did not deny this; but, as I find continually, this people often admit a truth one minute, and deny it the next. Nor do they seem aware of the inconsistency; for they are accustomed from infancy to attribute to Jesus only the mere name of Saviour, and to trust to the Virgin, or priest, or themselves, for the rest.

These two individuals may be taken as fair specimens of the thousands whose only language is the Irish. They may be also regarded as types of what all the people would be under the priests' teaching exclusively, for they have had no other. With that fact couple this other, that none of them, except the few taught by Protestants, have ever in conversation with me made any reference to the Word of God, either as the rule of faith, or even as to its existence. Their only standard of appeal was, "the catechism says so;" or, "I heard it read out of a book;" or, "the priest said so:" but never one word of "what saith the Scripture"?

Again: all this class—left, as we have said, to the sole guidance of Rome—looked chiefly to the Virgin for salvation. They did not directly reject Jesus; quite the reverse; but it was in the Virgin they trusted. This fatal error came out in every conversation; and it was so general and so deeply rooted as ordinarily to defy argument. It acted like a supernatural spell, of which no power short of the Divine could disenchant them.

Of this Mariolatry, let me give another example. A country-woman, with whom I had some conversation, finding that some of my children were sick, offered to get them cured. I thought she meant by herbs; but it was by miracle, for she said that a neighbour of hers had a "gift of healing." Of course, I declined the offer as superstitious; but she maintained that it was not, declaring that it consisted only in her breathing into the child's mouth three times, and offering prayers to " God, to Christ, and to the Virgin."

Here the Virgin was prayed to in the same sense as the Father and the Son! Can any error be more lamentable, remembering the awful denunciations of Scripture against all kinds of idolatry! With fear and trembling we should think of it.

But it will be objected that the educated Romanists are not so blinded; and in a degree that is true; still, they cannot explain away this fatal dogma of their Church. However, we shall let one of them speak for herself on that point, in the following conversation:—

A Roman Catholic Lady's Ideas of the Virgin, and of
" Holy Trout," Dreams, &c.

In B——, a lady got up on the stage-car beside me, and, after we had begun to converse, made an abrupt allusion to Garibaldi, as if to ascertain which side I took. I told her I was not a Roman Catholic, but that as to Garibaldi, many of her clergy in Italy had joined him. This elicited a general conversation on the usual disputed points; but all was spoken in a kind spirit. When I admitted that the Roman Catholics and we held many precious truths in common, she alluded to Rev. Mr. ——, who, travelling with her in the train, had ridiculed every thing connected with her Church, especially the nuns. This she seemed to feel deeply. She also complained that he said "the Virgin Mary was no better than his own mother." From his view I dissented, saying that the Virgin Mary was an eminently-holy woman, and, according to Scripture, should be called "blessed" by all generations. But I asked her was she aware of the hope that many of her Church reposed in her—in fact, looked to her for salvation, as I myself had heard some of them confess at Galway. This she denied, and said that they only sought her intercession. "If," said I, "you are a Roman Catholic, "you are bound, under pain of mortal sin, to believe with St. Liguori, in his Glories of Mary, that she is often a better hope for the sinner than Christ Himself! That," said I, "is what we Protestants shrink from and abhor." She replied that she had never read the book; and she condemned my drawing down Scripture in conversation. I then besought her to read the Scripture for herself. After that she censured Rev. Mr. —— for his tracts against her Church, some of which she had read, but thought them "full of nonsense." She added, that at the great riot at G——, "the mob longed to tear him;" but she did not approve of such violence. After her thus denouncing Protestant tracts, she was surprised when I told her that I knew a priest to circulate Romish tracts; and that when I appealed to him to check his people, who were calling Protestants bad names, he refused to interfere. She then asked regarding the usual nickname "Jumpers," if there was any religion of that name; and was surprised when I told her there was not.

Afterwards she introduced a story of certain "holy trout" in a river under ground at Cong, and one of which bore the mark of a gridiron, which, as her mother told her, was caused by a County Clare man, who had carried it off and tried to broil it. At first she really appeared to believe this to be a miracle; but I showed her the folly of thinking that God would work a miracle for so useless a purpose. She also professed her belief in dreams, and mentioned two cases in which they had been remarkably fulfilled. She wished to know what Protestants thought on the subject. She also stated, as an odd circumstance, that she had one uncle, a Protestant archdeacon in E——, and the other a Roman Catholic bishop in America.

After much more of the same kind, I told her our great principles were, that Jesus was the only Saviour, and that the Spirit of God alone could renew the heart, making us true believers; and that except in this way there was no salvation. She professed to believe this too; on which I begged her to act on this belief, and I assured her that while there was only one way to heaven, (which was Christ,) yet all were welcome to Him, whether Protestants or Roman Catholics.

2. *The poverty of the lower orders.*

That considerable improvement has taken place in this respect, is undoubted. But the change is more apparent than real; for if wages have risen, so also has the price of provisions. Employment, too, is very uncertain; and in remote districts remuneration is still very small. Thus, I have known a mower employed at a shilling a-day; whereas, in some midland counties, he would have got for the same hard work from half-a-crown to four shillings. And as to the increased trade of the town of Galway—which is one of the most encouraging "signs of the times"—that is only a local benefit. Beyond that locality it has had no appreciable effect, at least so far as I have seen. In consequence there still remains a great mass of squalid poverty. Indeed, the wonder is how most of the lower orders can exist at all, or, in their own words, "keep soul and body together." And if their condition is only tolerable at the best, what is it when sickness is superadded, as will appear from the following

Scene of Misery in a Cabin near Galway.

On this morning the weather was very severe; so for shelter I walked out on the M—— road. In returning, I felt strongly inclined to enter a poor cabin on the way-side. Having stepped in, I could not at first see any object distinctly, as there was no window. The only light entered through the chimney, and that was very dim; so I called out, "Is there any one here?" I was answered by a weak voice in a corner; and looking in that direction, I noticed in the shadowy light the figure of a man half naked, and cowering over a hearth, for no coals were visible. He seemed of middle age, but was bent down like an old man. As my eye became accustomed to the weak light, I noticed behind me a place apparently for tying a cow, also the *debris* of the animal—though the whole cabin was only a single room. After a few common-place questions to the man, which he answered in a broken, querulous voice, I asked was he sick. He said he was—had taken a cold from a great wetting; it had settled on his chest, and was followed by a severe cough, with loss of appetite and emaciation. I pitied him, and asked how he lived, or had he a wife and family. He said he had not, but that his brother and himself lived together, and supported themselves by the labour of a horse, which was the occupant of half the cottage. He said that he felt his illness the more as this was the busy season, being spring time. I reminded him that God did it for a good end, which was to give him time to seek salvation. "And now," said I, "you know you are a sinner; so am I; and one sin alone deserves hell for ever. Do you know, then, how your sins are to be forgiven?" "Arrah, wisha, then, I don't know, Sir." Saying this, he clasped his two hands together, and raised them to his breast, as is their custom in prayer. That he was deeply affected, was evident from his whole appearance, which was dejected and woe-begone. Sickness and solitude, without the knowledge of the Gospel, had reduced his mind to the lowest ebb. In unaffected sympathy, therefore, and with thankfulness to God for this opportunity of speaking to such a sufferer, I opened up to him the way of salvation. I asked would it not be a heavy penance for sin, if he were to live thirty-three years in misery for it, and at last to shed every drop of blood in his body? Now, this is the penance, said I, that a Friend in heaven has done for you. As a proof of this free salvation, I reminded him of the thief on the cross, who had only time to offer one prayer to Christ; but, having done so in faith, was instantly saved; while the other thief, though in other respects no worse than he, was, by his unbelief, eternally lost. I then quoted John iii. 16; and, that he might understand it the better, I repeated it in Irish, adding, "Have you not heard of this Jesus?" He replied that he had; and all the time that I spoke on the subject, he listened most attentively, sometimes raising his hands clasped together, and exclaiming, *Moladh le Dia!* "Praise be to God!" In conclusion, I said to him, "You and I may never meet again; and I am a stranger to you; but being desirous of your salvation, I beg you to pray to this Jesus for His Spirit, to give you a new heart—that is, a heart truly sorry for sin, and loving God; without which we cannot enter the kingdom of heaven." In reference, also, to his present sufferings, I added, that the thief on the cross, now in heaven, praises God most of all for his crucifixion, as it was the means of bringing him to Jesus, only for which he had been lost for ever. Such, also, I hoped was God's object in his present affliction. After much more of the same nature, I left; and he followed me to the door with blessings.

Hard work and small pay.

After reaching B——, on the sea-shore, I turned westward, and went some distance in that direction. On the way, I overtook a young woman heavily laden with a creel on her back. Having saluted her in Irish, she started, and said, "What is it, Sir?" being surprised, I suppose, at my accosting her in that language. I repeated the Irish salutation, when she civilly responded in the same. We then got into conversation, and she, loaded as she was, quickened her pace to hear me; still, however, keeping a little behind me, out of respect. Having learned that this burden was potatoes, which she was carrying to town for sale, I remarked that they would be dear bought, after such a long carriage. "But the worst of it is," said she, "that they are not my own either." They belonged to a family with whom she lived, and who gave her but four shillings a quarter as wages, and even that was not regularly paid. I was really astonished at such hard work for such pay; for the town to which she was carrying the potatoes was more than two miles distant, and she was literally bowed down under the weight. Her dress, also, was scanty and tattered; and she had no shoes or stockings on her feet; but that is a common case amongst the poor here, and thought nothing of. Commiserating her condition, I prayed in Irish that God might help her. "And now," said I, "there is a burden heavier than what you carry; that's sin. Don't you know you are a sinner?"

"I hav'nt done any thing out of the way."

"You have, against God. Our sins are more than the hair of our heads; and one sin deserves hell for ever. Do you know how your sins may be pardoned?"

"By ——, I don't know."

"Well, it is by means of a Friend in heaven — Jesus Christ, the Son of God; who, from love to our souls, and taking on Him our nature, died to obtain for us a pardon."

"Oh! yes; Jesus that died on the cross for us."

It may seem odd that she should thus know of Christ's dying for us, and yet not have understood, a little before, how sin could be pardoned. But the matter is easily explained. The mere fact of that death she knew; but not the doctrine connected with it, and to which it owes all its value. And so of nearly all the Roman Catholic poor whom I meet here. They, too, acknowledge that Jesus has died for mankind; and that, in some sense, this is beneficial to us. Nevertheless, they believe that our sin remains to be atoned for by ourselves; but how we are to do so, no two of them exactly agree.

Before parting with this girl, I, in my usual way, explained to her fully the plan of salvation; and assured her that Jesus was now looking at her from heaven, and willing to save her; and that this was the only way of salvation. On her part, she seemed greatly to relish the conversation, following close after me all the time, that she might catch every word. Nor did she object to any thing that I said.

Walked to the hill on the S—— road. Beside a small lake here, is a number of cabins. With a woman who came out of one, I got into conversation. We spoke first of the bad weather, and the rot in the potatoes. Then I alluded to the cause of all our misery being our sin against God. On this, she asked me directly was I a Protestant. I replied in the affirmative, and expected a rebuff. Instead of that, however, she asked me civilly into her cabin to rest myself. But while thus favourable to Protestants, I found that she was still a Roman Catholic.

Within, we had a long conversation, and very interesting, showing the state of the poor in this country. The following are the principal particulars of it. Her married name is C——. She has six children at home, and one in England, a servant-maid, at £9 a-year. Her husband's only support is working with Mr. D——. The family have only two meals a day, and the husband no more. Their chief food is potatoes, generally without milk or any thing else; sometimes they eat India meal. She once had a brother who made money in England; he took ill there; and though attended by "six doctors," died in the Isle of Wight. She got nothing from him, or any other friend abroad; though she has, in America, "two score of cousins," male and female. She is a Joyce by birth, therefore her clan is large. Her husband has been often annoyed, and sometimes threatened, for sending his children to the Mission School; but he persists in doing so. On one occasion, two men attempted to beat him for this in his own house; and when he took up the pothooks to defend himself, one of them drew a prong of it into the palm of his hand, tearing off the flesh. By this means he was disabled for work a whole spring; but a lady visiting at Mr. D.'s, supported them. She thought even worse would have been done to him only that his clan are too strong to meddle with; "and, indeed," said she, with some pride, "the C.'s, or the L.'s, or my own people, the Joyces, are not to be touched in Connemara." I was amused at this spice of old clanism.

As a further example of the persecution, she told me that

a Reader was lately arguing with a man on the road before her door, when, "Father Tom," came up, and said to the Roman Catholic disputant, "Didn't I tell you not to speak any more to the devils." After that, one of the Roman Catholics present attempted to strike the Reader; and would have done so only she rescued him. She also spoke indignantly of having seen Mr. D. himself insulted at the late trial at ——, and denounced such ingratitude; for she said that he had saved many of their lives in the famine.

During this conversation, I directed her mind frequently to the way of salvation; first in English, and then in Irish. Specially I showed that it was not our good deeds, or the help of priests or saints, that could save us; and, in proof, quoted John i. 29, "Behold the Lamb," &c. As she was so teachable and afflicted, I felt drawn to speak to her largely on this subject; and she seemed most grateful. In conclusion, I assured her that though she, in this poor cabin, was despised and unknown to the world, Jesus was near her, with a purchased pardon, which, if accepted, would entitle her to an everlasting inheritance. When I was leaving, she prayed often and fervently that the Lord might bless me; having first earnestly inquired my name and situation in life. These prayers I sincerely reciprocated; and I felt thankful to God for the refreshing interview.

A Galway Shopkeeper reduced to Beggary—his Religious Opinions.

On the hill beyond B——, I got into conversation with a poor Roman Catholic. We spoke first in English; and when I introduced Irish, he at once became most civil. When I spoke of the value of salvation, and the duty of seeking it before every thing else, he assented; and, looking up to heaven, said very earnestly, "This is what I daily seek from God." He then put his hand into his breast, and pulled out his prayer-book, to show me how he always carried it about with him. When I asked how he hoped to be saved, he replied, "By a good confession, with right dispositions." I told him only One could save us; and that it was from no deserving of ours; and as proof quoted Isa. liii. 5. But, before giving the words, I said that I knew a Priest who forgave His people their sins without penance, because He did all the penance Himself. I asked him did he ever hear of such a priest. He looked puzzled, and replied that he did not; and that "such a clergyman must have been a very good man." I then quoted the above passage, and applied it to Jesus—"He was wounded for our transgressions; he was bruised for our iniquities; the chastisement of our peace was upon him; and with his stripes we are healed."

Having inquired how he became so poor, (for he begged,) he told me that he was once in good business in Galway, with a shop of his own; but he "was broke" by the failure of a mercantile house in Dublin, which took from him £130. We then returned to the subject of salvation, when he told me that a little before I had come up, he had been annoyed by some "jumpers" who met him on the road. Who they were I did not ask, but only told him not to mind other people, but to seek his own salvation, repeating that Jesus was the only Saviour and Mediator. To this he assented, without referring to the Virgin. I then prepared to leave him; and, pitying his poverty, gave him a penny. He was thankful, and requested me to hear how a man was once rewarded for his kindness to the poor.

The substance of the story was, that a certain farmer, though a bad person in other respects, took pity on a poor man whom he saw one day trembling in the cold; and so, taking off his own coat, he wrapped it round him. Some years afterwards, this farmer died, and, at the bar of God, was asked how he had lived. He confessed that he had not done his duty, and that he had no excuse to offer for himself. Being then asked to recollect if, on a certain occasion, he had given a coat to a poor man, he said that he had; and this gift, it seems, was accepted as an atonement for his sins!—and so he was saved. Such was his idea of atonement for sin!

After this, I explained to him more fully the way of salvation. He then asked my name, that he might "put it in his prayers," and forthwith began to repeat the Lord's Prayer and "Hail Mary." Already I had warned him against trust in the Virgin, but this he had soon forgotten! But I must only persevere in witnessing to these poor people for the Lord's truth, and look to God to make it effectual, which, no doubt, He will do, sooner or later.

Poverty and Sickness.

Walked on the B—— road. The day became wet; so I was obliged to shorten the walk, by descending from T——'s Hill to B——. Here I got into conversation with a young woman, who was very sickly looking. Her face was thin and pale, and her lips white as paper. In answer to my inquiry, she said that she laboured under a severe pain in her side and chest; in fact, she had all the symptoms of consumption. She added, that all her support was derived from selling small pedlar's ware—chiefly match-boxes; and at the same time, she showed me a little basket of them which she had hid under her cloak from the wet. Thinking her time for this world would be brief, I asked her solemnly what was her hope of salvation. She said her hope was in God, nor did she mention the Virgin. I replied, that it was well to trust in God; but that many who did so had only a false hope, which would not serve them in the hour of need. I then warned her against expecting pardon of her sin from any creature, or her own good works. She said, she did what she could, and that she often prayed God to have mercy on her soul. I replied, that God cannot have mercy on us but in one way, which He Himself has explained to us, and I hoped she would not be offended if I warned her against any other hope. I said I was myself exposed to death as well as she, and that if I were to die this night, my hope is what I would now make known to her. I then opened up to her the unmerited love of Jesus—His incarnation, death, and atoning sacrifice. I dwelt also on John xiv.—"No man cometh unto the Father but by me;" and Matt. xi.—"Come unto me all ye that labour," &c.

During all this time, we were standing beside a wall for shelter from the rain; but when I went on my way, she followed me part of the road. I then repeated what I had before stated, begging her, for the sake of her soul, to act accordingly. And when I spoke of the cleansing influence of the blood of Jesus, I pointed to the bay before us, saying that her sins, if a hundred-fold greater, would as easily be washed away by that blood, as a drop of milk would be dissolved in the bay. All this she heard with the utmost attention; but I must admit, that she asked relief also for her temporal wants, pleading that it was very hard, in her extreme weakness, to walk about all day for the mere chance of earning a few pence; and she complained of the want of warm clothing. Having no change at the time, I asked her to call at my house, which she did soon afterwards, and I gave her an old shawl and a few half-pence. Poor creature, she will not long need such things.

These are a few illustrations of the poverty which I saw amongst this people, and which, I must say, they endure with amazing patience. They suffer more, perhaps, than any other peasantry in Ireland; and yet, to their credit be it spoken, they are not guilty of these agrarian outrages so common elsewhere. But while their misery so seldom leads to the commission of crime, oftentimes, in the absence of the comforts of the Gospel, it crushes out of them all energy and self-reliance, for which they are to be pitied rather than blamed. In one instance I knew it to overturn reason itself, which, as it was a very sad case, I cannot pass over. The following is the account of it in my journal:—

"To-day there was a painful scene behind my garden. A widow, called ——, generally reported as a person of bad temper, having been ejected from her cottage, had returned to it to-day, as some of the people told me, 'to curse the neighbours,'—meaning, I suppose, the present occupant of her cottage. A quarrel ensued between her and the latter, and, sad to say, blows were exchanged by the two women. Being worsted, the poor widow ran off to my well to drown herself! She was so determined on this, that with difficulty two men could hold her back. The noise having attracted me to the place, I found her, as I came up, violently struggling in their grasp, and attempting, like a maniac, to bite their hands! Then they got angry with her, cursed and beat her. It was a painful scene, especially when I noticed that her cap was clotted with blood! Eventually they got her off, though with much ado. Nor was it possible, amid the confusion, to get from her a hearing for a few words of Gospel admonition which I felt disposed to address to her."

Such scenes forcibly remind us that we are in a fallen world, and should stimulate us more fervently to pray, "Thy kingdom come." In Scripture it is said, that when

"Jesus saw the multitude, He had compassion on them,"—that is, when He saw their wretchedness. May this description of the misery in the West have a similar effect on the reader; and in that case these pages will not have been written in vain. Meantime, we close with the following aspiration for a better state of things, which was written many years ago, but never before published:—

THY KINGDOM COME.

Earth-wanderers, with a weary breast,
And longing for a place of rest,
We pray—with sin and woe oppress'd—
    Thy kingdom come.

This kingdom 'twas the Hebrew seer
Saw high on mountain tops appear:
Oh! that we knew it yet were near—
    Thy kingdom come.

When comes this kingdom, every knee
Throughout the earth shall bow to Thee;
And Thou the King of kings shalt be:
    Thy kingdom come.

Thy grace outpoured then shall bind,
In union sweet, each heart and mind
Of Jew and Gentile—all mankind:
    Thy kingdom come.

Peace, like a river, then shall flow;
Then truth shall like a palm-tree grow,
And love in every bosom glow:
    Thy kingdom come.

Oh! haste Thy kingdom, Lord, we cry:
How long for it, ah! must we sigh?
Oh! why delay Thy coming—why?
    Thy kingdom come.

CHAPTER V.

CONVERSATIONS AND DISCUSSIONS CONTINUED.

Use of these Conversations—Openness of Romanists to conviction—Turf-cutters taught Repentance and Faith—A Man goes on his knees while taught Salvation—Another receives the Truth on Baptism and the True Church—Ribaldry Rebuked with good effect—A Tradesman Denounces the Reformation—A Devotee Vilifies the Protestant Bible and Discusses in the open air at night—Love of Learning in Boys—A Professed Romanist, and yet a True Believer in Jesus—His Experience, and several interesting Conversations with him.

THIS chapter is written at a season when tourists love to wander by the sea shore. There they will be struck with the aspect of the beetling cliffs, whose wave-worn sides disclose the under-lying strata elsewhere concealed. It is as if a hill were sliced in two to show the materials of which it is composed.

A similar insight into the world of mind is presented by a missionary's conversations. On the most important of all subjects, they expose to view men's thoughts, otherwise hidden. And as it is the " mind that makes the man," these disclosures are more valuable—or may be made so—than the discoveries of the geologist. The one excels the other, as much as mind excels matter. This fact is admirably brought out by the celebrated E. Irving, in the following remark on the fall of man. " God, after making Adam—a creature for an image and likeness of Himself—did resolve him into vile clay, through viler corruption, when he sinned; proving that one act of sin was, in God's sight, of far more account than a whole world teeming with beautiful and blessed life, which He would rather send headlong into death, than suffer one sin of His creature to go unpunished. . . . . This was a sublime exaltation of the moral above the material, showing that material beauty and blessedness of life is but, as it were, the clothing of one good thought, which, if it becomes evil, straightway all departs, like the shadow of a dream."

We have said that these conversations may be made useful. We allude to the help which they may afford to believers willing to aid in this mission, but unacquainted with the right mode of addressing Roman Catholics, or with their peculiar feelings and opinions. How necessary such knowledge is, need not be stated. Indeed it is the want of it that has led so many to regard the Roman Catholics as impracticable, and to give them up in despair. The cause of this failure was, that the instruction offered to them, though it might be true and Scriptural in itself, was not of a kind that Romanists could understand or appreciate. Differing from us on so many essential points, and generally ignorant of Scripture, they must be taught in a different way from ignorant Protestants, and with that way, no one can become fully acquainted without experience. That is the ground on which we claim some value for these conversations.

3. *Their openness to conviction when suitably addressed:*

Conversed with three men whom I employed to carry in turf. They were rough-looking, and unwashed, apparently, for many weeks, and one of them was barefoot notwithstanding the late cold. They spoke but little English. One of them, when he saw a child of mine coming to me, quoted to his fellow-workmen an Irish proverb, that people were twice children, meaning in youth and old age. Hearing this, I related to them our Lord's way of settling a dispute, by putting a child in their midst, and saying, "Unless ye be converted, and become as little children," &c. I explained, also, how little children are examples to us, and said that it would have been better for thousands if they had died in infancy. "Yes," said one of the men, with more knowledge of theology than I had expected, "for in that case they would have no sin but *peacadh na sinsear*"—original sin.

In the evening we talked of the trials of the poor, when I showed that Christ Himself took to His *choice* to be a poor man. I then related the case of a farmer, whom I once met in great distress, as he had been "Noticed to Quit" his home and land; but, on my asking him if he had not—for the present at least—" a place to lay his head," he was greatly moved when I told him that Jesus, when on earth, had not even that much; and he replied, " I did'nt think of that ever before; it is a very feeling word." We then spoke of the shortness of life, which we all admit so easily, and yet in practice forget.

I then told them a story out of Dr. Gallagher. A hermit of the middle ages having consented, after great importunity on the part of his brethren, to preach to them a sermon on repentance, spoke not a word after entering the pulpit, but only burst into tears. On trying a second and third time to speak, tears still came instead of words. At last, finding utterance, he exclaimed—and that was the whole sermon—" Brethren, let us weep for our sins now, lest we weep for them throughout eternity." Following up the subject, I explained the true nature of repentance, as being sorrow for sin, versus penance; and I then showed that the only remedy for sin was the blood of Jesus. The men listened very attentively, but said nothing, and on leaving, they prayed for " myself and family."

A Man goes on his Knees while taught the Way of Salvation.

For the first time for some weeks we were blessed with a beautiful day. Accordingly I walked to B——, four miles. On returning, I got into conversation with a poor man in L—— wood. Like the "lame man" in the temple at Jerusalem, he had asked me for "an alms;" and from this I took occasion to direct him to something better. He spoke only Irish. Having told him solemnly that we were all sinners, and as such deserved eternal damnation, he became greatly affected. He seemed to tremble. I suppose he took me for a priest. I then proceeded to explain the way of salvation, when he instantly threw himself on one knee in the middle of the road, and listened with great reverence. I then told him of a Friend above who took pity on us—for our sake descended from heaven, assumed our nature, and died on the cross as a "penance for our sins;" and now, having atoned for us, He offers to us immediate pardon. I begged him to trust only in that Saviour. He replied after the Romish fashion, "I will, with the help of God and the Virgin." I then told him that Jesus alone should be trusted in, and that He alone could save us; and I begged him to ask Jesus for His Holy Spirit, to give him a new heart, so that he might hate all sin, and love God supremely. Meantime several other Roman Catholics appeared in sight, who, I feared, would interrupt the conversation; so I drew the matter to a close, and gave the poor man some help, as he seemed to be in distress. He was most grateful, and, as I left, he repeated the Lord's prayer in Irish, "*Ar nathair,*" &c.

After I had passed on a little further, I overtook a decent-looking woman of middle age. She carried a creel on her back, as is common here even with farmers' wives, when they attend market. After saluting her in Irish, I asked if the great rain had injured the crops in her country. "In S——, you mean," said she. I said yes. She replied that the rain had laid the crops, but had done no other harm. I then turned the conversation to the goodness of God in causing the earth to produce her fruit for people, most of whom daily broke His commandments, and some of whom insult His holy name by cursing and swearing. I then dwelt on the evil of all sin, and said that a hundred years of prayer and good works would not atone to God for one sin. This seemed to startle her, for, with an exclamation for "mercy," she put up her hand to her forehead, and "crossed" herself. I then introduced Christ's love, atonement, and free offer of pardon. All this she heard with the deepest interest. As an example of free, immediate salvation, I referred to the thief on the cross, asking her did she ever hear of him. She said that she had, but did not hear fully, and would like to hear it all. So I told her what a bad life he had led up to the hour of his death; but fortunately for him, he happened to be crucified near to Jesus, and finding out that He was the Son of God, he offered one prayer to Him; and that prayer being in faith, was enough for his salvation. "You would think, perhaps," said I, "that Jesus would say to him, 'You have spent your life in the service of the devil, and do you think I will take you now?' No: but Jesus' reply was, 'To-day shalt thou be with me in paradise.' So," said I, "Jesus can save you also this moment, without waiting for penances or any thing else." While I thus spoke, she listened with the deepest interest, and "crossed" herself repeatedly. She did not appear to doubt one word I said, but to feel as if it came from God, whose Word indeed it was. I was thankful for this impression, but regretted to notice people watching us from the fields with no friendly feeling. I feared, too, that we might be annoyed at the village of fishermen at C——. So, to prevent this, I apologized for haste, and bade God bless her, which she returned most cordially.

A Roman Catholic candidly admits the truth regarding Baptism and the true Church, &c.

During the early part of the day, the weather was very fine; so I took a walk as far as B——. The people, after the long rain, were busy drawing sea-weed, and spreading it on their potato fields; so the country presented a cheerful look, after the late wintry solitude and dreariness.

Met many men and women coming to town, some of whom I saluted in Irish. In one place I passed three people engaged in earnest conversation, one of whom, after my salutation, followed after me, as if desirous to converse. A reference to the late severe weather, suggested the remark that God gave us more good than we deserved. To this he assented, adding that God would give us many other good gifts also, only for our sins. He also alluded to the strife and divisions existing in society. On this point, I stated that much of true religion consisted in loving our neighbour as truly as ourselves; but that most people, of all sects, while admitting this duty, lived as if the Saviour had never taught it. He said he feared that no one practised it. I replied that some tried to do so; and that there was a great difference between doing willing service to the devil, and resisting him. At the same time I said that no man living has so obeyed this law as by it to deserve any thing from God; and that only the death and merits of Christ will avail for the pardon of any sin. Then I quoted John iii. 16; and stated that God could not pardon or bless any man, but for the sake of

Christ. He admitted this; but in a few minutes afterwards said, that we could not get the grace or favour of Christ, unless we deserve it! "In that case," said I, "no one will ever get it; for no one deserves it. We deserve only hell. Besides, the promise is not, 'deserve, and you will find,' but, '*seek*, and you will find.' And if it were not so, how could the thief on the cross have been saved." This example struck him very forcibly; so that he admitted the truth of the great doctrine which it implied.

The conversation then turned to Mr. Lever, and the Galway Packet Line—the success of which he was anxious to hear; the folly of trusting to representatives in Parliament, who did nothing for the country, but only for themselves; the singularity of Father Daly proposing a Protestant candidate for Galway; the opposition of the Limerick people to the Galway interests, of whom he spoke severely, calling them "brutish;" the hope of Ireland's prosperity, agricultural and commercial, &c.

After this, he made several allusions to sects, as if to ascertain to which I belonged. But I took no notice of it; only I told him that, in my opinion, the true Church consisted, not of one sect alone, but of some members of different sects, being those only whose hearts were renewed by God's Spirit. "Now," said I, "some Roman Catholics have told me that they depend on the Spirit of God guiding their clergy; but I tell you that, unless the people have the Spirit for themselves also, that will not avail them."

"But don't you mean by a change of heart, baptism?"

"No. There are two baptisms; one of water, and the other of the Spirit. The latter is evidenced by a holy life. But don't you know that most who receive water-baptism are not changed at all, but live in the practice of sin? But when a man receives the Holy Spirit, he is made to hate all sin, and to love God supremely. And this Spirit is given only to those who seek it through Christ, putting all their trust in His merits."

"Well, what I do is, I go to my clergy, and confess my sins to him; and when I feel sorrow for my sin, is not that what is wanted?"

"That sorrow is very well so far as it goes. But, in many cases, it is only sorrow that God will not permit people to go on in sin, while the love of it still remains. 'Tis like a drunkard throwing away the bottle when he has emptied it; but the reason is not that he hates the whiskey, but that it is all drunk. Now, do you not see from the way that people relapse into sin after confession, that such is the case with them; still the love of sin remains, and *that* no clergyman can change. They can but point the way to heaven—only God's Spirit can change the heart. Christ, by dying, has opened heaven; but what of that, if people will not enter in? What good were it to you if you were drowning, and I threw you a rope, if you did not lay hold on it? That laying hold on Christ is the true faith. And if any man, of any sect, do so, he will be saved. If not, he will perish."

"There is no use in going to a clergyman, so. What is the use of confession if we do not get pardon through it?"

"Can any clergyman give you pardon on different terms from Christ? Now, Christ says that no man can enter heaven till his heart be changed. If, then, a clergyman can pardon you without that change, this is a new way to heaven! And as for your sorrow for sin—till you get the Spirit —'tis like cutting off the top of a weed in a garden, while the root remains in the ground, ready to spring up again. That's the reason why so many are ever relapsing into sin: they have not the Spirit. And I advise you to ask for it.

We may not ever meet again; but I beg you, for your own soul's sake, to go to God; on your knees tell Him you are a lost sinner, deserving hell, and that you put all your trust in Christ. And for His sake, ask God to change your heart, making you hate all sin, and love all His commandments."

"Well, these are good words, I admit. And what you say of sin is true. Now, I am a sincere Catholic, and believe my religion is the best; and that without any offence to other religions. Was it, Sir, in the Catholic or Protestant Church you were baptized?"

"In the Protestant; but I do not agree with many Protestants in some things. [meaning those whom he knew.] The true Church, I believe, is not confined to any sect, but is composed of all whose hearts are changed by grace—to whatever Church they belong."

"Capital doctrine! What you say is very fair. And I am glad you're not any of the Jumpers who leave their own Church."

"I belong to the same Church as the ancient Irish saints—as St. Patrick, and St. Columbkille. And my wish is, that the Irish people would not have any foreign Church, but a pure Church of their own."

I then begged him to read the Bible for himself; and said that one of the priests of his Church—Martin Boos—held the same view (substantially) regarding the way of salvation as I did; and that it was also his opinion that only few would be saved. Indeed he once said he feared that, of his large congregation, not more would be saved than would fill the "sacristy," or little room for the vestments. We then conversed on the blessings of education; and he regretted that the Archbishop of Tuam had prohibited National Schools in Connemara. He also admitted, notwithstanding his dislike to converts, that some of them had become very intelligent since they began to study the Scriptures.*

An Aged Fisherman, poor and nearly blind, knows not how to die.

In the evening, walking by the sea-shore, I met an old man, who told me that he lived in the C——. Gave me his name, and stated that he was now quite alone in the world, having neither wife, child, or near relative. Formerly he lived by fishing, and by going out sometimes as a sailor to the United States; but in one of these voyages his eyes were injured by a cold, and now one of them is quite blind, and the other defective in sight. He was out all this day looking for help; but had got only three potatoes, which he showed me in his pockets. As might be expected, he ended by asking an alms.

As he spoke English imperfectly, I answered in Irish; and said that I could do him a greater favour than to give him a little help for his bodily wants. "You are now," said I, "an old man; and if God were to call you, do you know where your soul would go? How could you appear before Him when your sins are more in number than the sands of the sea shore, [pointing to it,] and one sin alone would send your soul to the bottom of hell?" This solemn address seemed to startle him. He said that it (the charge) was true; and that he did not know what he would do if he were called to die. Then, in allusion to what I had stated of the awfulness of death, he told me of a monk who once lived in the C——, and who, after all his austerities, said before his death, that

---

* As some of the above conversation may seem strange coming from a Romanist, I have only to assure the reader that it is accurately reported; and that, on the most important points, it is nearly verbatim.

"he was now more afraid to die than he was in his youth." From this he appeared to infer that there was no possibility at all of dying happily. "Well," said I, in reply, "all this fear proceeded from his trusting in his own works; for in that way no man can find peace." Then I explained to him the unmerited love of Jesus, and his atonement; also faith. He heard all attentively, and thanked me for my instruction. I told him that my only object was his good; that having read in God's book what I had stated, it was my delight to explain it to all who would hear me. On parting, as the man was in such want, I gave him a little help. The more I see of the Romanists here, the greater do I find their spiritual and temporal disadvantages; and that makes it so difficult to do good amongst them. They are constantly at starvation-point; and this so absorbs their thoughts as to leave little room for the Gospel. And should they embrace it, they then lose the little means of support they have, and so become perfectly helpless.

Profane Singing Rebuked, and Palliated on the ground of a previous "Absolution."

As I was walking home near B——, a young woman who was carrying a pail of water began to sing a profane song. This is often done out of disrespect to me. But I would not have noticed it in this case, only as I passed, I heard another girl ask her would she attend the chapel to-night. It was "Holy Thursday," when the chapel is splendidly decorated. Stopping for a moment, I asked the singer might I put a question to her. She replied civilly in the affirmative. "Well," said I, "if you sing profane songs in the morning, is it any use to hear hymns in the chapel in the evening? That is, to serve the devil one half of the day, and God the other half?" By this pointed question, I did not mean to offend her; nor did she seem vexed. She only denied that the song was profane; and said that she had no sin to answer for, as the priest had forgiven her all. Neither did she practise any sin whatever. After saying this, she stopped suddenly in the middle of the road, and, raising her voice, prayed solemnly to the Virgin Mary to "direct us, keep us from sin, and guide us in the right way." I suppose this was part of her daily prayers; but it was all to the Virgin; in it was no word of God or of Christ—at least, that I heard. I replied that I joined in every word of the prayer; but would direct it only to God in Christ. "You know," said I, "that it was Christ, and not the Virgin, who died for us." To that she made no reply; but the other girl shouted that, "if the Virgin did not die for us, she did what was as good.' What that was, she did not explain; and in speaking so loud, her object was, I believe, to attract the attention of some sea-weed cutters who were passing by; but they took no notice of it. Both girls then added—still in a loud voice— that if they had any sins, they confessed them to the priest, and he forgave all. I also raised my voice that others might hear; and said that I could show them, from a sermon by one of their own priests, that most "absolutions" were useless, because the people had not the right dispositions; and I said that if they had, they were forgiven already. But by this time they had reached their own house; or, at least, they took occasion to cut short the conversation by entering one. And so the matter ended.

Ribaldry of Workmen severely rebuked with good effect.

This morning, in my garden, I overheard Father D——'s workmen conversing in Irish behind my garden, when very obscene language was used. That it was done to annoy me, I have no doubt, for they spoke so loud as to be heard a great way off. Under these circumstances, I considered it my duty to interpose. So opening the gate, I walked over to one of the men, and I asked him in Irish if it was he who had spoken the bad words. He admitted it, when I told him plainly that no man could so speak unless instigated by the devil. He had made no scruple of speaking evil, so I resolved to be equally plain in my rebuke. "And now," said I, "your own priest, Father D——, or any other, would give you the same opinion of it as I do. Besides, I have read in the sermons of Dr. Gallagher, one of your priests, that whoever lives in the practice of any known mortal sin has the devil every night for his bedfellow!" "Oh!" said he, "I know it was wrong." "Well, then, remember, as our Lord said, 'What would it profit you to gain the whole world, and lose your soul?' One day in the place of torment would make you feel the evil of sin for ever." I then exhorted him to repent, and to ask the Saviour's forgiveness, and the gift of His Holy Spirit, to cleanse his unholy nature and make him pure. I added that I gave him this advice for his good, and not from any unkind feeling. He replied meekly that he took it so, and thanked me for it. I said I was obliged to him for taking it in that light, and then left. On thinking over the affair afterwards, I felt surprised that the extreme severity of the rebuke had not vexed the man. I believe some other Roman Catholics, if they were in his place, and God did not restrain them, would have struck me with their spades. However, this man's own conscience seemed to smite him.

Such are a few examples of the openness of this people to conviction when suitably addressed. That there were many exceptions, has been already stated; specially in time of persecution, when very few dare to listen at all. For *that* the missionary must be prepared; but he may console himself with the reflection, that in matters affecting salvation a little success is a great gain, just as the dealers in pearls consider a single precious one an indemnification for years of toil. But, alas! how many of us, by neglecting the salvation of our neighbours, daily trample on better pearls, and know it not. Still further to show that this people, if left to themselves, would, as the rule, give a fair hearing to the truth, I subjoin the following account of the work of a single day. If that state of things had been allowed to continue, I could not conceive of a more delightful occupation than that of the Irish missionary; but even a few of such sun-blinks are very encouraging, and should excite his praise to God for thus employing him even occasionally as the successful dispenser of spiritual good to a people, with all their faults, so interesting and so grateful.*

After walking over T—— hill, a shower came on, to escape which, I went to a cabin that stood near the road. I stood outside, waiting to see if I would be asked in. Very soon a woman and girl came to the door, and civilly invited me to sit down till the shower would pass over. Within was a man eating his dinner, who turned out to be the master of the house. Suspecting what I was, no doubt, he looked very sulky. Without ceremony he asked where I came from; and when I told him, he abused my country, saying that it was a place full of poverty and pride. I answered, that

* They have been charged with a habit of assenting hypocritically to whatever is told them; and no doubt, there are many instances of the kind, which, however, are often owing to a natural politeness, rather than to hypocrisy. But whatever temptation some of them might have to act the hypocrite to masters or employers, they had none to do so to an unfriended, persecuted missionary, as I was in Galway; and, in fact, they generally did the very contrary.

likely he was but slightly acquainted with it; and, as to pride, I said all men were born in sin.

Again he began abusing my country, as if resolved to pick a quarrel; but his wife interposed with a few kind words. He then changed the subject, and denounced the number of sects, and specially those who "scattered tracts on the roads." I denied that I did so, on which his wife explained that he did not mean me. He then demanded if I ever knew a turn-coat who, when dying, did not send for the priest. I assured him that I did; but he maintained the contrary, saying that they all turned for money. "Take care," said I, "of judging men's hearts; God only can do that; and He will one day be your Judge; and He says that they who have no mercy on others will receive no mercy for themselves." This remark softened him a little, for he added, "I have no objection to one born a Protestant, but only to turn-coats."

He then introduced some arguments, such as that there was only one true Church, and only one Mass. My answer I need not give, being of the usual kind. After that I proceeded to show, that according to our belief, there was no atonement for sin but the death and merits of Jesus; that we depended not on saint or angel; and while we honoured the Virgin as a holy woman, whom all "generations should call blessed," yet we looked not to her for salvation, nor worshipped her. This last observation might appear sufficiently respectful to the Virgin, but it fell far short of his exalted ideas on the subject. He could bear no more, but started up from his seat in anger. He did not order me out, but hinted it significantly. In leaving I merely regretted his uncharitable disposition towards me. To this he made no reply; but his wife, ever anxious to drop a kind word between us, exclaimed, "that he had no bad heart to me or to any one else."

Walking on towards ——, I overtook a man who had his coat off, and hanging on his arm. Him I saluted in the usual Irish phrase; but, as he stopped to talk to another man, I passed on. Soon, however, he overtook me, and asked what o'clock it was. He then proceeded to speak of the weather, of improvement of the country, and wages, &c. When he alluded to the former poverty, I said it was a sad thing to be poor in both worlds. I also quoted the remarks of a dying man :—" How miserable a thing it is, that we so seldom inquire why we were sent into this world, until we are leaving it." Finding that I was a stranger here, he wondered how I knew Irish, when I made some remarks on the beauty of the language. We then returned to the subject of religion, when I stated that there was only one Saviour, who was able and willing to save all who seek Him, because He had Himself " done penance" for their sins on the cross. He said that was true, but that " God liked help." I replied, that in working out our salvation Christ needed no help of ours; that His merits alone atoned for sin; but that after our becoming His by faith, we get grace to do good works. He then introduced the Virgin Mary, as having power with God through her intercession; but he had scarcely finished the sentence, when, on a sudden turn of the road in a wood, two priests on horseback made their appearance. They looked at me very sharply; and one of them rode up as if he would accost me. Instead of doing so, however, they beckoned to the man beside me; and he, falling back, went off with them in the direction they were going. He had told me a little before that he was going home towards the village of ——; so this sudden change was at the instance of the priests. No doubt their object was to interrogate him respecting the subject of our conversation.

After this I walked as far as B——. On returning I had come nearly as far as where the priests met me, when I saw a woman weeping and crying out, "Oh! what will I do! what will I do!" I asked her what ailed her; as I suspected that it was a trick on her part to get alms. But it was not so; for, on pointing to her donkey, a half-starved creature, loaded with turf, I saw its knees and other parts of its body cut and bleeding. It had fallen under the load. She said that her husband was sick at home, and that they had not a penny or morsel of food in the house; and that all her dependence was placed on this load of turf, which she feared the animal would never carry to the town. With that she beat him again, trying to drive him on; but again he fell! Pitying her sad condition, I gave her a little help; and I was going to say a few words to her regarding salvation, but a carriage coming up at the instant, she was obliged to use all her efforts to get the donkey out of the way. So I passed on.

A young woman, who had been looking on, followed me. She spoke good English, and corroborated the account which the other had given of herself. She stated that this was the second wife of her husband, and that he had three children by her, besides two others by the previous wife; and that he had become so sickly that he could do no work for their support. With this young woman I had an interesting conversation also on the need of seeking salvation; the shortness of time; our inability to save ourselves; the death and merits of Jesus; the nature and source of the new birth, and the promises made to those who seek it. All this she listened to with great attention, and without making any objection.

After my return home, I walked out again in the evening along the sea-shore. Rain came on, to escape which I knocked at a cabin door on my way. The door was bolted inside, the common entrance being by the back door. It was opened by a decent-looking woman, who received me kindly, and wiping a long stool asked me to sit down. I thanked her in Irish, when she became still kinder, and wondered to hear the like of me speak Irish. Soon after, I introduced the subject of salvation, and told her that "Jesus was the only name given under heaven whereby we must be saved," and I bewailed the neglect of seeking His salvation. As evidence of this, I referred to the number of people drunk yesterday; (Patrick's Day;) and, with regard to swearing, I asked her to walk through the markets or fairs, and hear all the sins committed in that way. In regard to this latter sin, I added that, in one sense, it was the worst of all—a man gained nothing by it. If he stole, he had some gain; but that not being the case with regard to swearing, it was a gratuitous insult to God. She said she had heard the same from the priest in the chapel, and was much struck with the coincidence. I then explained to her my view of the way of salvation, and she prayed the Lord to bless me for it. "But," said she, very solemnly, "I suppose you do not honour the Virgin as we do. I think that is the difference between us." "That is our chief difference," said I. "We believe that Jesus alone saves the soul. He, only, died for our sins; and I believe, if the Virgin were now on earth, she would give us the same advice as she gave the servants at the marriage of Cana—'Whatever He saith to you, do it.'" She, in reply, dwelt on the fact of her being our Lord's mother, and that a son honours his mother. I said that, as God, He had no mother; and that, as such, He had created the Virgin herself, as well as the sun and sea, &c. "A thousand praises to Him," said she. "He has all power." "Yes," said I, "and needs no help." Still, however, I saw that she adhered to her hope in the Virgin's intercession.

Changing the subject, she asked, had we "baptism in our

Church?" "Yes," said I, "but we use only water." "You dont, then, use salt, like us?" adding something else, which I forget. I said, "Nothing but what God has ordered." "Then," said she, "your view is to use nothing in worship but what is ordered in Scripture?" "You have just hit it," said I; "that is our principle. We add nothing to what is ordered, and take nothing from it." And I asked her was it safe to interfere with God's appointment.

In this way we went over several other points, specially the way in which the thief on the cross was saved, who had no time to do good works, but only believed in Jesus. I explained also that great Gospel text, John iii. 16. Meantime, her interest in the subject seemed unabated. As I rose to depart, I prayed God to guide us into all truth by His Spirit; and told her, if we wished to be right, we must pray daily for His teaching; and that we must also live on the grace of Christ daily, as we take daily food for our bodies; and I assured her, that if we asked this in dependence on His merits, we would get it. So I left, and she stood in the door blessing me.

4.—*The Arguments of Educated Romanists.*

It has been already remarked, that the great majority of Western Romanists are not competent for regular argumentation, nor should it be forced upon them. At the same time, however, there are individuals amongst them, who, by superior education and study of the question, are very clever controversialists, and who, confident in their abilities, often challenge discussion. In such cases, of course, the missionary has no excuse for avoiding it; but even then he should ever remember, that all controversy is lost labour that has no bearing on the salvation of the soul. Of the arguments used by these disputants, a few examples will suffice.

An Intelligent Tradesman Discusses Image-worship, and fiercely Denounces the Protestant Reformation.

Though the weather was still wet, I took a walk between showers across the hill. Overtook a man carrying a bundle in his hand, who was better dressed than the peasantry, and spoke English well, being a man of considerable education.

We began by referring to the weather; and when I remarked that it was better than we deserved from God, he replied—" I believe I am addressing a Protestant minister." He then added, ironically—" If we were what we ought to be, we would not need clergy at all." This sally amused him greatly; but I waived it for something more useful. " Well," said he, " there is one wrong that you and others of your persuasion do us. You say that we worship images; but that is not the fact. Thus, when we look at the picture of the crucifixion, it puts us in mind of Christ dying for us, and that is all." I answered that I did not class all Roman Catholics together; but that while he and other intelligent persons might not worship the images, might not the ignorant do so; and was not the use of images in churches calculated to lead to this abuse? Hence, we condemned the practice; but I would be sorry to charge all the Roman Catholics with intentionally worshipping images; on the contrary, I wished to think as charitably as I could of Roman Catholics. This pleased him, for he replied, " I never before met so civil a Protestant minister."

He then assured me, that the principles of the Church of Rome were—love to God with all our heart and soul, and to our neighbour as ourselves. These principles I approved highly, saying that they were true Christianity; but I asked, if we had not lived up to them, how could we get pardon?

This brought him to a stand; but, after a little hesitation, he replied, that the way to get pardon was to repent, and to take the sacraments. I said that the sacraments were like food for a living man, but not able to impart life or pardon at the first. We must be born again before we could be Christians at all, and I explained in what that consisted. After I had dwelt on this point, he got angry, and for the first time I noticed on him the appearance of drink; but on further observation I suspected that this was only "put on," as a pretext for the insolence that followed. Be that as it may, he told me that he had once to avow a tenet of his Church, the denial of which would be mortal sin; so that, if he died in the denial of it, he would be damned! This tenet was, that out of the pale of the Catholic Church there was no salvation. I replied, that I belonged to the Catholic Church, properly so called. "But not," said he, "to the Roman Catholic." "Nor is it said," I replied, "that there is no salvation out of that Church. The word is, that "whosoever believeth in Jesus will be saved, and whosoever believeth not shall be damned." I then advised him to study the Scripture in order to find out the truth on the subject. He replied contemptuously, "How could I choose amongst the fifty thousand Protestant sects?" Then he got excited, and raising his stick in the air, fiercely denounced the Reformation. "The bloody Reformation," said he, "the founder of it ought to have been crucified." "And so," I replied, "the Founder of my religion *was* crucified." This allusion increased his rage, so that he exclaimed—"In five years, not one of your persuasion will be in existence." I thought it now time to stop; so taking advantage of a cross-road, I bade him good-bye, telling him I was sorry that he had so soon forgot his principle of love to his neighbour. This reminiscence softened him. He put out his hand, which I cordially shook, wishing him in Irish "God speed." On hearing this, he, in the same language, wished me "seven thousand blessings," and then shook my hand over again—and so we parted.

A Devotee Discusses the Way of Salvation, and curiously accounts for the Origin of the Protestant Bible.

This man, of his own accord, introduced the subject of religion, after hearing a remark which I made to some workmen, that in matters of business "we should obey conscience." "Without obeying conscience," said he, "there is no salvation." From this we were led to speak of the commandments of God, free will, and the possibility of our keeping the whole law of God, which he affirmed, though he admitted our need of God's grace. He then, nearly in the words of our Lord's parable, compared the state of a sinner to that of a tree, which is manured, and dug round, and pruned, in order to fruitfulness, and failing in that, it is at last cut down and cast away for ever. Such, he said, was the condition of every sinner. And when I added, that after this life there remained no possibility of any more probation, he assented, saying, "No man can have two lifetimes." He seemed not to perceive that this upset purgatory. He then alluded to the temptations of the devil, and said that the permission of such was the only thing that stumbled him in the providence of the Son of God. Indeed he used a stronger Irish word than stumble—something implying displeasure—but I believe he did not mean that, for he appeared to be, in his way, a devout man, and whenever I mentioned the name of Christ, he reverently raised his hat.

When talking he ran along with great volubility, being an excellent Irish speaker. Seldom could I get him to pause that I might put in a few words of explanation; and he still begged me to hear him patiently. However, we did not differ much until I quoted Dr. Gallagher on the small number that will be saved. After this he broke out into a fierce tirade against Luther and Calvin, as the authors of Protestantism. He denounced them as apostate priests, and charged them with forging a new Bible of their own. "First," said he, "they wrote it out privately and buried it in the ground. Then they waited till the grass grew over the spot concealing it; after which they gathered a crowd of people, some of whom believed their doctrines, while others did not; but all were deceived by the trick, so as to receive this forgery as the real old Bible of the Church." After he had finished this story, I merely remarked that there was not one word of truth in it. As he did not profess to have any proof, I proceeded to explain the way of salvation out of the Scriptures; but he ran away, saying he was in haste. He still, however, remained within hearing distance, and came back occasionally to have a few "more last words." He insisted, as before, that keeping the commandments was the way to heaven; and when I told him that God gave but ten commandments, to which his Church had added six, he, in proof of her authority to do so, quoted—"hear the Church." But I said that the Church herself must "hear God," otherwise her words were only the words of man; and that, in fact, it was the Word of God which I was now speaking to him, and which he would not hear. He replied that the Church of Rome was the only Church, and would never fall. I undertook to show from Scripture prophecy that the Church of Rome would fall; but as he was in such haste to depart, I requested him to come to my house at any other time to conclude the subject. He said that he doubted not that I would make him welcome, but it was only to convert him. I said I considered it the greatest honour on earth to be the means of turning a soul to the right way. But he repelled the idea of the possibility of conversion in his case, and imputed my zeal to mercenary motives. However, he said he would not blame me, as I was brought up in that way. He then left abruptly. Excepting this last imputation he treated me civilly throughout, and he took all I said in good part. In leaving, too, he expressed his best wishes for my welfare.

This Discussion renewed and carried on after nightfall in the open air.

In the morning I had a long conversation with a Claddagh man. There was another man present from the same place, but he only listened. We spoke mostly in Irish. I began by referring to drunkenness—the evil and prevalence of which I set fully before him, giving examples of it that had come under my own observation. Meantime one of the men happened to swear; so I took up that sin next, and said, that while all religions condemned the practice, it was very common. The man admitted this, and said, "We know very well it is wrong, and yet we do it." In reply, I warned him that any sin persisted in against conscience, would cause God to withdraw His light from us, and to leave us in darkness. Still further to show the wickedness of cursing, I quoted Dr. G——, who says, that since no gain is made by it as by stealing, it is a gratuitous insult to God, and therefore the greater sin.

I then alluded to the way of salvation. At this, the man started up suddenly, and asked—"What is that way?" "Christ," I replied, "who died for us, and who alone can save us. To Him all are welcome; and He can instantly cleanse the sins of all—both of Protestants and Roman Catholics alike." That," said I, "is my entire hope for myself, and not any thing I can do, or that man can do for me."

After hearing this, the man reflected a good deal, but said nothing. We then spoke on other subjects, after which I left.

Soon after my leaving, three priests came to the place, and spoke for a while to the men; so I was informed afterwards, but I was not told what they said. In the evening, however, when I returned, I found before me the devotee with whom I had the former discussion. As I came up, one of the men remarked to him in my hearing, what good advice I had given them in the morning. N—— replied sharply, "Perhaps himself wants good advice, too." "Yes," said I, "I always need advice from above." Then he at once launched into argument, or what he considered such, for it was only a string of quotations from his Irish catechism. I was glad, however, to hear him admit, at the outset, that "according to nature we had no good in us, unless God by His Spirit inspired it into our souls." To this I cordially assented. We then spoke of the Saviour; but he said that to get the benefit of His salvation "we must follow His rules," which also I admitted, if properly understood. "Well, then," said he, "we admit one God, one faith, one Saviour, and (with emphasis) one true Church." "Yes," said I, "if you understand what that Church is. It is composed of all men, from the beginning of the world, who have accepted Christ as their Saviour, and whose hearts have been renewed by the Spirit. That is the one true Church, out of which there is no salvation." Running off again from the point in hand, he quoted from the catechism the "seven sins against the Holy Ghost." I admitted that these were great sins, but said that the one damning sin was omitted, and that was unbelief, quoting our Lord's words, "He that believeth shall be saved, and he that believeth not shall be damned."

Next he quoted the catechism on "penance." I said that

some of this was very good; but that I altogether objected to the part which required us to "satisfy God" for our sins. "That is impossible," said I, "sin being so hateful to God;" and, as an example, I referred to the eating of the apple by our first parents, which to us would seem a small thing, but for which Adam could never atone. This point I explained fully, and was glad to find that the workmen assented to me more than to him; for they were listening all the time sitting on their creels. This disconcerted him, so he seemed at a loss for an answer. Indeed it was now late: the night had insensibly darkened around us, and the moon had shone out on the bay. But still the men, after their day's labour, seemed not in the least tired of the controversy. Encouraged by this, I solemnly besought them all not to trust their immortal souls to any thing but the atonement of Jesus; and reminded them that His sufferings were thrown away if we could for ourselves "satisfy God," as this catechism required. "No," said I, addressing N——, "if you were all your lifetime shedding tears, and at last shed every drop of your blood, it would not do; for Christ alone can save us. Remember," I added, "that not only Adam, but the fallen angels were shut out of heaven for a single sin."

As if to turn the subject, N. caught at this last idea, and confidently maintained, that the reason why the devil was cast out was, because he refused to humble himself to the Mother of God! I told him she was not then in existence; but his answer was ready: "God foresaw that she would be, and ordered all the angels to bow to her. Proud Lucifer refusing, was cast out with all his followers." At this odd notion, I could not refrain from laughter, saying, that I would not give ear to such "old wives' fables." But he insisted that it was all true. I told him that I would adhere to whatever was in his own Bible, but that this was not.

Having quoted Dr. Gallagher, he asked me had I read his sermon on "Confession." I said I had; and then I cited what he says of those who after absolution relapse into sin; that their absolution, in such a case, was null and void; and that such a confession was only a mockery of God, and instead of conferring spiritual benefit, only increased their guilt and sealed their damnation. All this was admitted by N——, but the workmen seemed quite startled by it, specially when I added, "Now, after what that honest priest has said, how can Roman Catholics tell me that, as a matter of course, after confession they are as free from sin as when they were born?" To this they could make no reply,

By this time it was too late to speak any more, and all the while we had been standing in the open air. On leaving, both N—— and the men prayed for me.

The grounds on which an intelligent Romanist excuses the persecution of Converts, and condemns Protestant Missions.

To-day when in the room of H——, we got into a conversation on the late outbreak of the mob. He said that my being a sufferer was owing to a mistake; that Rev. Mr. —— was in the habit of posting up offensive placards before his own door, one of which was headed, in large type, "Roman Catholic idolaters;" that when the Roman Catholic missioners were here, he went amongst certain women who were selling crucifixes, circulating his tracts, and interfering with their worship.* He also stated that he would forbear with Protestants, but not with "Jumpers." I said that the latter were equally entitled to toleration as the others; but he

* These statements are given here merely as part of our conversation. From my own knowledge I could not either affirm or deny them; only I am aware that most Romanists are predisposed to take the worst view of all Protestant missions.

denied that, insisisting that they all turned from corrupt motives. I said I knew some at least who were sincere, and if they were not, I attached no value to the change. I would, indeed, consider it the greatest honour on earth to be helpful towards the salvation of a Roman Catholic; but, at the same time, I considered I had no right to go further than, in a kind manner, to explain the truth to him, after which the matter lay wholly between himself and God. I then showed what it was to be a true Christian and a member of the true Church; that it consisted chiefly in saving faith in Christ and renewal by the Holy Spirit, evidenced by "newness of life." On that point he did not like to enter; still he was civil and rational from first to last. In conclusion, I advised him to read God's blessed Word for himself, having seen a few numbers of a new commentary on it lying on the table. He replied, with a laugh, "How could I understand it without a teacher: see all the sects there are for want of that." I replied that God has promised His Spirit to teach us, and would fulfil His promise if we ask it. Still, however, he repeated the same objection as before. I again urged the same advice, saying, that "surely whatever our religion, we must admit it is right to ask God to teach us: on that point we cannot differ." But he said no more, appearing still to hold his own view: and so we parted.

Another Discussion with the same on the Way of Salvation— the " Bearing of the Cross"—Doctrine of " Intention," &c.

To-day had another conversation with H——. Seeing in his room some numbers of Haydoch's Bible, I remarked, " I'm glad to find you read this blessed book. Continue to do so, and we will agree." He assented to my estimate of the Bible, and said that indeed it was the best of all books. " My confession of faith," said I, " may be given in one of its verses—

'God so loved the world, that He gave His only begotten Son, that whosoever believeth in Him should not perish, but have everlasting life.'"

"That is very good. But will a man be saved, nevertheless, who goes on drinking and cursing?"

"You mistake me. In saying Christ saves us when we believe, I mean He saves us *from sin* as well as punishment. He does not save us *in* sin, but *from* it. In fact, that is an essential point of our salvation."

"But *we* have something to do. Does He not say in another place, 'If any man come after me, let him take up his cross and follow me'"?

"Certainly. We cannot be saved, but in following Jesus. That is the test of faith, and what proves it genuine."

"But what do you say of those turncoats? I would not believe any one that they turn from conviction. Not one of them but turns to get gain.

"I differ from you. I know there is chaff among the wheat, but I am as sure as that I sit here, that some of them turn from right motives. Remember your charge is nothing new. Ages ago, the devil said of Job, 'Does he fear God for nought'? That is, he is religious only for gain."

"Well, what do you say of a Protestant gentleman who told Mr. H——, in my hearing, that if he turned a Protestant, he would get three times the business he now gets?"

"I would say of that Protestant that he was a bad man to hint such a motive, if he meant it seriously."

"Well, that is not all. I know officers in the army who, through shame, would not go to Mass, because it was not respectable. And so of the old Irish families who turned to save their properties."

"Well, I condemn that as much as you do. It was a dishonourable and sinful motive. But you are wrong in classing all converts together. There was a Judas amongst the Twelve:

no wonder, then, there are bad men calling themselves Protestants. But returning now to your assertion, that no Roman Catholic can turn except for gain: what do you think of this text of the Bible, 'There is one God, and one Mediator between God and men, the Lord Jesus Christ'? Now, I know a man, originally a Roman Catholic, who turned when he read that verse. He would not at first believe that it was in his own Bible, but when he got one, and found it so, he changed to Protestantism. Now, I ask, was not that an intelligible and rational motive? Was there any thing incredible in a man turning after that discovery? But that is not all. I heard in a place where I was travelling of a Protestant lady, whose husband, a Roman Catholic, got the priest to argue her into his religion. She asked the priest would a person be saved without baptism, and he said no. 'Well,' said she, in hearing of her husband, 'is it not a doctrine of your Church, that unless the priest *intend* to baptize, there is no baptism?" He had to admit this; and from that hour the husband became a Protestant, for he saw that there was no possibility of being certain of baptism or any thing else in the Church of Rome."

"I don't know about that." (doctrine of intention.)

"You may rely on it that such is the doctrine of your Church. I can show it in the priest's Missal, of which I have a copy. It is as sure as that you sit there. And see the effect. Besides rendering it impossible to know the certainty of a valid baptism, neither can you tell what it is you worship on a Sunday. Unless the priest intend to change it, you are worshipping a wafer! How can you be sure of another man's intention?"

"We know the priest does his duty as he ought."

"That you cannot tell. You are aware that many priests, in the time of the French Revolution, turned infidels, and some of them confessed that they had been such long before in heart, in which case they did not intend to consecrate at all; and what was the people worshipping in that case?"

Here he seemed puzzled, and changed the conversation.

"Well, about this people that turn, they're only weeds the Pope throws out of his garden."

"Why is he so angry, then, when they turn? Why all this persecution of them? As, for example, in T—— at present. On the other hand, what insult or injury has been inflicted on the Protestant ministers in England that have turned Roman Catholics?"

"No matter; we know what kind of people they are who turn. Don't they all gain by it? And look to the Reformers, who began your religion. Wer'nt they —— ?"

"Oh! that is a long story. I know what you are told against these men, and of course you believe it. Neither would you take my word on the other side. But to show you how little mere abuse is worth in these matters, if you ever go to London, step into a synagogue, and you will hear far more against our blessed Redeemer Himself! And in Jewish books, it is awful how they abuse Him!"

"Well, but what do you think of the Quakers. Will they be saved?"

"Having known some of them, I do not doubt but they will. I know that they believe in the one Saviour, and die in that faith."

"And the Unitarians?"

"I don't consider them Christians at all. They don't believe in the Saviour, when they deny his divinity. They do not believe in the Trinity."*

---

* Their right to call themselves Christians is not denied here in any offensive sense, but on the principle plainly laid down by Paul, that baptism into the name of a creature is unlawful; consequently, they are bound either to give up Christian baptism along with the Christian name, or to admit Christ's divinity.

"Well, but there is only one true Church. And does not Christ say, 'Whosoever hears you hears me'?

"True; but, mind, he said *that* to the apostles, whose words are in the Scriptures. So it is we who, in the true sense, 'hear the apostles,' because it is we who circulate and abide by the Scriptures."

"But it is said that we are to obey the Church."

"Not the Church of Rome. To her it is said, in the epistle addressed to herself, that she was liable to fall. (He seemed to doubt this.) Look to the 11th chapter of Romans, and you will find the place."

"Oh! I know it. And it has so happened." (By this, as afterwards came out, he meant, not that she fell into error, ut had lost her former power.)

"Fall from the truth I mean. We are not then to depend on that Church. And what do we want here in Ireland with the Church of *Rome?* We had our own Irish Church before she came here at all, and it was a pure one. It prized the Bible. St. Patrick used constantly to recite the Psalms. And so did the holy fathers, as St. Augustin and Cyprian. Cling to the Bible, then, and we will soon agree." Then rising to leave, I added, "I hope you will not think that I have said any thing to offend you—I said it only in kindness."

"I know that; and nothing was said that is any way offensive."

A Third Discussion with the same on the Pope's Temporal Power and his Supremacy, on Sects, and on Bearing the Cross, &c.

He introduced the news of the day regarding the Continent. We spoke of the Pope and his subjects. I said I feared that, being a Protestant minister, he would not receive my testimony on that point, but it appeared to me, that the

Pope, as a clergyman, had no right to organize armies, or to have a "Minister of War," or artillery, or rifled cannon, &c. He maintained, however, that the Pope had a right to his provinces as well as any other ruler, and therefore was at liberty to enforce obedience on his subjects. At the same time he did not deny, that not one in a hundred of them would vote for him, but said that, nevertheless, every true Catholic in the world would fight against them in this quarrel. I said I thought that strange, when clergymen were prohibited in Scripture from intermeddling in political matters; and on that ground, the Pope was bound to accept a support peacefully, rather than go to war. And as to his provinces, I did not see how he could claim them as head of the Church, when the Lord Jesus said of Himself, that His kingdom was not of this world. What Christ had not, no one can claim under pretence of succeeding him. And to show still further the incongruity, I supposed the case of Peter organizing an army in Jerusalem, and ordering them to slay all who should oppose his claims, &c. In reply, he said twice, "Well, no matter, the Pope has got his kingdom honestly." The reverse could be shown from history; but wishing to avoid useless questions, I discussed the matter only in the light of Scripture. He quoted, "hear the Church," and "on this rock I will build my Church." I said I would here take him on his own ground, and accordingly I demanded of him to "hear the Church" herself in explanation of this Rock. I pledged myself to produce the authority of Chrysostom and other saints, to show that this Rock was Christ, not Peter. And as further proof, I quoted Paul's own words—"Other foundation can no man lay than that which is laid—the Lord Jesus Christ." Besides, whether Peter was the foundation or no, I showed that this had no reference to Rome at all, as Peter, being an Apostle, could not be the bishop of any one place, nor is there any Scriptural evidence that he was ever in Rome! He replied that the Church must have some visible head to guide it, as an army must have a general. I said this was true, but that Christ is that head; that no body could have two heads without being a monster; and that as to the guidance of the Church, Christ Himself says His Spirit is given for that purpose, and thus supplies the want of His own visible presence. I begged him to seek for himself this Spirit, as the only means to guide him in these questions and disputes.

After a great deal more to the same purpose, he asked me, if he should cease being a Roman Catholic, what sect of Protestants he should join, inquiring if I had read " Evans' Sketch of all Religions." I replied that salvation did not depend on the sect we belonged to, or on the opinions we held on minor points; but that all, of whatever name, who believed in Jesus alone, and were renewed by His Spirit, were true Christians, and the true Church, even though they erred on other matters.

Again, as on last day, he maintained that more than faith was required for salvation, such as taking up our cross, &c. I replied that this was true thus far; that faith was proved by works, of which the " cross" was the chief. But what " cross?" If it meant only a crucifix, what trouble was it to carry that? But suppose that I, in this town, for following the Bible, were hooted, insulted, called " Jumper," and stoned to the risk of my life—that, in my opinion, is carrying " the true cross." In reply, he candidly admitted that it was to some such troubles for Christ's sake that the " cross" referred.

After discussing other points of the same kind, and in the best temper on his part, I promised to lend him " The Life of M. Boos," and I earnestly prayed him to seek the guidance of God's Spirit, but he would not give a direct promise to do so.

5. *Their Appreciation of Knowledge.*

The progress of Ireland, educationally, during the past twenty years, is the brightest star in her horizon. True, as regards the religious element of this education, it is often indifferent. But in other respects it is excellent, and any useful knowledge is surely better than ignorance. It is also a stimulus to the acquisition of more, creating a thirst, which will not be satisfied with the first fountain from which it has drunk; or, to vary the figure, it resembles the lighting of a candle, which goes on to burn of itself, and were it only a rush-light in a cabin, it is better than darkness. There is also this consideration to console us for the defects of this education in a religious point of view. Had it been better, then, for certain reasons, it would be less diffused. It would be good done on a square inch, compared to a square mile.

The superiority of the present education to the old, can be understood only by those who remember the "hedge schoolmasters," immortalized by Carleton, with their smattering of knowledge, and ridiculous pretensions—their ready wit, and extreme pugnacity; not without a touch of genius too. But as to solid and useful information, they knew little. Nor was that their fault, poor fellows; it was their misfortune., Well I remember a teacher of this class, whose acquaintance I made twenty-one years ago at Clonmacnoise, near Athlone. In the open air, amongst the tombs and ruins of its ancient "seven churches," I found him one summer day instructing, as he best could, his ragged disciples. After we had conversed for a while in Irish, I, by his direction, grasped my arms round an old stone cross there, when he gravely assured me I was now a doctor. He alluded to a legend which connected with this feat the miraculous power of healing in certain cases. The truth of this he seemed firmly to believe; and from that fact alone an estimate may be formed of his educational qualifications.

But that is only one instance. Long before that, I remember a dispute between two rural disputants, I presume of this order; and one of their posing questions was, "What is the diaméter of my waistcoat button, that is only three barleycorns in circumférence." Again, in the County Kerry, a friend of mine passing a hedge-school, overheard its teacher threatening his boys—"I'll cut the meat [flesh] off a' yees!" By another friend I was assured that he heard two others arguing about the proper pronounciation of the word rhinoceros; one maintained that it was "rhisoneros," and the other that it was "rhonseroros"!

The present improved system of education has imparted to the peasantry an increased desire for it. We say, an increased desire, for they have always appreciated it. The most ignorant of them have respected learning in others, and earnestly coveted it for their children. That their expectations in that way were moderate, is true—"As soon as my son is able to read his prayer-book, I'll take him home." But, at that time, little more could be learned; and even that little was often the labour of years, owing to the bad teaching. But now, with the increased facilities for a better education, their desires have proportionately risen; so that they bid fair to distance other nations in the race. Surely such a people ought not to be despaired of. We do not over-estimate mere education; nor commit the atheistic mistake of attempting to "regenerate society by the multiplication-table." Only God's truth, applied by His Spirit, can do that. But He works by means; and one chief means is education. Nor do we withhold the name from even an ability to read; for after that, a man can obey the Saviour's command—"Search the Scriptures."

Love of Learning in Boys.

To-day visited F——, in the neighbourhood of Galway Bay. When there, I got into conversation with two boys, in Irish. They were remarkably intelligent, and very civil. In course of conversation, they told me that one of them attended school, but the other did not. This loss the educated boy deplored, saying that there was "no prosperity in after life without learning in youth. With that," he added, "one might get to be a steward." I was struck with this aspiration after social elevation, being a new thing in the class to which he belonged. They were much pleased when I admired their bay, which, seen from this place of a fine day, is very beautiful, and might even be called sublime. As in a picture, one beholds at a glance the bold headlands of Clare, on both sides of Black Head, one trending south till it is lost in the dim horizon. Westward, the three isles of Arran stud, with their blue outlines, the "ocean's wide expanse." To-day, also, the whole scene was lit up with the brightest sunshine. From this, I remarked to them how great was the Being who had made all, and who, from these bright skies, was now looking down on us. This sacred allusion did not alarm them, as it sometimes does; but neither were they disposed to follow it up. One of them, returning to my praises of the locality, said that it was the wholesomest place in Ireland; and that the gentry came long distances to dine on a table-rock, a little further on, and which, by their description, seemed intended by nature for the purpose.

We then spoke of the employment of the people. They told me that some of them took great numbers of lobsters on this coast in the summer, fishing for them in their "corachs," meaning small boats, once made of wicker-work covered with hides, but now composed of a wooden frame covered with canvas. They added, that for these lobsters the fishermen got in Galway six shillings a dozen. I then returned to the subject of education, and asked the boy who did not attend school what was the reason. The other replied that his father lived by his day's labour, so that it was hard for him to send his children to school. I then suggested a night school in winter when there is no employment; but they said that poor boys had to work even then. Happening to have in my hand a Hebrew Psalter, I showed it to the educated boy. He asked me was it a prayer-book. I told him that it was printed in the language anciently spoken by the Jews, the people of God; but he had not heard even their name. To be more explicit, I said it was the language spoken by Moses, supposing that all had heard of him. But they said they had not; and one of them, after a little reflection, asked me did I mean Adam. That seemed to be all he knew of Old Testament history. I replied that likely it was the language spoken by Adam; and then I praised the Irish language, too, which seemed to please them, and they wondered how I knew it.

Returning to religion, I asked them the first question in their catechism, "Who created you, and put you on the world?" This they answered correctly. In brief terms I then explained to them that all mankind were sinners, and as such deserved hell-fire for ever: that from this we could not deliver ourselves; that Jesus was the only Saviour, &c. In conclusion, I reminded them of our Lord's words, "What would it profit a man," &c. They listened attentively; and after I had left, they came running after me with a handkerchief which I had left behind. I praised their honesty, and rewarded them with a small donation, for which they were most grateful.

Appreciation of General Knowledge.

In the evening a Roman Catholic lady, with whom I had some worldly business, entered into conversation on subjects of general knowledge, specially on natural history and geology. In regard to the latter, she at once started the difficulty of harmonizing it with the first chapter of Genesis. This gave me occasion to speak of the solution of Hugh Miller. Of him she had heard; and she also spoke highly of his genius. I then added, with regard to the object of the Bible generally, that it was only to guide us to a better world, and consequently it should be viewed only as a guide-book. Now, in a guide-book to Dublin, suppose, we would not expect a description of Belfast or Cork, or indeed of any places not lying in the direct route, or within sight of it. So of the Bible: its revelations are intended to bear upon our journey to a better world, and to this all other matters are made subordinate. I also showed how it was contrary to God's providence for Him to reveal to men what they, by the proper use of their faculties, could discover for themselves. And, as cases in point, I reminded her that Jesus in raising Lazarus, did what man could not do—imparted life; but He would not do what man could do, that is, to take away the stone from the grave's mouth: so also the servants at Cana had to draw the water which He changed into wine.

She seemed satisfied with these explanations; and I hope they may tend to her spiritual benefit. She is well educated, and intellectual beyond what I have met with in this place. It is pleasing to notice how the general enlightenment of the times is reaching their minds.

The opinion of an educated Roman Catholic Lady in a disturbed district on the causes of it—on Political Priests—on Nuns, &c.

My route lay through B———. Being delayed here for an hour, I got into conversation with the people without their knowing who I was; and I ascertained that the papers do them no injustice in the accounts of their turbulence. Father L——— was expected to accompany us on the public car; but when we were starting, a messenger came to the office, saying that he had gone off to Dublin. The same individual, in answer to an inquiry of one present, stated that to-day there were no less than twenty-six cases to be tried at the court for "trespass on a mountain." I suppose at the instance of Bishop P———. For this litigation one of them abused him, saying it was only a "trespass on rocks." At the same time several looked at me to hear what I would say, but I kept silent. I perceived clearly that they all approved of the priest's violent conduct. Meantime a well-dressed lady, of middle age, sat up beside me on the car. She was also well-educated, and, as I afterwards ascertained, was a Roman Catholic. After some general remarks on the extreme severity of the weather and on farming, we spoke of the antiquities on the road to Cong, and on ancient Irish history. In the latter she said she took no interest, not considering it reliable. We then spoke of the heathen sages, specially Socrates, of whose sentiments she had read something. She had also read Zenophon's History of Cyrus. This gave me occasion to show how far short of truth were the best guesses of these men, and how great the advantages conferred on us by Christianity. I told her also of the awfully degraded condition of the Australian savages, with some anecdotes of their habits; also of the South Sea Islanders, and their wonderful change by the Gospel. This introduced religion generally; and when I alluded to the present disputes in B———, she blamed the "Jumpers" for it all; condemning all missions on principle. She was greatly surprised, however, when I told her that the Roman Catholic Church, too, has her missions in England and other Protestant countries. I added that, for my part, I would not resent any attempt to convert me if made in a kind spirit: in fact, that if I am right myself, I am bound, if I can, to bring my neighbour for his good to the same path, but only by kind means. She declared, however, that the Scripture-readers had "insulted the Roman Catholics;" but when we referred to the priests, she said aloud, determinedly, "Indeed, I've not a bit of respect for our clergy; for they're not preaching peace and good will, but only dissension." I was surprised at this opinion, and specially at her expressing it so fearlessly. She still, however, avowed herself a staunch Roman Catholic, only she preferred representing her Church by the nuns. Of these she spoke most highly, but did not care for the monks. She said that one of the nuns in B———, a Miss L———, had £10,000 fortune, yet gave herself up to a life of devotion; that at the convent school she has taken poor girls into her room, and there washed their faces lest they should be dismissed from the school for untidiness, agreeably to a rule on the subject. She complained that notwithstanding this, a Protestant friend of hers had called the nuns "idle women."

As a set-off to this, I told her of the Ragged Schools of Protestants, and their usefulness; and while I acknowledged the good done by the nuns, I said the evil lay in their taking on them unscriptural laws, and making a merit of it. I then stated my view of salvation as being altogether of grace, through the merits of Christ, and that, before we can do any thing really good, our hearts must be changed by God's Spirit. I told her, also, that M. Boos, a priest of her Church, held similar views, and I advised her to read his life. And I explained that it is not sects, as such, that will be saved; but only those of them who are thus changed, and who, I feared, were few. That some of her clergy, also, believed the same, I showed from Dr. Challoner's "Think Well On It," where he speaks of the " small number of the elect;" also from Dr. Gallagher. And as to these persons who fight for religion, while open sinners in other respects—swearing, lying, and stealing—I said that all such were manifestly children of the devil, and had no religion whatever.

All this she heard with only an occasional objection. She then told me that a man on the opposite side of the car was a "Carmelite;" that in speaking he always "weighed his words;" and that he had induced most of the people who lived near him "to enter his order," and had thus done much good. When she was leaving, she held out her hand to me, which I shook, and she bade me good-bye in the kindest manner. I regard her as a good specimen of the intelligent Roman Catholics, and so give the conversation at large.

These conversations might be greatly extended, but the above will suffice as specimens. We conclude with one case more, the most interesting and encouraging that we have met with for many years. The individual referred to was a gentleman, still nominally a Roman Catholic, and yet, as the event proved, a sincere believer in Jesus. "Can any thing good come out of Nazareth?" will be asked by many Protestants. In answer I shall just lay the facts before them, not colouring or over-stating in the slightest degree, and then let them judge for themselves. I need only premise, that this gentleman, as I afterwards learned, had risen by his talents from a humble rank, to fill an important Government situation, from which, however, he had been obliged by ill-health to retire, before I made his acquaintance. It will also appear, that when he made himself known to me, I had suffered severely from the mob at Galway, who, excited by others, and acting, it is said, under mistake, had fiercely assaulted me, striking me several times, and when I fled, wrecking houses in order to get at me for further vengeance. At one time I was rescued from their hands by forty policemen with fixed bayonets; but in my greatest straits I owed my escape to the kindness of two Roman Catholics, who, though personal strangers to me, rescued me at the peril of their own lives.*

Though I dare not enter the town during the present excitement, I ventured to take a walk on the shore road beyond B———. A fisherwoman whom I met, and with whom I got into conversation, condemned greatly the attack yesterday, but said that the people of C——— were very peaceable. When I spoke of the sin of it, she acknowledged that; but in praying for their conversion, she applied only to the

* While I make it a point thus gratefully to record the kindness I have so often received from the Roman Catholic laity, and am generally silent as to the very different conduct of their teachers, yet, I cannot pass over a case of this latter kind which occurred on the day after this assault. Walking out, I met a priest who must have known me well, for he had often followed me on the road-sides when I conversed with the people. Nor could he have been ignorant of what I had suffered the day before. Indeed I still bore traces of it; for there was a large black mark on my face, imprinted by the fist of an angry assailant, and I was lame in one leg by the blow of a stone on the ankle. But how did he recognise my altered appearance? He first rudely stared me in the face, and then positively burst into laughter, and continued laughing till he bowed down near the head of his horse! Never while I live shall I forget the malignant triumph of that man's countenance.

Virgin Mary! "*Go leasaidh Muire iad,*"—"May Mary mend them!"

I was met by groups of people who had been gathering sea-weed on the shore. I saluted some of them in Irish, but they made no reply, and looked very sullen. None, however, offered any insult, except at a house that was repairing at S——, from which, after I had passed, a very savage shout was raised after me.

At this sudden closing of the door of usefulness, I felt downcast, as I walked along; but my mind was relieved by reading Psalms xxv. and xlvi. I thought, also, of that passage in Mark, where it is stated, as one great object of the preaching of the Gospel, that it would be a "testimony *against them.*" This result no Christian would desire for its own sake; but it is well to know that men's rejection of the Gospel will not defeat God's object in sending it. Besides, this very opposition may attract more attention to it.

After these reflections, I was not a little encouraged by a most unexpected incident, showing how easily God can overrule the wrath of man for the advancing of the truth. A gentleman whom I met in the pathway, and a total stranger to me, accosted me in the kindest manner, asking if I had recovered from the blows of the mob, and adding, "I hope that you will not suppose respectable Catholics approve of it. They do no such thing." I replied that I was fully assured of that; and to show the sin of all persecution, I added that if I supposed a man fatally astray in regard to salvation, I would pity and not hate him on that account. This sentiment he highly approved, and said that if a man wished to change him by insult and bad treatment, it would have the opposite effect. He admitted, also, that having travelled many Protestant countries, he had never been insulted for being a Catholic. He added that it was the duty of every man to read the Bible; that for his part, he read not only the Douay, but the Protestant version also; that he did not believe salvation confined to his own Church; that the question God would ask a man at the last was not the sect he belonged to; and that salvation was for all who sought it. "Through Christ, the one Saviour," said I; and to that also he assented. In reference to his statement, that the true Church consisted not of one sect alone, I explained that such was my own view also; but that by true Christians, I meant only those whose hearts were renewed by God's Spirit. To this he agreed. I then referred him to Martin Boos, who was a priest of his Church, and yet held substantially the same view as I did; and I begged him to read his life.

Thus conversing, he accompanied me all the way from the shore to my own house, though we met a priest on the road. I confess I could have scarcely then expected this, when even many Protestant friends shrink from publicly recognising me! Surely the Lord must, in some degree, be working in his soul. Gladly would I have invited him in for further conversation, but I thought it wiser not to do so for the present.

Second Interview with the same.

After walking to the shore, I sat down on a stone, leaning against a ditch, when the Roman Catholic gentleman before referred to came up. I was reading a little Hebrew Psalter, but when he approached, I laid it aside on the grass. He sat down on a stone near me, and we had a brotherly conference, as I may truly call it. We talked over a great many subjects, doctrinal and experimental, on which scarcely a shade of difference existed between us! With this result I was gratified beyond measure. Surely, there are in Babylon souls looking to Jesus, like Simeon, amid the mass of Jewish formalism, "waiting for the consolation of Israel."

Having spoken of the Psalms, he told me that it was the book that he enjoyed most, and that he had got some of it by heart. Then taking up the book which had the English version bound up with the Hebrew, he read from the former some of the best psalms of the collection, stopping occasionally to point out the beauty of their language. I directed his attention to the twenty-third; and as we had just been speaking of the sad loss of the poor people here in not having the Bible, I told him of a party of Scotch Highlanders emigrating to America, who, in passing the graveyard of their ancestors, could not tear themselves from the spot, till an aged patriarch of their number poured forth in Gælic psalmody the thrilling words of Psalm xxiii. I said what a blessing it would be to our own countrymen if, in their wanderings, they enjoyed the same consolation. In this respect his feelings were as warm as my own; and he stated that since his mind had opened to the Gospel, the two things that grieved him most were the desecration of the Sabbath, and the withholding of the Scriptures from the people. This sentiment he repeated two or three times during the conversation, appearing to feel it deeply.

Regarding the spiritual change which had passed over him, he stated that it had originated in hearing an address from an aged clergyman in England on Palestine, into which much Scripture truth had been interwoven. "I may, indeed," said he, with emotion, "ascribe to that man my conversion." This led us to converse on Scripture generally; and I asked him had he remarked, in his reading of it, how many of the conversions which it records had taken place instantaneously, without previous preparation or worthiness in the subject of them; and how, in such cases, there was, from the first moment, a consciousness of complete pardon, and a sure hope of final salvation; and how all this had resulted from their believing something concerning Jesus; and this something was the simple fact of his having died for sinners, with the free offer of all its benefits to all who would accept them. He replied that he had remarked this peculiarity of Scripture doctrine, and that he believed it. I then quoted some illustrative passages, as, "whosoever cometh unto me;" I also cited the case of the penitent thief, and of the Pentecostal converts. With all this he fully agreed; and this I consider the essence of saving faith.

After a great deal more to the same effect, I begged him to accept a copy of the "Life of M. Boos," which I had brought in my pocket for him. He took it thankfully, and promised to read it.

Third interview with same.

Walking to-day to B——, as I passed over the stile, I met Mr. —— again. He was walking with a friend; but, on seeing me, left him, and accompanied me. We had another conversation equally interesting. Having alluded to the great vegetation since last rain, we spoke of gardening, in which he felt much interest; and I remarked what a beautiful simile of saving faith is afforded by the process of grafting. On this point I quoted an observation of Dr. Chalmers, to the effect that the engrafted branch, if it could speak, would say of its fruits, "These are not mine; the sap by which I bore them comes from the trunk of the tree. In myself, I have none; I live every moment by what I get through my union with it." So of the believer's dependence on Jesus. This I had verified in my own experience; for, as I told him, I had long lived content with the mere form of religion; and when I discovered my unregeneracy, I tried to reform myself; but, failing in that, I was driven to despair, till I cast myself wholly on Jesus, and then I found peace.

Nothing else could give me solid footing. In confirmation of this, I quoted the Scriptures, "Able to save to the uttermost," and, "By whose stripes ye are healed." And to meet the common objection—but not his—that these terms of forgiveness are too easy to be true, I quoted the reply to Naaman, "If he had told you to do a great thing," &c.

We then spoke of infidelity, and its prevalence; when I told him that the easiest way to meet it was the plan proposed by a Christian lady, a Miss Graham, "Ask, and ye shall receive"—that is, prayer for Divine direction. This plan is equally available for the disbeliever of the Bible, if he only acknowledge the existence of a Creator, all-wise, powerful, and good. And if he do not, he is hopeless, as regards reasoning with him.

Walking on together, we reached a headland stretching into the sea, and there we sat down on the stones. He here related how he had lived, for some years, a dissipated life in London, frequenting balls, and dancing till the morning; but was by no means happy. On the contrary, when he heard the criers in the streets as he returned home in the mornings, he often wished himself one of them. This reminded me of Colonel Gardiner wishing himself a dog under similar circumstances. He said that he had read the life of that gentleman. He also condemned modern dances, as fatally seductive; and said that, in private life, there was much dissipation in Galway. This led us to speak of the opposition of the world, in all its forms, to spiritual religion; and of the absolute necessity of Divine grace to enable us to overcome it. On that point, I quoted the saying of St. Augustine, "*Quam suave,*" &c., "How pleasant it is to want such pleasures." And then, as to our moral inability, I quoted another of his sayings—"Give what thou commandest, and command what thou wilt."

In respect to the Life of Boos, he apologised for not returning it, saying that he had lent it to a gentleman "to break down his prejudice." We then walked home together, still conversing on the same subjects, and with unabated interest on his part as well as my own.

It only remains for me to state regarding this excellent individual, that having soon after left that country, I found, on my return, that he had gone to live in England. He foresaw, I doubt not, the consequences of avowing his change in Ireland, and to that step he should come at last. It has been my invariable rule to advise inquirers, before making such a profession, to wait till they were prepared by knowledge and grace. But in the present state of the West, they are forced either to come out at once, or fall back altogether. That my friend foresaw this, I have no doubt; and I feel assured too that he would abide the test. It is also my earnest request, that if these pages should ever meet his eye, he will communicate with me, as I still feel a deep interest in his welfare, temporal and eternal.

How far God has blessed any more of these conversations I know not, as I did not often meet the same parties twice. Literally, then, it was "bread [or seed] cast on the waters." But the sowing alone I consider success in its way, for the fruit will follow some time. God's order in the case is, "One soweth, and another reapeth;" but each succeeds when he does his own work. And this is a truth which I think it well to repeat—partly to relieve anxious missionaries who burden themselves unnecessarily with care for the results, and partly to meet the cavils of objectors who cry out failure, merely because that, in the missionary Calendar, seed-time and harvest do not immediately succeed each other.

CHAPTER VI.

IRISH PREACHING IN WEST CONNAUGHT IN 1841.

Best Means of Ireland's Elevation is the Gospel—Irish Sermon at Galway, and Good Results—Visit to the Isles of Arran—Intolerance there and Superstitions—Joyce's Country—Great Ignorance—A Strange Congregation—"Patterns"—"Joyce's Will"—Recess—Lough Ina—Meeting at the Marble Quarry—Conversation with a Smuggler—Roundstone—Opposition—Clifden, good reception at first—Personal Assault on a subsequent visit—The Killeries—Scenery—Poetry—Improvement of the Country—Irish Sermon at Salruc—Sunrise on the Killeries—End of the Tour—The Missionary future of Ireland—Great Opposition to be expected—Grounds of Hope—A Missionary's Comforts—Testimonies to this Mission and to that in Kerry—Concluding Appeal.

THE subject of this chapter is Irish Preaching in West Connaught. This took place in 1841 and 1842, after which we removed to Kerry. Having, however, gone over this country again in 1859 and 1860, we are enabled, in these "Sketches," to take in its altered state at that time, showing what great progress it had made in the interval. The result of this missionary tour, even according to the lowest estimate of it, will show the value of presenting the Gospel to our countrymen in their own tongue, and therefore will cause regret that, in past ages, it was not more extensively employed. Had that been done when Irish was still universally spoken, and the public mind unembittered by political strife, the history of our country might have been of a far brighter complexion. The past cannot be recalled; but let us learn from it the needful lesson of availing ourselves of all remaining opportunities of atoning for former neglects. Nor will this narrative be without its use, if it show that the Gospel of Jesus, properly presented, is, after all, the most likely appliance for Ireland's amelioration. That it was the instrument used by God for the elevation of the rest of the United Kingdom is a matter of history; why, then, did it fail in Ireland? We answer, that it did not fail; for it was not presented to the Irish people in a way they could understand, but for a long time, instead of it, legal compulsion and penal enactments. We know the results. But in this case, alas! failure did not teach worldly men wisdom; and so other expedients, equally unscriptural and anti-national, were tried in quick succession. Their success was the same. It seemed as if God, after honouring His own Truth for the enlightenment of the sister countries, had, in judgment, left Ireland to the politicians, that by their wretched failures, they might show the absolute necessity of the pure Gospel, for national as well as individual regeneration. God grant that this lesson may not be lost on the present generation as well as the past. That many now are sincerely desirous of Ireland's conversion, and that some of them are willing in earnest to labour for it, we rejoice to know; but we fear that few yet recognise the duty, or will kindly take the pains, to adapt their mode of instruction to the feelings and habits of the Irish people, as is done in all other missions. This is not said from a desire to find fault, but for the removal of what has been hitherto the chief stumbling-block to the spread of the Gospel in Ireland.

This tour of preaching began at Galway in 1841. At that time, this town was not the scene of such frequent religious disputes as at present; and yet, party-spirit does not appear to have been then less bitter; for, not long before my visit, a Protestant controversialist had been obliged to fly for his life through a window of his place of meeting!

Under these circumstances, my friends in Galway seriously dissuaded me from running a similar risk; and I confess, that in their apprehensions, I somewhat shared. But I resolved, at least, to make a trial, leaving the result to God.

My first operation was a series of visits to poor Roman Catholics, in their own homes. The place I selected for this purpose was the western suburbs, called Newcastle. Here I stood before the first open door that I met, and introduced myself to the family within by asking leave to read for them a portion of God's Word. In a Protestant country, this request would have appeared intelligible enough; but here it seemed in the highest degree novel and perplexing. They knew not what to reply. True, they evinced no repugnance to the Scripture, as is sometimes the case, but neither did they accept my offer to read it for them. At length, however, the mistress of the house walked over to the door where I stood, and, still hesitating, asked me, "Sir, what will you charge us?" Having relieved her mind on that point, she cheerfully pulled aside the half door between us, and begged me to come in and read for them, and "God bless you."

So read I did, seated in the best chair. Her children gathered round me; and, with herself, listened with attention and surprise, for to them it was all new. This was all the fee that I desired for my trouble, and I felt richly repaid.

In other houses also I was received with equal welcome, and in one my words seemed to be blessed. Here I found only one person, an aged woman, for whom I read part of a well-known tract, "Do you want a Friend?"—meaning Jesus. And certainly, as the event showed, no subject could have been more appropriate to this poor creature. As I read, her feelings became so excited that she interrupted me, exclaiming, "Oh! I do want a friend. I had only one son; he went to England, and was killed in a mill, and now I am a poor lone creature." I need not add that I took all pains to direct her distressed soul to this "Friend that sticketh closer than a brother," and not, I hope, without success. In leaving, I felt thankful to God for having honoured me, even in this one case, to dry a mourner's tears. The pleasure was enhanced by remembering that probably she had never before heard so much respecting Jesus as the true comforter of the afflicted.

Still more encouraging was the result of the Irish sermon. This was duly announced by placards posted over the town; and the hour selected was seven o'clock in the evening, being supposed the most convenient. This sermon was a step of great responsibility. I do not mean merely in reference to the apprehended riot, but still more to the fact that this was my first public address in what was to me for the most part a foreign language. Only those who have made a similar trial can understand the difficulty; especially as the theme being a sacred one, any mistake, or even mispronunciation, would have been very injurious. There was nothing for it, however, but to cast myself on the promised aid from above. So at the hour appointed I was duly in my place to meet my expected audience. To my delight the house was crowded, and what was equally gratifying, they were mostly poor people, the very class whom I wished to see. Many of them, as I was afterwards told, were from the Claddagh, which is inhabited only by fishermen. Thus it was that I for the first time opened my commission in the Irish language. My text was John i. 29.—"*Feuch uan De a thogfas peacadh an domhan*—"Behold the Lamb of God that taketh away the sin of the world."

How I treated this subject will appear from an extract of a letter which I wrote to a friend soon afterwards.

"Forgetting all human distinctions I addressed them as sinners together with myself—as creatures partaking of the same evil nature, and involved by sin in similar guilt and misery. I then dwelt on the great remedy provided in the Gospel."

Thus the sermon was not what is commonly called controversial. It had to do only with the great controversy between God and the sinner, while he is unsaved. And yet is not that the root of all other controversies, and does not the settlement of it smooth the way for agreement in all other points? Only let men come to Christ as a Saviour, and soon their judgments as well as their hearts will be blended in sweetest harmony. Impressed with this sentiment, I directed the undivided attention of my audience to Jesus as the only and all-sufficient Saviour, avoiding all irritating topics. And if it was in this spirit that I preached, certainly it was in the same spirit that my audience heard. Instead of riot, or other species of opposition, they behaved with the greatest decorum; and at the close, one man, standing in the aisle, prayed aloud to God to bless me. Nor was this all. Two others of them, after they had gone out, were overheard saying, "Well, we gave him a fair jury at all events." "Yes," said the other, "and he deserved it;" alluding, I suppose, to my having used no irritating language.

Perhaps some readers will charge me with exaggerating the importance of this occasion. That my statements are true, however, will be attested by Christian men still living in the place, and who were present during the service. Nor can it be denied, considering the difficulties of mission work in the West, that even this much success was a matter of importance. As such I felt it at all events. It was one of the happiest days of my life. After several years of preparation, and many fears of failure, I was now for the first time enabled to preach to my beloved countrymen, in their own tongue the "unsearchable riches of Christ;" and what was more, they had heard me with attention and respect.

This success at the outset was very encouraging; but, as will appear from the sequel, it was succeeded by many an experience of an opposite character. Nor should we omit one great lesson taught by it. No altar denunciation had yet been issued against me; and in this instance we see how little the people were of themselves disposed to hostility. This is a fact that should ever be borne in mind in connection with the opposition to missions in the West.

The next place to which I directed my course was the Islands of Arran, which lie off the bay of Galway.

With this object in view, I presented myself between six and seven o'clock on a fine summer's morning, on the quay of Galway. At that time there was no regular passage-boat, except what carried the mail, and which sailed only once a month. For a passage, then, I was thrown on the civility of the Arran boatmen, who, in a small fleet of schooners, at this season of the year, carried over their seaweed to sell it on the mainland. Just as I arrived, the tide was beginning to turn, which was their signal for departure. So, without loss of a moment, I went up to a boat, and asked the owner for a passage, offering to pay for it. But no: I was rudely repulsed, and no explanation given. Evidently there was some secret objection against receiving me. This I could not discover, till one boatman, more civil than the rest, when pressed to tell me the cause, replied, "Sure we're ordered not to take any Jumpers into the islands." This offensive term for Protestants was then new to me; so I said angrily,

"I'm no Jumper, but a minister." But the man, by his looks, seemed to regard the two words as synonymous, and so refused me admission. However, in doing so, I saw that he acted with reluctance. Taking courage from this circumstance, I stepped on board without further ceremony, saying in Irish, *Racha me asteach an ainm De.* Never did that language serve me better; for at the instant another boatman, who had stood by, came up to him and said, "Don't fear, Andrew—myself thinks he's a priest after all!" Hearing this, the owner of the boat approached me with a smile, and said in Irish, "Now, Sir, I'll take you over without charge." These are small matters in themselves, but they illustrate the strange state of society as late as twenty years ago.

This difficulty surmounted, I recollected that in my hurry I had forgot to take provision for the way. So having got leave for a few minutes, I ran to the first shop that I found open, and procured a small loaf and an egg. But of neither did I taste one morsel the whole day, for a reason that will appear. During the voyage we were sometimes driven before furious gusts coming down from the Clare hills; and, on their abating, we were becalmed for hours. The swell of the waves continuing long after, tossed our frail bark most unmercifully. Thus I fell a martyr to that disease for which there is no sympathy; and, under its influence, I was obliged, in want of a better place, to lie prostrate in the bottom of the boat. Our whole voyage was only twenty miles; and yet it was eight o'clock in the evening ere we landed. Twelve or thirteen hours sailing twenty miles!

In my sickness the boatmen treated me with much kindness, specially the wilder-looking of the two. This man could not speak one word of English, and he wore, instead of shoes, a queer kind of slippers called "Pampooties." These were composed of pieces of cow-hide, rudely strapped to the feet with cords or thongs. This fashion I supposed to be peculiar to these islands; but recently, an officer, who had spent much time on the shores of the Mediterranean, has told me that it is common also amongst the Sicilian peasantry.

Just as I approached the village of Kilronan, which was our landing-place, it being now dark, I was startled with a curious natural phenomenon. This was caused by a ledge of breakers, which shot out a long way into the sea in a straight line. The billows dashing on this ledge diagonally, caused a high ridge of foam suddenly to rise at one end, and to run, with the rapidity of a race-horse, along the whole line. It then as suddenly disappeared, but at regular intervals was renewed. Really it seemed like a thing of life. With the aid of a little imagination, one could manufacture out of it such a fiction as that of King Donaghoe on his white steed, with silver slippers, careering over the waters of Killarney on a May morning.

In parting with my boatmen, they directed me to the only place where I could get lodging or food. It was a small cabin; but I was glad of any place to cover my head. After leaving me, by way of excusing themselves for bringing me over, they reported that I was an invalid priest, visiting the island for the good of my health. But I soon undeceived the people on that point.

Next morning, after going out I found the village in commotion. A storm was blowing down their cabins, or unroofing them; and it threatened to sink their boats in the harbour. As my object always is to describe things as I found them, no Roman Catholic can be offended at my mentioning that, amid this storm, an old woman, attempted to stop her thatch being blown away by pouring upon it a bottle of holy water! Nor was that all. With still greater faith—or credulity, as the reader will have it—another woman sent a boy, to immerse in the sea a bag containing two temperance medals and a scapular, believing that this would calm the troubled waters.

Such were the people between whom and the Bible their teacher had placed an impassable barrier. For I ascertained from one of the coast-guards that no communication whatever was allowed by him between any of his flock and Protestants. Even a common salutation by the way was not to be answered. In the house of this coast-guard lodged a Methodist missionary, who had come here with a similar object as myself; but he was barely permitted to exist on the island, nor could he find access to any of the people.

The next day was Sunday; and as I had come so far to do some good there, I liked not to return without a trial. Accordingly I attempted to arrange for preaching an Irish sermon, hoping that some at least would attend. In this intention, however, I was overruled by the parties last referred to, who represented to me that, even if the people were willing to come, they durst not, so dreadful was the persecution that would ensue. Defeated, then, in this object, I took a step which, under ordinary circumstances, might seem over-zealous. With an Irish Testament in my hand, I went through the village, from door to door, asking permission to read God's Word. In every instance I was refused; but as no abuse or insult was offered, I concluded that the cottagers would hear me if they were permitted. When I had done, a man accosted me in a private house, and seemed desirous of a discussion, starting some of the usual topics. Suspecting that he was only trifling with the subject, I opened my Irish Testament, and read for him Luke xiii. 3, "Except ye repent, ye shall all likewise perish." "That," said I, "is the main point, which we must take up first—how to be saved." I then explained what true repentance meant, and pressed it on his conscience. Not prepared for this sort of argument, he at once withdrew.

Satisfied that I could do no more under the circumstances, I retired to a lonely place among the high rocks, which overhang the sea; and there, in view of the great Atlantic, I spent my solitary Sabbath, reading, for my comfort under failure, those passages which predict the universal spread of Christ's kingdom, be the existing obstacles ever so formidable. At that glorious era, I rejoiced to think, Arran also, notwithstanding its present darkness, would come in for its share of blessing. And in anticipation of that day, I read with delight the following lines from one of our Scripture paraphrases:—

> "Let Kedar's wilderness afar
> Lift up its lonely voice,
> And let the tenants of the rock
> With accents rude rejoice;
> Till, midst the strains of distant lands,
> The islands sound His praise,
> And all combined, with one accord,
> Jehovah's glories raise."

Finding no door of usefulness open in this place I resolved to leave it; but an unexpected difficulty presented itself. No boatman would carry me back to Galway, or admit me into his boat on any account. One of them said as much as that he would not take half the full of his boat of gold, and receive a Jumper. In this way I was detained on the island about eight days; and at last I owed my escape to the providential circumstance of two Galway gentlemen landing on the island, who, on hearing of my detention, compelled their boatmen, partly by persuasion, and partly by force, to carry me with them to Galway. One of these gentlemen, to his credit I say it, was a Roman Catholic.

My detention, however, served one good purpose. It enabled me to learn more of the people. By this means I can show the uttter inexcusableness of that system of intolerance to which they were subjected by their clergyman. For such intolerance the only plea he could use was that himself had sufficiently instructed the people in the great truths of Christianity. But was that the fact? Let us remember that at the time referred to (1841) the language of all the people was the Irish. Let us ask, then, were they supplied with means of enlightenment through its medium? Was the Irish Scripture, or any portion of it, put into their hands? Or was there any school established to teach them to read it?

In reply to these questions, let the writer here record his solemn testimony; for the matter is one of the greatest moment as a test of churches. During the last twenty years he has travelled much in the West and South; and yet never in one case has he found an Irish Bible or portion of it put into circulation by a Roman Catholic clergyman. Nor has he ever found one Irish school set up by them for the benefit of those who spoke only that language. Never, in one single instance. Whatever has been done in that way is the work, exclusively, of Protestant churches.

But it may be replied, that people may be taught the way of salvation snfficiently without any Scripture books. Again we ask, was it so here? The contrary appears from the gross superstitions already alluded to; and is still further proved by the following statement furnished by an acquaintance who spent a year and a half in this island, and who, consequently, had opportunities of witnessing what he describes:—

"There are at the village of Onagh the remains of seven churches, as they are called. One of these buildings is entire, with a burying-ground attached to it. Here is a place called 'the Holy Ghost's bed!' It is about six feet long and four feet broad. Round this bed the Romanist performs his 'station,' repeating each turn so many rosaries, and at same time dropping a pebble in the bed. When all the pebbles are exhausted, of which there is a definite number, then the 'station' is finished. It was on a Saturday, in the month of July, 1840, that I visited this spot. In the waning twilight there were assembled at it about sixty men, women, and children, some of whom were 'going their rounds,' others repeating rosaries, and others lying on the ground. Those of them who desired the cure of diseases must sleep all night in the 'bed.' And this must be repeated for three successive Saturday nights, otherwise the benefit of the 'station' is lost.

"Arran is a very craggy place, and amid its beds of flags are found holes filled with rain water. These are called Bolans, and are supposed to be very holy. The islanders have the utmost veneration for them, and never pass them without bowing or crossing, and sometimes prostrating themselves on the ground. Amongst the virtues ascribed to these Bolans is that of curing diseases. As memorials of such cures, one of them, near Kilmurry, is strewn with votive offerings of nails, sticks, shells, and rags. One day, when I was walking along a road, conversing with a woman whom I had overtaken, I noticed that she suddenly knelt down and crossed herself. I waited till she got up, when she asked me 'Why did you not humble yourself before the blessed Bolan?' I asked, in reply, what claim such a thing had on her or me to bow before it? She answered that some old saint had blessed it, and that all that came before her had done as she did.

"This people place such faith in the fairies that scarcely one of them will ever venture out after night. But if they are obliged to bring in water they will first light a wisp of straw and waive it three times over the vessel, repeating each time, 'In the name of the Father, &c.' This is done to expel the fairies out of the water."

With another of their superstitions, I myself came in contact. During my detention, I visited the lighthouse which crowns the western shore of the island. Here I was applied to by one of the keepers, a member of the Established Church, in order to perform for his wife the ceremony called, "Churching of Women." For a long time no Episcopalian minister had come this way; and he was suffering great inconvenience on that account, owing to the superstitious veneration of the natives for this ceremony. They considered the poor woman unclean while "unchurched," and they would not even sell milk to her; and some of them went so far as to say that the very grass on which she trod would wither up! Greatly, then, was her husband disappointed when I told him that the Presbyterian Church did not sanction such a ceremony.

In detailing the superstitions of this people, let no one suppose that our object is to hold them up to ridicule. Far from it. Rather they are entitled to our deepest commiseration. But while they are to be pitied, these details are forced upon us in order to establish, in opposition to gainsayers, the absolute necessity that existed for a Protestant mission in that country.

From Arran, the scene changes to Joyce's Country. This is a mountain district on the western shore of Lough Corrib. At that time it was seldom visited; but, ere long, a railway projected from Galway to Outerard, will introduce that greatest of modern improvements to the border of this district and of Connemara. Who that saw its wildness twenty or thirty years ago, could have imagined its re-echoing, in this generation, to the railway whistle?

Of the tribe that inhabited these glens I had heard much. Some early tourists represented them as a remarkable race, larger in stature than ordinary men. For my own part, however, I saw nothing to warrant such representations; but their history was romantic. They were descended from an Englishman of that name, who, on his voyage to the west of Ireland, in the thirteenth century, touched at Limerick, and there married Honora O'Brien, the daughter of an Irish chief. Settling at first in Partry, by permission of the O'Flahertys, his offspring, in the course of time, swelled into a powerful tribe, who long contested ascendancy with their former patrons, but now implacable enemies.

It was amongst this clan that I now tried to introduce the pure Gospel; and certainly they needed it. In no other part of Ireland, perhaps, have I found any people whose spiritual state was more deplorable. Even their own Church seemed to have neglected them. Perhaps I was misinformed, but, at all events, I was told that a priest who had occasionally read mass for them, discontinued his visits until they should make up the price of a silver chalice—a sum of money very difficult to extract from a mountain region. Be this as it may, however, there appeared to be no resident clergyman of any Church nearer than Cong or Outerard; and as to other means of instruction, such as Irish school or Scripture Reader, none such was known in the district till several years afterwards.

Having obtained the use of the Hotel of Maam—the only slated building—I resolved to preach an Irish sermon there that evening. With this view, I visited a number of the nearest cabins, inviting the people to come and hear the Word of God. Great was their surprise at so unusual an announcement, and various were the answers which they returned. One man asked me what would I give him—that is what remuneration. He might have meant this in mockery; but, as he appeared in earnest, it is not unlikely that this demand proceeded from his being so unaccustomed to public worship that he viewed it as a secular work, and he expected to be paid for his trouble.

But a still more singular case of popular ignorance, was that of a middle-aged woman whom I met on the road, and with whom I held the following conversation, introduced by my invitation to hear the sermon.

"*Cia's ciall do shin?*" said she, for it was in Irish we spoke. "What does that mean?"

"Why, is it possible you do not know what a sermon means?"

"No," (with an oath.)

"Well, we will have prayers."

"What sort of prayers? Is it the blessed prayers?"

"Yes; we will have blessed prayers out of the Scriptures."

"What's that? What's the meaning of the Scriptures?"

"Why, have you never heard of the Scriptures?"

"No," (with another oath.)

Having explained to her the meaning of the Scriptures, I again invited her to come and hear it.

"Are you one of our priests?"

"No; I am not a priest, but a minister."

"Then, [with an oath again,] I'll not go a step to hear you." And so we parted.

All this was discouraging. It exemplified the melancholy truth that the more the Gospel is needed, the less it is desired; or, as the same sentiment is technically expressed, that the desire for the Gospel is in the inverse ratio to the want of it. How true is this! Seven years afterwards, when the famine deprived this people of food, how keenly did they feel their loss, and how earnestly did they seek a supply! But now, while they were perishing from a "famine of the bread of life," they were altogether unconscious of their want, and satisfied with it.

But in all cases I had not been unsuccessful. A few promised to attend; but in arranging with them the hour of meeting, I encountered another difficulty. Of time, as measured by our watches and clocks, they had no idea; consequently, it was useless to appoint any special hour. So great was their ignorance in this respect, that I have heard of some mountaineers counting as high as seventeen o'clock, or even more! How, then, to get over this difficulty I knew not, except by changing the time to sunset, which was too strongly marked on nature's own dial to be misunderstood by any one.

Accordingly, as the evening began to darken, I was prepared to receive my hearers in the largest room of the hotel. It was furnished with all the available seats, and a table was put in the middle, on which, besides the lights, was placed an Irish Bible. But now followed the strangest scene of all. The noise of feet ascending the stone steps outside, led me momentarily to expect the appearance of the Joyces. But, no; only one face looked into the room, when a panic ensued, and the next thing I heard was the same heavy tread dying away in the distance! Not a soul remained!

Such was my visit to the Joyces in 1841; but many have been the changes since. Gaunt starvation swept many of these poor people to their graves, and scattered others to the four winds of heaven. The blackened gable, or dilapidated wall, serves as a monument of once comfortable families, now either dead or wanderers in foreign lands. But, "in wrath, God remembers mercy;" and so this same dreadful scourge was made the means in His hands of spiritual good. Moved with sympathy, Christian people at a distance not only sent food to the survivors, but by supplying them with Scriptural instruction, blessed their souls with the "bread of life." In this way, it is said that several hundreds were brought to some degree of acquaintance with the Gospel; chiefly through the instrumentality of a pious lady in connection with the Established Church. What has since become of these inquirers, I know not; for on a late visit to the place, I found no trace of them. Probably they, too, were obliged to fly to foreign lands. At all events, this country, once so populous, is now turned into a pasture for cattle. In the words of the Prophet—"The Lord has removed men far away, and there is a great forsaking in the midst of the land."

Mysterious are the ways of God! Because this people were greater sufferers than others, it does not follow that they were greater sinners. But the fact that they did suffer, shows that spiritual disadvantages destroy not accountability. This excused their not knowing much of God; but nothing will excuse their not *seeking* God, or not *accepting* the knowledge of Him when it was offered. "This is the condemnation," says our blessed Lord, "that light is come into the world, and men loved darkness rather than light, because their deeds were evil."

But if they, in their unfavourable circumstances, were justly punishable for sin, how much greater reason have we to fear who, from our youth up, have enjoyed, "Line upon line, and precept upon precept"?

Some readers may be surprised at the condition in which I thus found Joyce's country so late as twenty-one years ago. I do not wonder at such a feeling on their part, as I myself could scarcely have believed it, had I not been an eye-witness of it. Indeed the fourteenth century still lingered there on the skirts of the nineteenth; just as, near the summits of the

Alps, you can touch with one hand a flower, and, with the other, the eternal snows.

The celebrated Hannah More, in speaking of a remote parish in England, states that the sun shone there only twice a-year, and the moon only once a-week. By the sun she meant the rector, who made his appearance only at Christmas and Easter; and by the moon she meant the curate, who being also non-resident, attended only on Sundays. This was bad enough, but still worse was the condition of these glens; for during the twelve months their spiritual luminaries shone only once; in other words, instead of regular Sunday services, they were favoured only with a great annual festival.

This festival was called a "Pattern," or more correctly, a "Patron." The latter is the title given by the Roman Catholic calendar to the tutelary saints who are supposed to preside over particular localities—a belief, by the way, which pervaded Europe long before it was visited by any apostle. In this case the "patron" was St. Patrick, of whom an ancient tradition reported that he slept one night to the west of those glens, on the shore of a lake called Loch-an-da-aon, or "Lake of the Two Birds." This name it received from the circumstance—real or imaginary—of two birds being always seen on its surface. Why this was so, or what was the superstition connected with it, I never learned. At all events, such was the general belief; and so, also, that the depth of the lake was unfathomable. This idea was embodied in an old Irish distich, which, with all its hyperbole, we shall here preserve from oblivion—

> "Ni fuide suas neamh na neul
> No iachtar sios Loch-an-da-aon.
>
> Not higher the cloudy heavens above,
> Than deep the bottom of Loch-an-da-aon."

Another local reminiscence of St. Patrick was, that this was his terminus in his progress westwards. He would go no further. But what the West thus lost of his presence, it gained in his blessing; for standing here, and looking in that direction, he exclaimed, "Fertility and prosperity to all the land I see; and double fertility to all the land I don't see!" So far the legend.

This Pattern was held on the last Sunday of July. The number of people who assembled on the occasion might be eight hundred, and the tents about twenty. A priest or friar being always in attendance, the proceedings opened with a Mass. This was celebrated in the open air, the lighted candles, with their feeble glimmer, forming a strange contrast to the summer sun; like an age of ignorance outshone by a brighter era. On a small table adjoining, a plate was laid to receive the offerings for the clergyman. The custom was for each to contribute either a sixpence or a shilling. This worship was followed by a sudden transition, characteristic, in all ages, of the religion which man himself originates, and which he loves. Amusement became the order of the day. The pipers struck up their merry tunes in the tents, and the dancing began. Nor was there any lack of "creature comforts." Bread and cakes were abundantly supplied by pedlars, and whiskey flowed on all sides. Under such circumstances, we may conceive the uproarious hilarity of an excitable people. Nor did it cease till the Sabbath sun "sought the western wave." But it seldom ended well; like all other unhallowed joys, it left a sting behind. In the words of my informant, "'S annamh la air bith nach mbeidh troid ann"—" Seldom a day that there was not a fight in it." At length these fights became so serious, that influential parties were obliged to interpose; and finding all other means for their suppression ineffectual, they got the Pattern removed to Tullochbee, near Lough Ina, in Connemara.

Such an odd combination of devotion and dissipation suggests many reflections to the Christian mind. Of these we shall particularise only one. Against the circulation of God's Word, many object that it causes strife and quarrels. We do not stop here to refute this objection. In reality it is an imputation on the Author of that blessed book. But to show that it is no less false than profane, we need only ask, where could a Bible-reading district be found which equalled this place for cut heads and broken bones?

Another way in which they wasted their Sabbaths was in "goaling." This amusement was conducted upon a great scale, and in accordance with an established rustic ceremonial. By previous appointment, two parishes met at a given place, each man carrying his long crooked stick with which the game was played. The first step was to take down the names of the richest individuals in the respective districts, and on these lots were cast. The two whose names were drawn, were required to treat the whole assembly to whiskey, which was the beginning, middle, and end of most entertainments. What quantity was ordinarily consumed at such times, I cannot say; but I know, on reliable authority, that on one such occasion two farmers presented between them no less than seven gallons of gin! To this fatal indulgence, even their ordinary occupations were made subservient. Thus, a farmer sends six men to cut turf in the bog. He is well liked in the place, and his neighbours embrace the opportunity of showing their esteem. So they assemble to aid, and presently, instead of six cutters, there are four and twenty. Grateful for this kindness, the farmer sallies out with a five-gallon keg and a piper; so to dancing and drinking they go. The day is far spent before resuming work; but so hard did they labour afterwards, that before night turf enough was cut to supply fuel for the whole year, with a very large surplus besides.

Various were their other social "reunions," and the amusements connected with them; and amongst the latter may be included their ingenious—and generally successful—stratagems to cheat the revenue and outwit excisemen.

Altogether, then, they enjoyed what many would call a merry life. The country, indeed, was wild, but it was their home; and if the land was barren, their rent was small. Their common food, too, was better than that of the lowland peasantry. From the time of sowing their potatoes in February, they ate no more of that root till the new crop. In its stead they used oat or barley meal, which each family ground for themselves in the querns or old hand-mills. Bread of this kind, with milk, formed excellent food; and of both they had abundance. At dinner, too, they always had meat of some kind. It was so cheap, that an old man assured me he never, in his young days, saw it weighed; it was always sold by the bulk.

Thus, then, between good fare and good fellowship, the Joyces got through life pretty comfortably. But, alas! they sought not the comforts which alone endure. When famine came, they had no "Covenant-God" to fly to for help. In the second year of the blight, one man, when he found it re-appearing in his potato-field, went home and hanged himself! Worse than Famine—Death came. But there was no Gospel to extract its sting. Hence arose a melancholy wail, which I can fancy still wafted to my ears from these wild glens. By this I mean an Irish dirge, which at that solemn hour one of these Joyces composed upon himself, describing and lamenting his misery. This poem begins with the words, "*S domhan m'osnaigh*," and is called "*Uacht a' Tseoigich*, or the Will (Testament) of Joyce;" but who he was, or when he lived, I know not. Did my readers understand the original, I think they would agree with me, that in point of naturalness and pathos, it has seldom been equalled. And that this is no rare excellence of such poems, is testified by no mean judge, the celebrated Macpherson. "Their elegies (the Irish) abound with simplicity and a wild harmony of numbers. The beauty of this species depends on a certain *curiosa felicitas* of expression in the original, that must appear much to disadvantage in another language." This latter remark is most true, and deters me from attempting a translation of the whole poem. But as a specimen, I shall give, in an English dress, the opening verses, which I translate as literally as the genius of the two languages will permit.

"JOYCE'S 'WILL.'

"My sighs are deep, my sufferings great,
  To me in pain the day seems slow;
While none on earth knows what I feel,
  Or sympathizes with my woe.

A sinner guilty and depraved,
  Wrestling with death I long have been:
My body wasted with disease,
  And no part sound, because of sin.

Should I resolve my soul to cleanse,
  One day would prove the effort vain;—
As to the pool the ducks return,
  So I'd relapse to sin again.

Alas! the sight has left my eyes,
  And from my hands the strength is gone;
And from my limbs the power to move,—
  The very marrow from the bone," &c.

In the same melancholy strain he bewails the utter emaciation of his body, the falling off of his hair, and the blackening of his skin like a "coal," &c. To alleviate his sufferings, oh! that there had been near him one of these hated "Men of the Book," (as the South Sea Islanders call missionaries,) to read for him the Divine promise to dying believers—"Who (Jesus) shall change our vile body, that it may be fashioned like unto His glorious body, according to the working whereby He is able to subdue all things to Himself." This resurrection-body, exempt alike from sin and suffering, is surely a glorious hope, and the confident expectation of it would reconcile the mind to the dissolution of its present frail and corrupt clay tenement. That Joyce was not altogether ignorant of this hope, we know; but it is only when it is guaranteed to us by the very Word of God, that we can realize its truth, or enjoy all the comfort of it. Then, and not till then, is complete victory obtained over death; not only divesting it of its terrors, but transforming it into an object of desire, agreeably to the prophecy of Isaiah xi. 8; where, comparing believers to children, and death to a serpent, he says—"The sucking child shall play on the hole of the asp, and the weaned child shall put his hand on the cockatrice' den."

But the most remarkable feature of this poem still remains. Remembering that this man was a Roman Catholic, who probably had never seen a Bible, it is singular that in it he never once alludes to the false dependencies of his Church. He asks not the intercession of the Virgin, nor even mentions her name. He says nothing of his own works, except to condemn them; and as little allusion does he make to the powers of his Clergy. Like a Protestant, he placed all his hope in Jesus, whom he affectingly styles, *Mo Liagh agus mo Shagart*, "My Physician and my Priest." And his last words are a prayer in that Name, for pardon to himself and to "all men." That he still seems doubtful of salvation, is what might be expected in one ignorant of the Scriptures, and their sure promises; but God is merciful, and makes allowance for unfavourable circumstances. So in parting with Joyce, we cherish the hope that, amid all his fears, his prayer was heard, and his soul saved.

For we, Protestants, having no desire to narrow the way to heaven, do believe that some who are called Roman Catholics will be saved; but, if Scripture is true, that is not possible unless, like Joyce, they put all their trust in Jesus as the only Saviour and Mediator, and are renewed by His Holy Spirit. How far such a trust can exist in the modern Church of Rome, is another question, and one which its own advocates almost unanimously answer in the negative. Sometimes, however, as if to show the omnipotence of Divine grace, a few such believers are found there; but not so much in its cloisters or palaces as in its prisons and dungeons. Though they are in Rome, then, they are not of it; they are Roman Christians, not Roman Catholics. And now that Rome's errors have culminated in the Immaculate Conception, or deification of a woman, (for that is the consequence,) the call of God to them is louder than ever—" Come out of her, my people, that ye be not partakers of her sins, and that ye receive not of her plagues."

We must now bid farewell to these glens. Were our object mere sight-seeing, we would pass right through them to the north-east, where they debouch on that sublime bay called the Killeries. The long and romantic valley thus formed, is quite unlike those in Connemara, being clothed in grass, while they are covered with heath. It resembles rather the Vale of Cona on the west coast of Scotland, and which is celebrated over the world for its connection with the great Celtic bard.

Intent on duty, we take the opposite direction, and through a dreary moor proceed to the Clifden Road, and thence to

Recess. On our way we pass a small farm-house, which, by its white-washed exterior, and air of comfort, indicates, on the part of the inmates, a higher stage of civilization. In connection with this family, I was told an anecdote which amused me not a little. As regards religion, they are Methodists, and they were accustomed to lodge the preacher when he visited the place. One of these preachers was an Englishman; this was his first visit to Connemara, and having never seen so wild a country before, he knew not what to make of it. In this gloomy mood he called at the cottage, where, after making himself known, he was kindly received, and seated at the kitchen fire. It was late in the evening, and candles being scarce, Mrs. L—— prepared to make rushlights instead. With this view, she placed on the coals a pan containing grease, in which she "dipped" the peeled rushes. Meantime the stranger looked on. He had never before seen such an operation, nor could he divine what it meant. At length, an unpleasant thought struck him, and he exclaimed—"Oh, Ma'am, if that's for me, I beg that you'll not mind it; for I have never eaten *fried straws!*"

At my first visit to Recess, it was almost a wilderness. Now it may be called a village, having got a hotel, post-office, police barrack, and schoolhouse. The latter is connected with the Wesleyan body; and in it, during a recent visit, I held two services. These, however, were attended only by Protestants; to the Roman Catholics I found no access but by means of private conversation.

Wishing to see Lough Ina, which lies embosomed in mountains to the north of Recess, I took as my guide an intelligent little fellow, of about twelve years of age, and a Roman Catholic. During our walk together, I asked him who made all things, which he answered correctly; but I regretted to find that he knew not who was the Son of God, nor what it was to be a sinner, nor how to be saved. As to other matters, he was not wanting. On the topography of the place he was well made-up, having learned it on nature's own map. He was also acquainted with the natural history of the badgers and other "fauna" of the mountains. Of the eagle, he related what was new to me—that it built its nest, not on the high hills, but rather on the flat moors, if remote and unfrequented. He added that one of these nests was lately found to the south of Recess; that the eggs in it were not larger than those of a hen; and that the eaglets were carried off successfully by some boys, though fiercely attacked by the old birds. If so, they were more fortunate than a man in a similar encounter, of which I was told twenty years before. He happened to come suddenly upon an eagle on the ground, and before the bird could spread his broad wings for flight, struck at him with a stick. The eagle adroitly parried the blow; and then, with one stroke, drove his powerful beak through the man's wrist-bone! This ended the combat.

Returning to the subject of religion, I found that my guide knew not who was the first man; but, when told his name, he remembered that his wife was Eve. That was the extent of his theological studies. However, he received instruction with much docility; and, after I had explained to him what was a new heart, and how to seek it, I understood him to promise that he would do so.

This opportunity of explaining salvation was all that I gained by my journey. For we had not quite reached an elevated spot which commands the best view of Lough Ina, when, as if moved by envy, a dark mist-cloud, hitherto "capping" the adjoining "Pins," suddenly descended on the lake like night, and dissolved in a drizzling rain. Of this beautiful scene, therefore, I beheld only as much as showed my loss by not seeing the whole. No inapt figure of the tantalising pleasures of this life, and, it is feared, of the deceptive hopes which many indulge, in regard to the life to come.

The rain continuing, we were obliged to seek shelter in a cabin. There I had an opportunity of explaining the way of salvation, both in Irish and English. When I first touched on this subject, indeed, the family became shy; but they heard it all respectfully, and on my departure evinced a most friendly spirit.

On our way back to Recess, we passed the well-known marble quarry. Here a rich vein of the green and variegated species "crops out" on the surface, but it has never been worked to any extent; and at present the only use made of it is for ornaments and trinkets. The manufacture of these is carried on by a native artist in Clifden; and it is only justice to him to say that many pieces of his handiwork are truly beautiful, being set tastefully in silver and gold. How far this marble would suit for artistic purposes, I am not qualified to judge. But to show that it has not got a fair trial, I may mention that, before my first visit to this country, Mr. Martin, after attempting in vain to overcome the prejudices against it, as being Irish, got a ship-load of it sent to Italy, and thence back again to England, as Italian marble; by which *ruse* it obtained a ready and lucrative sale! At all events, this story was current at the time; but, further than that, I cannot vouch for its truth.

A few days previously I had an interesting little meeting at the same place. Having gone to see the quarry, an old woman approached from the village beneath in order to sell stockings. In the conversation that followed, she told me that she suffered greatly from sickness, especially night palpitations. Of this latter, her description was most emphatic

—"It does be thumpin' within me." If she expected medical relief from me, I regret that I could not give it; but I did what I could, by directing her for comfort to the "balm of Gilead." Meantime we were joined by a considerable number of young persons from the village, forming a small extemporised congregation; so, standing on a piece of rock in order to be heard by all, I gave them an address, mostly in Irish. Alluding to what the old woman had told me of her sickness, I began by stating that sin was the cause of all suffering, and Christ the only cure; that for this He died; that for the same purpose He lived thirty-three years in misery and poverty; that by His death He satisfied God's law, broken by us; that if we got our deserving, we would all go to hell; &c. As I uttered the last words, one of the girls devoutly crossed herself; which she did a second time, when I repeated them. After this, I explained faith in Jesus, and the promise of the Holy Spirit. Still further to arrest their attention, I asked the old woman a question bearing on what I had said. Her reply was very melancholy—"*Neil aon sgil agam ann acht oirid leis na bethith.*" "Of that I know no more than the beasts." Nor was this the first time that I received the same answer from a western Roman Catholic. In another place, a middle-aged man, who could not speak English, told me, in reply to a similar question—"Sir, I know no more of that than the dog there!" Having again repeated part of my address, I pressed upon them all to seek from God a new heart for the sake of Jesus. To this, as well as my other statements, they assented; but the old woman slipped in the name of the Virgin also. And here a little incident occurred which impressed me in her favour. Whilst I was speaking, I overheard her say in a whisper to one of the girls, "Ha, you fell asleep, and let the cows into the potatoes." The mild tone in which this rebuke was administered, spoke well for her temper. In conclusion, I asked if any of the young attended a school. They replied that some did, but that the school was now closed, owing to the measles. I then asked if they could all repeat the Lord's Prayer, but found that only some of them could do so—it was not said how many. As their faces indicated much intelligence, I could not help reflecting how like they were to the marble beneath my feet—at present a shapeless mass; but capable, by proper moulding and polishing, of the most useful and ornamental developments.

Before leaving, I bought a pair of stockings from the old woman, and scattered some pence amongst the children. Let not the censorious call this a bribe; it was no such thing. They had heard me attentively without any such inducement, and that was all I wanted. Small as the favour was, too, it elicited many thanks. But the best of all is, that in after life some of them may remember the precious truths of this evening; and then rubies or pearls would be nothing in comparison.

Of my conversations with Roman Catholics there, the following was held with a young woman, who may be regarded as a fair specimen of her class and sex in Connemara. Being asked if she had read the Scriptures, she replied that she could not read, but that a Mr. —— had read some of it for her; but she remembered nothing of it. Before the famine, her father had a farm and was comfortable; he possessed a "drove of ponies," six cows, and eighteen goats; he had also a good house. He died of the "famine fever;" then all was lost; her mother has no child but her, and they live by whatever work they can get; she is fond of dancing; while at R—— she paid two shillings of her wages to the piper, yet did not dance herself, but only looked on; is now anxious to get home to help her mother to thatch the house; it is thatched with sedge; gives her wages to her mother, and thinks she would have "no luck" unless she did so; she carded, spun, and dyed her own red dress; bought the wool for one shilling and four pence per pound; it took three pounds; it was woven for $4\frac{1}{2}$d. a yard; it took three yards; dyed it with a mixture of madder, bought in the shops at one shilling a pound, and the juice of blackberries, or the tops of blackberry bushes. She prefers living in this country, as being her native place; knows it is wild in winter, and would go anywhere else to "better herself;" she admits that the best of all ways to "better herself" would be to get salvation. Then I took occasion to explain to her very fully the way to be saved, especially the atonement of Christ, and a new heart by the Holy Spirit. I then pressed on her to pray for this great change.

The next conversation was held with a farmer who, for twenty years of his life, had been a smuggler. His appearance however, was not that of a desperado, but, on the contrary, he seemed a man of mild, thoughtful disposition. His age might be fifty. Of his place of abode I will only say that it was not at Recess. Our conversation began with religion, when I explained to him the way of salvation, and the necessity of a new heart. After this he candidly confessed to me, that for a long time he had been a smuggler, making and selling poteen; that it was a very lucrative business, and that he got great demand for it; that he never sold it to publicans, but only to gentlemen for their own use, and that they prefered it to every other drink, as it was free from mixtures. He added, however, that his clergy condemned the traffic, and that it could not now be followed with safety; yet he thought it not sinful as long as a man made it of his own grain, and sold it honestly. Nor did he believe that, if called before his Creator, the practice would be laid to his charge as a sin. Further, he told me that he had ten children, of whom the eldest was now married, and in his own house; that it was extremely hard to support them on such bad land; and that he regretted most of all, the want of a school for his children, but they had got a little learning from a tutor, who was employed by a gentleman in the neighbourhood.

We again returned to the subject of religion, in regard to which he seemed to feel deeply. Sitting down together on a heather bank, though the day was squally and showery, we spoke first of the atonement. On this point I explained to him several times that Christ on the cross did penance for the sins of all who believe in Him, and that in consequence pardon is a free gift, which I pressed on his immediate acceptance. Though he went not fully with me in this view, yet he admitted that the priest's absolution was useless when not received with a "right disposition" and followed by renewal of life. He also believed that in the latter case the penitent was pardoned by God whether absolved by the priest or not. He seemed much impressed, by the words of Isaiah liii. 5, " With His (Christ's) stripes we are healed," (not with our own stripes.) And here, incidentally, came out an instance of his conscientiousness; for in speaking of the communion, he stated that he had not taken it for some years, because he felt resentment against a neighbour who had stolen from him. In connexion with this I again explained, and pressed on him, the doctrine of the new birth, the need of which he fully admitted, also the fact of its being the work of God's Spirit alone. But he still denied the sinfulness of smuggling, till at last I put the matter in this light; suppose the practice doubtful, yet considering the unspeakable value of the soul, is it not better to choose the safe side? In proof I quoted our Lord's words—" What shall it profit a man if he should gain the whole world and lose his own soul?" This solemn utterance greatly impressed him. We parted in the most friendly spirit.

Returning now to my first tour (1841), my next attempt at Irish preaching was at Roundstone. Accordingly, I got placards posted there announcing a sermon in that language on the following Sabbath. How far the Roman Catholic people would have responded to it if they had been left to themselves, I know not; but such was not the case. A counter notice appeared on the walls threatening death to any of them who should attend. So at least I was informed afterwards. Therefore I had to preach to an audience exclusively Protestant. Thus the place where I least expected it, showed the greatest hostility. But that is no unfrequent occurrence in missionary life.

Being on the subject of intolerance, I may relate another example of it which had occurred at the same place. A horse belonging to the Episcopalian minister had fallen into a marsh, and was in danger of drowning. At such times the peasantry are generally prompt in rendering assistance. But in this case there was an exception. One man, when asked to aid, bluntly refused, saying of the animal, "*Tha an diabhuil air*"—"The Wicked One is on him." But the other parties proceeded in their humane efforts without him, and not unsuccessfully; for which the owner, pulling out his purse, handsomely rewarded them. The sight of the money sorely mortified the bigot, and extorted from him this humiliating confession—"*S orm fein do bhi an diabhuil*"—"Ah! on myself was the Evil One!"

Of the two roads to Clifden—my next destination—that by the shore, though not the best, is the most picturesque.

Besides glimpses of the open Atlantic, it presents a succession of islands, bays, sand-hills, and promontories. Of the places on the route, the most remarkable is Bunowen. Here are the ruins of an old castle celebrated in its day for its eyrie of hunting hawks. Worthy of notice, too, as we pass along, is a kind of seaweed, thrown up on the shores after great storms. It is called "Sargossa;" and by those learned in such matters, it is pronounced to be entirely different from other Irish or British algae. They suppose that it has drifted from a vast distance in the West—probably from the American coasts. In the same way I would account for nuts of a strange kind which I have picked up on this shore; and still more common are pieces of white coral. The latter, though not always of the same colour, strew all Ballyconree Bay, to the north of Clifden; and in one place, where they are ground down by friction against the rocks, they form a literal and most beautiful "coral strand." This I had not expected to meet with on our Irish coast.

Nor should we omit noticing the extraordinary fact, as regards the temperature of this ocean, that in winter it is warmer by several degrees than the atmosphere. Of this the cause is now generally known. The great "Gulf Stream," originating off Mexico, and making the circuit of the northern seas, carries with it this vital warmth to our otherwise cold and barren country. Hence the genial clime and verdant fields of the Emerald Isle, instead of nine months' frost and snow, as in Labrador of the same latitude. Once the system of heating houses by hot water pipes was supposed to be a new invention; but here a similar plan has been at work for ages, blessing our countrymen, while they knew it not. What infinite wisdom in thus employing the surplus heat of one country to correct the otherwise excessive cold of another! By this contrivance the sunshine of the Mexican Gulf produces salubrity and fertility in a country three thousand miles off! Ere this, moralists have found "sermons in stones;" but now we find one in "caloric."

In Clifden my reception was all that could be desired. By the kindness of H. D'Arcy, Esq., then of Clifden Castle, I got the use of the only school-house that was in the town; and there I had a good congregation. No threats, as at Roundstone, had been issued against Roman Catholics attending, so they formed part of the audience, and conducted themselves with great propriety. Next day, too, I was informed by a Protestant friend, that at least one of them spoke approvingly of my doctrine.

Nor was that all. Eighteen years afterwards, when on a visit to Galway, I met an aged man, with whom I was then unacquainted; and he, after asking me was I the minister who had preached the Irish sermon in Clifden, repeated the text and the most striking part of the sermon. It was a place in which, to illustrate the efficacy of Christ's blood to take away sin, irrespective of any worthiness on our part, I compared it to the blood of the paschal lamb sprinkled on the lintel and door-posts of the Israelites, and of which the Scripture says, "When He seeth the blood . . . . . . the Lord will pass over the door," &c. (Exod. xii. 23.) Mark, "when He seeth the *blood :*" not any thing done by the Israelites— not their prayers, feelings, or good works. The latter, indeed, have their place; they are part of our sanctification, without which "no man shall see the Lord." But they are always preceded by pardon, full and free; and that is the effect solely of the shed blood. This vital doctrine formed a chief part of all my Irish preaching; and hence its being remembered by my friend for eighteen years!

In connection with this instance of long-deferred encouragement, I may mention another of the same kind, which has but lately come to light. Two years after this visit to Clifden —that is sixteen years ago—I wrote a tract for some converts in Munster, setting forth the great doctrine of justification by faith. What was its effect on the persons for whom it was intended, I never heard; but in the spring of this year I, to my surprise, was told of its usefulness in a different and unexpected quarter. A Protestant gentleman in Galway, who has been many years a consistent believer, confessed to a friend of mine that this tract was the first thing that opened his eyes to the doctrine in question. Surely this " was drawing the bow at a venture." What was intended for one party was blessed to another. Thus our feeble efforts to do good may fail in the object aimed at, and yet succeed in another way. Neither, indeed, should we ever suppose that such efforts, if scriptural, are a failure. God's " Word never returns void; " but it " prospers " only " in the thing whereto He has sent it;" and of that, the only sure test is the event. Without giving way to despondency, then, let us, when unsuccessful, still " work and wait."

One word more on this incident. Though I have known the gentleman referred to a long time, yet, singular to say, he never to myself personally made known the benefit which he had received from my tract. But was this silence right? That it would not be well for us to know in this life all the fruits of our labours, however small they may be, is admitted; our heads are too weak to bear it. But is not the opposite tendency also to be dreaded? To have no fruit, or to know of none, is calculated to produce despondency. That it ought not, is granted; and it is very easy to say so; but, except in a few rare cases of very robust faith, our hearts will speak differently. "Hope deferred maketh the heart sick;" and though this will not drive a faithful workman from the field, yet it will retard his progress and sink his spirits. To borrow the quaint illustration of an old divine, a net for fishing purposes requires leads to keep it low enough in the water; but if it have no counterbalancing corks at the top, it will sink to the bottom. A similar counterpoise of experiences is necessary for that happy spiritual equilibrium, which is not elated on one hand, nor dispirited on the other.

My next visit to Clifden was in 1860, that is nineteen years after this tour. Great was the change in the interval. Then no mission existed to the Roman Catholic people; but now,—under the Rector, Rev. Mr. D'Arcy,—an efficient staff of Readers and other agents were actively engaged in that work. And not without fruits, judging by the large increase of attendance at his church. Having visited his schools also, I was much pleased with the instruction there given, and with the proficiency of the pupils; and no institution could be better managed than his Protestant Orphanage. Altogether, then, this place presents the best specimen I have seen of the Episcopalian missions in the West.

My two first visits to Clifden having been so agreeable, I regret that I cannot say the same of a third, which I paid to it the year after. Great irritation, indeed, then existed, owing to a lawsuit which had taken place between an Episcopalian minister and a priest, for an assault by the latter. As to myself, however, being a stranger, and having nothing to do with the matter, I considered that I had no cause of apprehension on my own account; and so, without fear, I walked about alone on the beautiful roads surrounding the village. But ere long I had reason to repent of my temerity.

A few days afterwards, when passing over the hill to the west of Clifden, I observed a young fellow running from a distant field where two men were working, and with whom he had been conversing when I first saw him. He ran in the direction I was going; and when he approached the road, he suddenly disappeared. Suspecting nothing, I took no further notice of the matter; but as I was passing the place, I was suddenly stunned by the blow of a stone through my hat, dinging it, and passing a little over the crown of my head. It was a few moments before I could recover myself so as to look about for my assailant, and then I discovered him flying back towards the workmen. Instantly jumping over the ditch, I pursued the fellow, but he soon reached his abettors, and hid there behind a hillock. That these men really abetted him, was evident from a menacing growl which they uttered as I approached them; so I thought it prudent to retrace my steps. Seeing this, the fellow re-appeared, shouting defiance, and dancing with joy. After my return to the road, I met some women, who condemned his conduct; but when I asked them for his name, one of them gave a scoffing reply.

As this attack was so unprovoked, I hoped, by an interview with the people, to convince them of the sin of it; and thus, in some measure, to abate the spirit of persecution. The result will appear from the following extract from my journal:—

"I took the opportunity to visit the scene of the stone-throwing on Monday last. Finding in the very field a boy resembling the fellow who had struck me, I went over to him, and gently laying hold of his collar, charged him with the act, demanding his name. He denied the charge, and said his name was M. Q. I then requested him to bring me to his home, that I might lay the case before his father, for I had no desire to have recourse to law. To this he consented cheerfully, still denying, however, that he was the party. He led me up the hill to a cabin, and left me at the door, while he entered to make known the affair. His mother then appeared,—for the father was dead,—and she denied most positively that her son was the offender. So I at once dropped the affair, merely remarking how close was the resemblance. I also recollected having met the same woman at the time of the assault, when she condemned it.

"Meantime, during our conversation, several persons from the adjoining cabins came to listen, some of whom entered in, whilst others stood at the door where I was; for, not being invited in, I stood outside all the time. The parties within held a conversation with themselves, the result of which soon after transpired. While this was going on, I took occasion to show the sin of injuring any one on the ground of religion, and specially one who was quietly walking the high road. No matter what excuse might be offered for such a thing, I declared that it was doing service to the devil. All churches, I said, held that love to God and our neighbour was the chief principle of religion, which such conduct violated. This I repeated in Irish. Neither, I argued, could any clergyman in Ireland forgive the offence but myself, as I was the injured party. Here a voice from within denounced 'Jumpers;' but I said that I was no 'Jumper,' if by that was meant one who had changed his religion. At the same time, I said I would give up my religion at once, if I found it to be wrong; for 'what would it profit me to gain the whole world, and lose my soul?' 'Oh, then,' replied the same voice, 'if you're not a Jumper, you belong to them.' Other bitter remarks followed; and then Widow Q—— asked my name, which I gave her. She repeated that her son had not struck me, and that the boy who did so belonged to another village. With that, a female voice shouted from within, that he wore a different dress, being 'bredeen.' It thus came out incidentally that they knew very well who he was—as I had suspected all along. In reply, I stated, that whether or no, I wanted not to punish the fellow, but only to make him come forward and ask my forgiveness. To this they consented, saying that it was very reasonable; and one woman cried out that 'I should be allowed to go the highway unmolested,' but that for her saying so on Monday last she had got 'plenty of abuse.'

"So far I seemed to have gained the main object of this interview, which was to convince them of the sin of injuring others for the sake of religion. But a change for the worse quickly succeeded. It was the result of the consultation held within the cabin. What was there said I did not hear, but its purport was shown by the event; for Widow Q—— coming again to the door, warned me, in a defiant tone, that only for her I would now get a worse stroke than on Monday, because I had presumed to bring such a charge against her son. At the same time, an old woman who had lately come up, and who seemed to be very fierce, raised a rod she held in her hand, and denounced all 'Jumpers.' In vain I reminded the widow, that I only brought the boy to her to examine into the case, and that I had given up pressing the charge. There was no use in further expostulation, but rather positive danger. So, after expressing my regret that they should cherish such a bad spirit, I retired from the place. The only one who followed me was the old woman, who walked after me in a surly mood till we reached the main road. There I ventured to make an appeal to her, saying, 'So I see you would allow me to be struck going the highway.' In a furious tone she replied, 'You may go to the d——,' &c. To escape the abusive and blasphemous language that followed, I hastened out of the sound of her voice, not returning a single word. When I was nearly out of sight, I ventured to look back; and lo! she was still standing in the same spot—still looking after me—and, I suppose, still cursing!"

Resuming my first tour, (in 1841,) I proceeded in the next place to the northern parts of Connemara. Here are no towns; nor were there yet the numerous villas which, with their reclaimed farms and tasteful pleasure-grounds, now adorn this once wild and desolate region. Not knowing how long I might remain here, or what course I might take, I set out on foot, unincumbered with any vehicle, and literally without "two coats or staves." Nor did I bring even a guide, hoping to inquire my way as I went on. The first place to which I directed my steps was Tully, being slightly acquainted with the Curate. This place lies on the sea-shore, about ten or twelve miles from Clifden. During this long walk, I met only one fellow-traveller; so unfrequented were the roads at that time. Nor did I get from him much information. To my inquiry respecting the distance of Tully, his only answer was, "A good while, Sir;" measuring the distance, not by miles, but by time, as is still done in the East. I then asked him why the flock of sheep which he drove presented so ragged an appearance, their wool being shorn in patches, which gave the creatures a most ludicrous aspect. The explanation was, that this was the work of thieves, who thus purloined materials for stockings, when the animals were grazing on the mountains. Soon after, he turned aside at a bye-road, leaving me to pursue the rest of my journey alone. But I found agreeable occupation in admiring the sublime scenery, both landward and seaward, and which at that time possessed the charm of being to me altogether new.

Prominent in grandeur, rose Mulrea, which seemed quite near though in the County Mayo. The day being fine, it stood out in sharp relief, in all its vast outlines; and appeared quite animated when shaded by the flying clouds. Still more to enliven the scene, the ocean burst suddenly on the sight, and its billows, broken on the rocky shores, sounded like " thunder heard remote." Alone in such a region, no wonder that my mind took a poetical turn, the result of which was the following verses; which, with all their demerits, are, so far as I know, the first tribute of the kind to this magnificent mountain-group :—

ADDRESS TO THE KILLERY MOUNTAINS AT A DISTANCE.

Ye lofty cliffs! whose summits tower
   In heaven's vast domain;
Whose naked heads, from ancient years,
   The storm has swept in vain :
From Nature's war in ages past
   Unscathed, unchanged ye stand,
As wild and free as the rolling sea
   That shakes your rocky strand.

In vain does thunder often break
   Your solitude profound,
And lightning fierce his horrid fires
   Shoot all your crags around.
With effort vain the ocean vast
   Heaves all his billowy tides,
And pours aloft his myriad waves
   White-foaming up your sides.

Their wrath is vain: ye mock their rage,
   And all their vauntings proud :
As little reck the hurricane
   As shade of summer cloud.
Man is the creature of a day—
   His time is but a span :
But ye, from age to age, abide
   Unchangeably the same.

To thee I call, O proud Mulrea!—
    Thee with the rugged breast—
With eye up-turn'd and wondering gaze
    I mark thy lofty crest.
By man untamed; his iron yoke
    Has never fettered thee;
To him no harvest dost thou yield,
    No herb or shady tree.

Though it is sweet, in sunshine bright,
    To trace the shades that fly
In chace amusive o'er your sides,
    And mock the gazer's eye:
But ah! how lone and desolate
    Your heathery wilds appear;
Your cheerless wastes the stranger sees—
    His heart shrinks back with fear.

But hush! the storm comes on apace—
    I hear its rustling sound;
At once the sun withdraws his beams,
    And midnight reigns around.
And louder still the ocean roars,
    Hoarse-grumbling, far below:
His crest, that whitens in the gloom,
    Flies high like flakes of snow.

The watery clouds, from ocean driven,
    Pour down the streaming rain,
And darkening still from west to east
    Shroud crag, and sea, and plain.
Thus brightest scenes on earth's fair face
    Are soonest overcast;
And he that knows but earthly joys
    Oft treads a wintry waste.

Assuring the reader that the storm alluded to in the last verses, was a real occurrence, and no poetic fancy, I shall now, for the sake of the gratifying contrast, quote from my journal some remarks on the great improvement which I found in this country eighteen years subsequently.

"As I approached Ballinakill a few miles further on, I was surprised at the great change in the place. For this I was not unprepared having heard of it long before; but it exceeded my expectations. At my first visit to Ballinakill it was nearly a waste. But now, besides some beautiful villas, it has got a fine church with a rectory and school-house: and I was told that the congregation on Sabbaths is most respectable. Farther on at Letterfrack is a colony of Quakers, whose characteristic industry has not forsaken them; for nothing could exceed the comfort and cleanliness of their habitations. What a change from the wild uncultivated glen when I last saw it!

"One cottage particularly pleased me by its neatness and its nice pleasure-grounds, flanked by as fine a fuschia hedge as I had ever seen. What was my surprise when the driver of the car told me, that formerly this was a filthy hovel where the cattle were housed with the occupants, so that with difficulty he could pick his steps to the fire-place to kindle his pipe! But the finest house of all is that which was built by Mr. Ellis, and is now occupied by —— Hall, Esq. This is a wonderful creation considering that the little glen in which it stands was, a few years ago, a mere bog waving its barren heath, where now the finest flowering shrubs and garden trees display their blooms and ripen their fruits. Having been kindly shown over the place by its worthy proprietor, I never before saw such a triumph of industry over natural disadvantages. Truly it is 'the desert rejoicing and blossoming as the rose.' With the extension of such industry over all Ireland, what a happy island it would be: and this is the great lesson taught by Letterfrack."

In passing, I must here refer to a visit which I, with a

friend, paid to a Methodist who lived in a wild and desolate moor adjoining. In course of conversation he told us of another visit he had received a little before, from a Scripture reader; and how they occupied their time while in each other's society. "We argued on election and free will all the night, while there remained in the house a grain of tea or a pipe of tobacco!" In such a desert one would have thought that these men would rather employ themselves in edifying each other. But no: the same rage for argument that has set on fire churches and nations, pursued them even into the wilds of Connemara! Truly human nature is always the same.

Another theological reminiscence of this visit is thus described in my journal:—"Returning to Letterfrack, I was followed by a boy who pressed me to buy a handful of Irish diamonds, which he had gathered on the mountains. In vain I refused; like other duns, he would not be put off. I then asked him who made him; and, when he answered correctly, I asked did he hope to go to heaven, or was he worthy of it. I then told him that, being sinners, none of us deserved heaven; and that Jesus was the only Saviour: and that these truths, if believed in, were more precious than real diamonds. But the little fellow was taken quite aback by this unexpected address; and so, after looking at me with awe, mingled with aversion, he suddenly disappeared! I did not mean to frighten him away; however, my address had that effect most thoroughly. What an indication of the old catastrophe to our nature six thousand years ago! How indelible in the human soul is enmity to what is spiritual; and thus how perceptible in Letterfrack the effect of the fall in Eden!"

Arrived at Tully, my clerical friend received me kindly; and, on hearing the object of my visit, advised me to proceed onward to Salruc, the seat of General Thompson. This gentleman treated me with great kindness; and even gave me the use of his own parlour for an Irish sermon. Intimation of the service was communicated by the Curate, who for this purpose visited the surrounding cabins, and soon collected a good audience. Being himself an Irish speaker, he led the singing; and, as the people knew not our sacred music, being Roman Catholics, he sang the hymns to national airs, in which they heartily joined. Of course, I would not approve of this practice as a rule; but that was an exceptional case. This being the first time that I had heard a congregation of my fellow-countrymen praising God in their own expressive language, I was deeply affected by it; and my interest in the service was still further increased by a little incident which occurred whilst I was preaching. After depicting at the outset our fallen condition, with our inability to save ourselves, I then asked, "Is there no remedy? or shall I describe it to you?" Here one man, apparently anxious to hear it, cried out in Irish, "A hundred welcomes before you!" Indeed they all listened with great attention, so that, next to the Galway meeting, this was the most encouraging one which I had yet addressed.

Having some time afterwards described the scene to a gifted Scotch lady—a sister of Miss C. Pringle—she made it the subject of a beautiful hymn, of which I give two verses:—

THE IRISH HOME-MISSION HYMN.

Tune—"*Erin go Bragh.*"

ALL power is thine, Lord, in earth and in heaven;
  And yet this green isle is in darkness sunk down:
To Thee all the isles of the Gentiles are given;
  Stretch forth thy hand, then, and make it thine own.

"Go to all lands," was thy large, wide commission;
(Was Ireland excepted, and left to perdition?)
Oh! then, let thy presence go forth with our mission,
And place this bright Emerald aloft in thy crown.

Hark to that sound!—is it mountain-winds whistling
Their sad lonely music in this Irish glen?
Or water's soft murmurs; or Autumn's leaves rustling,
Far from the haunts and the voices of men?
'Tis the voice of devotion, from hearts new and living;
'Tis the soft Irish psalm joins the chorus of heaven;
Behold the glad tidings in Irish are given,
Of glory to God and of good-will to men!

Next morning I was up early at Salruc, in order to ascend a hill that I might see the sun rise on the Greater Killery. Before reaching my destination, the sun had risen; but it had not yet shone out, being obscured by dark clouds. These, however, by degrees cleared off, sailing away in silent majesty towards the east, and disclosing on all sides the wonderful landscape. This might truly be called, in the language of a Hebrew prophet, "Morning spread upon the mountains." or, in the kindred words of an old Celtic bard, *Mar madain samhradh an gleantaibh ceo*—"As summer's morn in misty glens." The most prominent feature of the scene is a long, narrow bay, which runs ten miles into the country from the Atlantic, and which, in savage grandeur, has been compared to a Norwegian fiord. On the north side, and partly on the south, it is flanked by mountains, from the summits of which the bay beneath, though a quarter or half a mile wide, seems only a mill-race, or altogether disappears amid the hills. To complete the picture, overhead hung the splendid drapery of clouds already mentioned, and which a mountain region alone could produce. Pierced by the sunshine, these gradually become luminous, displaying a beautiful variety of colours, till they are dislodged from cliff to cliff, and lost in ether. In the dazzling effulgence which succeeds, the hitherto dark bay shines like a mass of solid silver; whilst the rivulets pendant on the mountain sides, catching the same radiance, sparkle like pieces of polished steel. Favoured by this increase of light, I now discover, for the first time, that the highest peaks are covered with snow.

Long I gazed on the wondrous scene. But after the first excitement had subsided, my principal feeling was that of a painful solitude. The only human being in sight was a little child, who, at this moment, stood gazing up at me from the door of a cabin which hung, like a swallow's nest, on a steep declivity. No other living creature was visible, except a few sheep like white dots on the heath, and some birds of a dark colour which were on the wing, far down between me and the abyss. With these exceptions, all around was a death-like solitude. The stillness was broken only by the rumbling of the distant waves, or by the sudden whirl of the mountain gusts. This awful wildness was increased by the unearthly shapes of the mountains, and the sombre hue of the heath, all forming a picture of terrible sublimity.

But suddenly the scene changes. From the Atlantic, new clouds roll along, and shroud Mulrea, and other high peaks; while the east, still bright, forms a striking contrast to the darkening west. Simultaneously, the wind rises, and sweeps in whirling eddies through the winding ravines, and round the beetling cliffs. Again the clouds obtain the empire of the skies, and all is dark. A heavy shower succeeds. In ten minutes the rain ceases, and all is bright as before. The clouds, after discharging their contents, again became beautifully luminous, and cover a great part of the sky with their dazzling drapery.

Ascending a higher peak, my view enlarges; and I now

behold, along with the former scene, the expanse of the great Atlantic. Seen from this Alpine height, words cannot describe its grandeur. It was visible at one glance, from the Isle of Innisboffin to Clare Island off the County Mayo, and even to Achill Head. Thus, every element of earth, air, or water, was present to complete this sublime picture. In reason's ear it was one concert of creation's grandest works, praising their Maker, while

" Ocean rolled the deep, profound, eternal bass in nature's anthem."

No wonder that, under these circumstances, my reflections mounted upward from nature to its God, and assumed the form of prayer. This I shall not withhold, though it never was intended for publicity, having been buried in the dust for twenty-two years, and being now exhumed, only from its connexion with this sublime scene :—

"Oh! Thou glorious Creator, who, of old, didst form of nothing these wonderful works!—Thou Parent of all, Almighty! may I, in view of Thy stupendous creation, address Thee unblamed? Thou Mysterious Being, whose hand did, in the beginning, mould those mighty masses into 'everlasting mountains;' Thou whose fingers did spin into a gorgeous canopy these fleecy clouds; Thou who didst first place that glorious sun in the east, and with one breath didst kindle his quenchless fire; and Thou who dost hold, in 'the hollow of Thy hand,' the world of waters; and, when they dash their foaming billows on the trembling shore, dost restrain them, saying, 'Hitherto shall ye come, and no farther, and here shall your proud waves be stayed;' On this hallowed morn, may I, an atom in comparison with these, Thy great works, address Thy Majesty? From so insignificant a creature, wilt Thou accept, on this lonely heath, my humble, yet fervent orisons? Yes, I know Thou wilt!

Thou art their Creator; but Thou art my Father. They have no spirit, as I have, to exalt—no soul to animate—their sluggish nature. They have no bond of union with Thee— no spiritual substance on which to receive the impress of Thine image. They have no eye to behold Thee—no heart to love Thee. But I have. For me, too, oh! mystery of mysteries! He has bled. For me 'a hand of clay smote the Creator of heaven and earth!' The fruits of this mystery, oh! let me not lose; but, by believing it, may my sins be pardoned and my heart renewed. Then, adopted into Thy family, I shall evermore enjoy Thy protection and be solaced by Thy love. Then, without any doubt, I shall, in child-like confidence, claim Thee as my covenant-God. Then I shall be one of those who will yet behold Thy face in Thy glory, having seen, as yet, 'only the hidings of Thy power.' O! glorious anticipation! my feet will yet stand on Thy hill of Zion, and I shall pitch my tent on 'the mount of God.' But even here, O Father! while I stray as a pilgrim on earth, let my soul be dwelt in by Thy Spirit, dispelling thence the mists of darkness and of sin. On this hallowed morn, in view of Thy stupendous works, and in the light of this glorious sun, oh! dispel every cloud between Thee and my soul. Bow Thy heavens, O God! and come down; and let the mountains of estrangement between Thee and me flow down at Thy presence! Through all my remaining pilgrimage, guide me—guard me. And at the close of life's uneven way, oh! let Thy voice cheer me in the 'dark valley,' and say to my soul, 'Come up hither.' Amen for Christ's sake, and Amen."

In leaving the hospitable mansion of the General, he assured me that whenever I should visit the country hereafter, his house and a horse would be at my service. But we never met again, and long since he has gone the way of all flesh.

As I could not requite his kindness while he lived, I hope that this grateful acknowledgment of it will serve as a monumental stone to his memory.

In returning to Clifden, the road for the first few miles was indifferent. It had no bridges over the streams, and in some places it consisted of unbroken rock, from one side to the other. But the General's pony, being used to it, picked his steps carefully, and carried me safely to the main road. Here, returning the animal with the servant who accompanied me, I, as before, pursued my way alone. Again my thoughts flowed in a poetical channel, and hence this :—

FAREWELL TO THE KILLERY MOUNTAINS.

FAREWELL, ye cliffs! Though proud ye be,
    Yet dearer far to me,
My humble cottage in the vale,
    Beneath the white thorn tree.

There ocean storm shall never sweep
    My shelter'd clay-built shed;
Nor wintry tempest, piping loud,
    E'er rock my nightly bed.

A little plot of native ground
    Shall all my wants supply;
Its daisied fields and grassy banks
    Shall cheer their master's eye.

There woodbrier sweet, its fragrant arms
    Around my porch shall twine—
A gay parterre before my door,
    With flowers of every clime.

The ivy's clust'ring leaves shall form
    A wall of living green;
And the oak, his branching arms shall spread
    To shade the rural scene.

There shall I range the summer fields,
    When gleams the purple morn;
And shake the pearly drops that hang
    Upon the mild white thorn.

The thrush, high perch'd on topmost bough,
    Shall raise his morning song;
While echoing groves and mossy glens
    The cheerful notes prolong.

And when, in noontide's sultry hours,
    The flow'ry meadows fade,
I'll lay me by the babbling brook,
    Beneath the elm tree's shade.

There, lull'd by hum of wand'ring bee,
    I'll muse till shades of eve;
Or pore upon the Sacred Page,
    Or wreath poetic weave;

While all around a brighter sun
    Shall heav'nly radiance throw;
And Siloa's brook shall warble by,
    And Sharon's roses glow;

And Zion's harp of "solemn sound,"
    On willows hung no more,
In melting sweetness on the gale
    Its melody shall pour.

Farewell, ye cliffs! Though proud ye be,
    Yet dearer far to me,
My humble cottage in the vale,
    Beneath the white thorn tree.

Here the "Sketches of the Irish Highlands" must terminate. This tour, indeed, had only begun; but having, after this, passed away from the mountains, it falls not within the present limits. Suffice to say, generally, that during its course, the following places were visited and preached in to

Roman Catholic audiences, viz. :—Westport, Knappagh, Roscommon, Turlough, Castlebar, Ballina, Killala, Sligo, Drumcormic, (near Ballymote,) Clogher, Buckhill, (near Ballaghadireen,) and Boyle. See General Assembly's Report for 1841.

In these places, my success, on the whole, exceeded that already described. No wonder, then, that my friends and myself hoped for great and speedy results. But that was not the Lord's will, nor was there any Divine warrant to expect it. For in this fallen world, spiritual progress must ever excite opposition, and that generally in an equal ratio. One object with the Lord in permitting this, is to distinguish between the real and the pretended friends of His cause. Most people favour it, when it "walks in silver slippers." But only those who love it for its Master's sake, and who implicitly believe His promise of its ultimate triumph, can adhere to it in trying vicissitudes. These faithful few are the future conquerors of the world for Christ. For it is not numbers, but faith, that "overcomes the world;" and faith does so simply by laying hold on Omnipotence, which alone is adequate to the work.

But even with Divine help, ordinarily to the human instruments, victory is no easy task, but demands from them sacrifices for which, at first, they are not prepared, and which drive them to the brink of despondency. Nor am I ashamed to confess, that at certain crises, it has been so with myself. But before censuring me for such weakness, one should know all my discouragements, the worst of which did not come from Roman Catholics. With sorrow of heart, I state this; but being the fact, it needs to be mentioned, for the warning of future Irish missionaries. So much did I suffer in this way, that, after long forbearance, I was at last obliged, in self-defence, to cast down, through the press, the following challenge to all enemies, none of whom have had the hardihood to take it up:—" If any man shall pretend, that during the twenty-two years I have been in the ministry, he can impeach my doctrine or character, otherwise than as regards those failings common to me with other believers; to such accuser I reply—*Mentiris impudentissime*."

No Missionary claims, on the ground of his office, immunity from censure, if he should deserve it. In such a case, faithful rebuke were a precious, as it is also a much neglected, proof of Christian love. But with that heavenly grace, who can confound the evil spirit, which, " like the pestilence, walketh in darkness"—which seeks not to build up but to destroy the usefulness of others—not to extend the Gospel so much as to prevent them from extending it. That few would intentionally lend themselves to this bad influence, is charitably hoped; but many friends of missions can bear testimony to its prevalence, as well as to its blighting effects on their labours.

Nor, after all, can that enmity be wondered at, considering what our nature is; for, as experience and Scripture testify, it is, till renewed, a nature fearfully and innately opposed to the Gospel; and, though not without its redeeming qualities in the sight of man, it is spiritually a ruin, and its best deeds only flowers of a weed. Even when favoured with Scripture light, and making a Christian profession, it is not less really, though not so openly, inimical to godliness, being the old quarrel begun outside the wall of Eden, and, under different names, continued ever since, whenever a regenerated soul comes into contact with an unregenerated one. Hence the painful alternative to which we are shut up—" We must either suffer from the world or with the world." And if suffering is thus the lot of all believers, how much more so of the Missionary. " The forlorn hope" of the Church, and alone amid a host of foes, he is exposed to a thousand shafts assailing him at once, in his character, his doctrine, his converts, nay, even in his very life. "I will show him," says God of Paul, "how great things he must suffer for my name's sake."

Is this the language of one repenting of his chosen work? God forbid. No man, unless he had entered on a mission-life from wrong motives, has ever regretted it; and for my part, I daily bless God that I was ever led to embark in it. Neither do I wish to discourage others from undertaking that work. God forbid. On the contrary, I never considered it so hopeful as at present. From the first, relying on God's promise, I regarded Ireland's evangelization as certain at some period; but now, in ways that I cannot stop to particularise, I see the harbingers of its approach. And even were existing agencies withdrawn, I believe that "deliverance would arise from some other place," perhaps from the Roman Catholics themselves. But at the same time, to prevent disappointment, I must candidly state that, in my opinion, final success will require much greater efforts and sufferings. It has been said of Connemara, that "few men like to spend a second winter in it"—that is, it is a pleasant place only when the elements are asleep. So of this mission; its summer time is very pleasant, but "a second winter" in it is what few will endure. And yet, such endurance is indispensable. To work it effectually, we must persevere in it at all seasons; and, at whatever hazards, carry in our own persons, as well as by our agents, the blessed Gospel to the homes and hearts of Romanists.

At a distance, and in imagination, it is easy to suffer for Christ; but in practice the thing is not so easy. And those who are called to it, though it is really a great honour, feel their need of all the strengthening influences of the Gospel. Of these, the principal is the assurance, that such sufferings are precious to the Lord. Jealousy for the doctrine of grace has led many to disparage the believer's services, of whatever kind, which is a very pernicious mistake. Because others would substitute good works for the Saviour, they practically discard them altogether. But not so the Lord Himself. The apostles had their failings as well as modern believers, and yet He tells them, " Ye are they who have continued with me in my temptations, and I appoint unto you a kingdom," &c.; thus attaching a glorious, though undeserved, reward to their sufferings for His sake. Nor is that blessed hope unneeded. Whatever the case with those " at ease in Zion," the persecuted missionary requires all its comfort; and, in great straits, when assailed, perhaps, from within as well as from without, he could not bear up at all if deprived of it. Whoever, then, undertakes this work should " arm himself" with this assurance; not resting on the uncertain favour of men, but on the infallible promise of the Master, who is his only sure Vindicator, and who will not permit the least thing done for Him to go unrequited. And let him remember, too, that his sufferings for Christ will not only be rewarded, but that they are short. This consideration comforted our Lord Himself in his trials. "This is your hour," said He, " and the power of darkness." Our suffering, then, is but for " an hour," as His was, and it is followed by an eternity of bliss. Reflecting on this great fact has suggested the following verses, which may interest some readers:—

" WATCH WITH ME ONE HOUR."

The night in which He was betray'd,
  When pangs unknown His bosom tore,
This one request the Saviour made—
  Ah! watch with me, my friends, one hour.

That they were willing, He confess'd;
  But they were " weak." The day before
They had toil'd hard, and sweet was rest;
  And so they slept that awful hour.

> How great the patience of the Lord,
>   Who meekly, thus, their sleeping bore;
> He utter'd no reproachful word,
>   Though left alone to watch that hour.
>
> In me too, Lord, the flesh is weak;
>   Yet, willingly I'd sleep no more.
> From carnal ease my soul awake,
>   That I may watch with Thee one hour.
>
> Should not indulgence be abhorr'd
>   Where Thou hast bled at every pore?
> The servant should be like his Lord—
>   Content to watch with Thee one hour.
>
> Oh! make it clear, the cause is thine;
>   And though with Thee afflicted sore,
> Yet, by Thy grace, I'll ne'er repine,
>   But gladly watch with Thee one hour.
>
> An hour is short—'tis quickly past—
>   One parting pang, and all is o'er;
> Then, while eternity shall last,
>   They'll reign with Thee, who watch'd one hour.

Next to these divine consolations—and itself also divine—is the sympathy of believing friends. Of this, no man receives so much as the missionary. Thrown upon first principles, in which all true Christians agree, he is received as a brother by converted men of all sects, and, for his Master's sake, treated with a kindness unknown to earthly friendship. This is one of the purest and most refreshing fountains of comfort. That Paul felt it so in his case, appears from his many grateful allusions to it. And every other missionary can say the same. For my part, I owe to such friends not only much of the comfort I enjoyed in the work, but even of its success. Therefore, I feel under deep obligations to them, " the greater part of whom remain unto this present, but some are fallen asleep." Neither shall their valued co-operation—including that of dear friends in my own Church—ever be forgotten by me, nor, I humbly trust, by my Master.

Thus, then, the missionary life is one of the "warmest friendships, as well as one of the bitterest enmities." And it was so with the Master Himself. In His presence indifference was impossible : by acquaintance with Him, every man was made a friend or an enemy; and usually those feelings went on increasing to the end. The more His own people knew Him, the more they loved Him; on the other hand, the more light His enemies received from Him, the more they hated Him. And so their worst treatment of Him was at the last. It is often thus with His people too; such as the "two witnesses" spoken of in Revelation, who were slain only when they had finished their testimony. But it is consoling to observe, that upon their death, they had "finished it." To human appearance, the only effect was to exasperate their foes, which certainly was not what they wished. On the contrary, they might have thought that undesirable result a proof of failure; but it was not so; they succeeded in the work "whereto they were sent." This great principle let the persecuted missionary ever bear in mind; for without it he could not stand, in some crises of his struggle; but with it, he is "more than conqueror." Defeated or disappointed in twenty ways, he ever succeeds, if faithful, in this respect. Why, then, ever despond ? "A thousand griefs pierce him; but every grief is the entrance for a balm."

As these pages will fall into the hands of many who have no personal knowledge of the author or his work, there is a necessity for his appending a few vouchers to the narrative. This is the more needful, as, for the work's sake, he has, for a long time, shunned publicity. Two vouchers, however, will suffice, as they proceed from quarters in which there was no possibility of private bias, while there was the most perfect competence to form a right opinion. One is that of the Missionary Directors of his Church, who in these matters represent the whole Presbyterian body. Their approving testimony was given at different times, and in different forms; but here I shall cite it only in reference to the years 1841 and 1842, being the time of my Irish preaching in Connaught. Alluding to its results in the former year, they state that " it is a matter of extreme gratification to them to lay before the Assembly the following report of Mr. M'Manus, their first missionary to the native Irish;" adding, that " it is the highest [agency] which God has appointed, and which the Assembly is privileged to employ." Again, in 1842, they state, " that it is a matter that should move the very heart of this Church with the deepest sorrow, that she has but one missionary among the myriads of our countrymen, who are destitute of a preached Gospel in their own language," &c.

The other testimony has reference to my mission in Kerry, and is that of the Presbytery of Cork, which includes most of the Presbyterian clergy in Munster, with their respective congregations. This reverend body, having personally visited my field of operation, and officially examined the whole work, came unanimously to the following decision, which their Moderator, at his own instance, published in the *Banner of Ulster* newspaper. He prefaced it with a letter of his own, which also is appended, except one paragraph, that was too complimentary to the author. It should be added, that on my first visiting Kerry in 1842, this district was pointed out to me, by Christian friends of different Churches, as being the most spiritually destitute in that country; and it was for that reason chiefly, that I selected it. It is a wide valley at the head of the Dingle bay, stretching from Sliav Mish, south of Tralee, to the

Iveragh mountains, west of Killarney, and embracing the villages of Castlemaine, Milltown, and Killorglin.

Visit of the Presbytery of Cork to Laherin, the principal Station of the Irish Mission in Kerry.

" We went to visit Laherin, (about ten miles from Tralee,) the principal station in Mr. M'Manus's interesting field, where, in the school-house lately erected by our Mission Directors in that place, we found assembled to meet us a congregation of between seventy and eighty. Of these, about twenty-five were converts from Popery—fully come out—the fruits of Mr. M'Manus's own labour, forty Roman Catholic inquirers after the truth, and the remainder persons who had always been Protestants. The meeting was commenced with praise and prayer, after which the converts were subjected to a close and lengthened examination on the most important and essential truths of Revelation, when the majority of them evinced a knowledge of the Word of God, which, for its extent and accuracy, considering their many disadvantages, gratified and surprised us. Several of the Roman Catholic inquirers, at our request, very willingly read portions of the Irish Testament, and translated it into English. That dread of truth, so universally manifested by the dupes of the priesthood, was no longer to be seen among these. There was a willing ear for every statement we had to make, and as much deep and devout attention as any Protestant audience could possibly evince.

" At the close of this most interesting interview with the converts, which lasted an hour and a-half, one of the brethren addressed the meeting in terms suited to their capacity, and brought before them a mass of essential truth, which they not only willingly heard, but to all appearance most cordially received.

"If even the twenty-five before-mentioned had not really relinquished the errors of Rome, what grounds for rejoicing and gratitude to see so many of our fearfully deceived fellow-countrymen, in the face of open day, in the heart of a Popish country, and with the prospect of persecution, assembling, on intimation given, to meet for religious purposes a whole Presbytery of Protestant ministers! Let but this one consideration have its due weight, and we have reason to 'thank God and take courage.'

"What a contrast that place now presents to what it was when our worthy brother first entered on his labours there! Then " darkness [literally] covered the place, and gross darkness the people." Then *none* (R. C.) would *even listen* to the truth; now *many* are *searching* after the truth. Then *all* were the benighted and willing dupes of Popish power; now *many* of them ' the free men whom the truth made free.'

"Instead of bowing a blind obedience to the dogmas and dictates of a self-deceived and bigoted priesthood, many are now, regardless of the reproach of the scoffer and the power of the persecutor, anxious and submitting to be taught the ' way of life.'

"Under these circumstances, the brethren found no difficulty in coming to the following finding—a finding expressive of the feeling of the hearts of all—called forth by facts submitted in evidence, and justly due to our respected brother, who, in the face of fierce persecution, and in defiance of many disappointments, has laboured far away from the society and sympathy of his brethren for the space of four years.

"The Presbytery having visited the scene of Mr. M'Manus's labours, and having seen and heard for themselves, have pleasure in recording their entire satisfaction with the measure of success that has attended his labours, express their fullest confidence in him as a laborious self-denying fellow-labourer, and assure him of their sympathy in his manifold difficulties and trials, and that he shall not be forgotten by them in their prayers.

"(Signed)   E. M. DILL,
"*Moderator.*"

This official approval of the work seems now providential, considering the obloquy subsequently cast upon it by hostile priests and others. But its publication at the time was prejudicial, having attracted the attention of enemies, and thus greatly increased the persecution. The attacks that followed, exceeded all former experience, and occasioned on my part so great an increase of labour and cares, that eventually my health sank under it. The strain was too great for my ordinary frame long to bear, and mine had never been robust. By the blessing of God I partially recovered afterwards, and even resumed work to some extent; but, after struggling for a while, I found myself unable for the task. With great reluctance, then, I was obliged to resign the superintendence of this mission, though afterwards, as far as my strength permitted, I resumed missionary labour without holding any office in our mission. After a few years, however, another breaking down of health disabled me for any work whatever.

But meantime what became of these fruits which had so pleased the Presbytery? There, alas! is the saddest part of my history. The Irish missionary resembles the builder of a lighthouse, who, after much progress with his structure, finds it scattered by one disastrous storm. So was it in this case. And hence, in the previous part of this volume, I have dwelt more on what I have taught Romanists than on any immediate fruits of it; for the latter, as painful experience has taught me, are liable at any moment to be scattered by persecution. Neither is it to be expected, that all converts will stand that ordeal. If this surprises any one, he knows little of human nature, or of other missions, or of primitive Christianity itself. The missionary is sent, "not to call the righteous but sinners to repentance;" consequently he must, in the first instance, expect to meet with deception as well as other vices, just as a physician expects to meet with diseases. And if the subjects of these vices should continue unimproved, he is not responsible for that if he has faithfully applied the Gospel remedy. In that case, their unregeneracy is his cross—not his fault; and any reproaches cast on him for their sake, would also apply (we speak with reverence) to his Master, whose first disciples sometimes turned out "stony-ground" hearers. That so self-evident a principle should be ennunciated so formally may appear unnecessary; but experience testifies the contrary; for the opposite notion, as absurd as it is unscriptural, has been made the ground, not only for unmerited censure to missionaries, but also for abandoning mission work altogether! According to this view, the Creator should send no more rain, because much of it falls on deserts; and the apostles should not have preached the Gospel at the first, because that confessedly, while it saved some, it hardened others.

Besides this, the mission of which we now speak was then but in its infancy, having been established only a few years. It is no wonder, then, that persecution should have caused defections in it. Two of the families which had come out of Rome relapsed, and many inquirers drew back. But others nobly stood firm. Their names deserve to be recorded, only that, under present circumstances, it would be no kindness to them; but they will be soon recognised by friends through the following brief notices:—

One of them, and the first to join the mission, is a farmer, still residing there, who, amid many trials, has ever since continued a consistent member of our Church, and his children, now grown up, happily tread in his footsteps. Another convert, who was obliged by persecution to fly the country, was afterwards met by me in Dublin, a zealous Protestant. A third, also a refugee, turned up in a distant county, where he joined our Church. A fourth, a clever young man, whom I had appointed Irish teacher, was heard of several years subsequently, in London, where he was usefully employed by the city mission, to read the Irish Scriptures to his countrymen. Several others, who owe their enlightenment partly or wholly to this mission, joined other Protestant Churches, and, as far as I have heard, they all continue steadfast, or have died in the Protestant faith.*

Thus, then, visible fruits were not wanting. But they came far short of my object, which was to form, in connection with our Church, the nucleus of a native congregation worshipping God in their own Irish language, and thoroughly Celtic in their sympathies, like the Highland congregations attached to the sister Church in Scotland. Could that project have been realized, it would do much to naturalize the Gospel amongst the native Irish. But this part of my work fell to the ground. The time for it was not yet come. However, the succeeding Superintendents—though not knowing Irish—were very useful in other respects, especially by their scriptural and industrial schools. The principal one of these was supported and personally superintended by a devoted Christian lady, Miss Banks, of Edinburgh, who laboured with the energy and self-denial of a Mrs. Judson. She left it only to die; but to her, " death was gain."

* All the above had been Romanists; but several Protestants also, on their death beds, ascribed their conversion spiritually to the instrumentality of this mission.

Finally, a few years ago, when the funds of our Church ran low, this mission was broken up — a sad necessity. But God did not withdraw His blessing with the removal of that instrumentality. This will appear from the following letter, which I have received while writing these pages, from William Lunham, Esq., a worthy merchant of Tralee. He there describes a revival that has taken place in that very locality, and in which I know that himself has been greatly blessed, though he does not say so. "I am happy to inform you, that the work of the Lord is going on prosperously. Last night I was at the weekly prayer-meeting at Castlemaine. I am rejoiced to say, the Holy Spirit of God was in the midst of it. I think there could not be less than sixty in attendance. It continued for two hours and a-half; even then, they were not willing to separate. God is doing wonders in our day. There has been a great shaking among the dry bones in this part of God's vineyard. It is really delightful to hear many of the young country lads offering up prayer and thanks at the throne of the Almighty, through our Lord and Saviour, Jesus Christ, for all His mercies, in bringing them from darkness into the marvellous light of the glorious Gospel of our dear Redeemer. Oh! let all who bear the name of Jesus hold Him up, and then He will draw all men unto Him."

In another letter, Mr. Lunham laments the giving up of the mission school-house, which I had got erected there twenty years ago; and he expresses his confident hope, that by this unlooked-for outpouring of God's Spirit, a Church must, after all, be erected in the place. In this great object, which involves the resuscitation of a useful mission, perhaps some brethren in the Lord, who read these pages, and to whom God has given the means, would kindly assist. If they desire further information on the subject, it will be willingly given by Mr. Lunham or myself; and contributions for the purpose will be entrusted to a Committee, whose names will be a guarantee for their judicious outlay. Should this appeal succeed, one great and cherished object in writing this book will be gained, many bitter trials sweetened, and, what is best of all, a deserted watch-tower on Zion's walls will be re-occupied, to the glory of God and the good of souls.

With this appeal, we close our notice of the Kerry Mission; but should the Lord continue life, and the public receive this volume favourably, an extended narrative of it will likely be given hereafter, forming "Sketches of the Southern Highlands." Meantime, we take our leave of that romantic country in the following verses, which we composed on re-visiting it, after an absence of twelve years, and which express our feelings regarding it, if not poetically, yet at least truthfully:—

THE KERRY HILLS.

CAN I forget the Kerry hills—
Their heath-clad rocks and foaming rills!
Hail, region of the wild and grand!
None can forget thee, Kerry land.
See Carntoul gleams from afar;
Of vales the pride, behold Glencar;
And lone Drunghill, where suddenly
The ocean bursts upon the eye.

From Ballybunian's fretted caves
Resounding with the Atlantic waves,
To Brandon Head and Blasket rocks,
Repelling the Atlantic shocks,

Thy winding shore I trace again,
To Skellig Isle and Derrynane;
Each headland with its cloud of spray,
And long withdrawing sandy bay.

But chief, Lough Lane,* the brightest gem
Of fair Hibernia's diadem,
The grand and beautiful combine
To make thy landscape half divine;
Thy Tomies' wilds, and Ross's glades,
O'Sullivan and Torc's cascades;
And, last to deck this lovely scene,
Glena's soft swell of purest green.

Unearthly wild thy echoes rise,
And crag to crag aloud replies;
Like fairy voices to the ear
Their dying cadences appear:
Again they rise, again they die,
As if expiring Nature's sigh.
Enraptured list the festive bands,†
And spread thy fame through distant lands.

Nor are the ties my soul that bind
To Kerry land, of earthly kind:
To me 'tis bathed in heavenly hues;
Holy remembrances diffuse
A nameless beauty o'er its scenes,
Like those oft pictured in our dreams;
Surpassing all this earth can show
Of what is beauteous here below.

---

* Old name for Killarney.   † Parties of tourists visiting the Lakes.

Though oft with sin and sorrow press'd,
And by the world allow'd no rest,
Yet many a Bethel I have found,
A holy, consecrated ground,
Upon its hills and in its dells—
Sweet solitary Peniels—
To memory dear till that great day
When heaven and earth shall pass away.

And if that day one child of thine
In the Redeemer's crown should shine,
And He my feeble efforts own,
As bless'd to save that single one,
I'll joy for hatred and for shame
Oft pour'd upon my humble name;
And praise the all-directing Hand
That guided me to Kerry land.

A Prayer from St. Augustine.

O Lord God, whatever of Thine I have written in this book, may Thy people, as well as Thyself, acknowledge; and whatever I have written of my own, may Thy people, as well as Thyself, forgive.

FINIS.

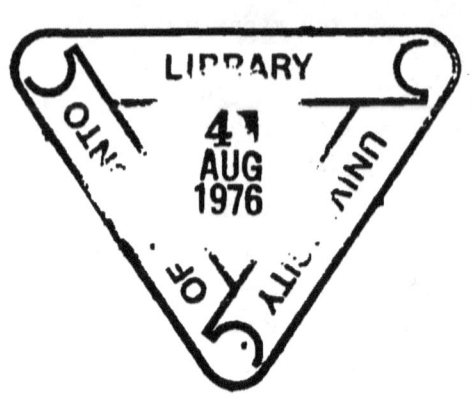

APPENDIX.

With a view to the diffusion of missionary information, a promise was made in the Prospectus of this book, that a free copy for the use of any Congregational Library, would be given to every person who would, at the time, send in a list of eight Subscribers. This appeal for aid in circulating the work was responded to by the following brethren, to whom the Author takes this opportunity of recording his gratitude. He would also publish the names of all the Subscribers, only they are too numerous for that, being between four and five hundred.

Rev. Robert Allen, Ballina,	16 copies.
J. H. M'Manus, M.D., Ballymahon	8 ,,
Henry Bewley, Esq., Dublin,	8 ,,
Robert Kane, Esq. Dublin	80 ,,
John Alton, Esq., Galway	8 ,,
J. Reid, Esq., Liverpool	25 ,,
A. M'Cutchin, Esq., St. Croix, West Indies	25 ,,
Rev. J. B. Huston, Randalstown	9 ,,
Rev. J. K. Leslie, Cookstown	16 ,,
Rev. H. Perry, Portglenone	14 ,,
Rev. J. Simpson, Portrush	16 ,,
Rev. J. Witherow, Maghera	13 ,,
W. Whitton, Esq., Athy	8 ,,
Rev. J. Edmonds, Tully	8 ,,
Rev. R. Harshaw, Mountmellick	8 ,,
James Morrow, Esq., Ballyjamesduff	8 ,,
Mr. Lamont, Parsonstown	8 ,,
G. H. Stuart, Esq., Philadelphia, U. States	20 ,,
Dr. Coulter, Tullamore	8 ,,

www.ingramcontent.com/pod-product-compliance
Lightning Source LLC
Chambersburg PA
CBHW021409230426
43666CB00006B/689